FEMINIST
PHILOSOPHY

FEMINIST
PHILOSOPHY

HERTA NAGL-DOCEKAL

Translated by Katharina Vester

Foreword by Alison M. Jaggar

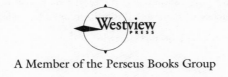

A Member of the Perseus Books Group

English Translation © 2004 by Westview Press

German Edition © 1999 Fischer Taschenbuch Verlag GmbH, Frankfurt am Main

Published in the United States of America by Westview Press, A Member of the Perseus Books Group, 5500 Central Avenue, Boulder, Colorado 80301-2877, and in the United Kingdom by Westview Press, 12 Hid's Copse Road, Cumnor Hill, Oxford OX2 9JJ.

Find us on the world wide web at www.westviewpress.com

Westview Press books are available at special discounts for bulk purchases in the United States by corporations, institutions, and other organizations. For more information, please contact the Special Markets Department at the Perseus Books Group, 11 Cambridge Center, Cambridge, MA 02142, or call (617) 252-5298, (800) 255-1514 or email special.markets@perseusbooks.com.

A Cataloging-in-Publication data record for this book is available from the Library of Congress.

ISBN 0-8133-4189-2 (hc.); 0-8133-6571-6 (pbk.)

The paper used in this publication meets the requirements of the American National Standard for Permanence of Paper for Printed Library Materials Z39.48-1984.

Typeface used in this text: 11-point Galliard

10   9   8   7   6   5   4   3   2   1

CONTENTS

Foreword by Alison M. Jaggar   vii

Acknowledgments   xi

Introduction:
    Feminist Philosophy Under
    Post-feminist Conditions   xiii

1   On the Anthropology of the Sexes   1
    Why there is no natural order of the sexes, 1
    Corporality as an issue of freedom, 9
    Are binary oppositions discriminating speech acts, 15
    Cartesianism: A reproach that needs further precision, 18
    Sex/Gender: *How a long-running debate could come
        to a conclusion*, 22

2   Art and Femininity   41
    Art is gendered, 41
    Sigmund Freud and the woman artist, 45
    Writing with white ink, 58
    Feminist aesthetics, 73

3   Reason: A Concept with Connotations
        of Masculinity   87
    One problem, many questions, 87
    Rationality and gender blindness in the sciences, 88

Is science founded on aggressive masculinity? 110
The criticism of Western Logos, 116
Is the subject shaped by instrumental reason? 122
Detached emotions, 127

4   For a Nonessentialist Politics   133
Moral foundations, 133
The feminist we, 141
*Women as citizens; or, Why the social contract theory
     should be reformulated,* 152

Notes   171
Bibliography   213
Index   237

FOREWORD

PROFESSOR DOCTOR HERTA NAGL-DOCEKAL is Professor of Philosophy at the University of Vienna. She is a pioneer in the philosophy of the German language, both as a woman and as a feminist. It is a philosophical honor and a personal privilege to present Nagl-Docekal's groundbreaking book to the Anglophone philosophical world.

Nagl-Docekal's professional career was influenced at an early stage by feminism in the United States. In 1970/71, when she spent a sabbatical year at Millersville State University, Lancaster, PA, Nagl-Docekal encountered the then-new aspiration among women philosophers to become full members of the academic philosophical community. At this time, no women philosophy professors in Austria existed. Nagl-Docekal decided to write her habilitation thesis in philosophy. She accomplished this in 1981 and soon became a philosophy professor at the University of Vienna. Since that time, she has been very supportive of younger Austrian women philosophers. In 2001, she was elected a member of the Austrian Academy of the Sciences.

Feminist philosophy has long been a central—though far from the only—focus of Nagl-Docekal's work. In addition to making her own intellectual contribution to this emerging field, Nagl-Docekal has encouraged the work of other feminist scholars. She was a founding member of an interdisciplinary group on feminist studies at the University of Vienna and helped to establish the first lecture series on feminist topics. In 1989, she co-organized a landmark conference on feminist philosophy at the University of Vienna, which brought together prominent English- and German-speaking feminist philosophers. Fluent in English, she has presented feminist debates occurring in English to German-speaking philosophers at many occasions. She has co-edited several volumes of feminist philosophy, translated from English to German.

Nagl-Docekal's study, *Feminist Philosophy*, is one of a very few book-length philosophical treatments of feminist topics in German. However, it is unique in Anglophone as well as German philosophy because it is deeply informed by the author's extensive knowledge of feminist philosophical work not only in German but also in English and French. The book thus brings together and analyzes critically contributions from several philosophical literatures. This rich synthesis offers a fresh and important perspective on the central issues of feminist philosophy, including topics in philosophical anthropology, aesthetics, theory of science and the critique of reason, and philosophy of law.

Nagl-Docekal's distinctive point of view developed through her attempts to discuss feminist philosophical issues in the Continental European perspective, an approach that is of significant influence in German philosophy. She contends that, against this background, the issues of feminist philosophy cannot be avoided. Her work draws especially heavily on Kant, despite his mixed reputation among feminist philosophers. Nagl-Docekal shows that Kant's moral philosophy and philosophy of law can—and must—be turned to feminist purposes, arguing that those who read Kant properly have to become feminists.

For Nagl-Docekal, feminist philosophy is not simply an academic enterprise. In her view, the ultimate aim of this field of research— whose point of departure is the fact of manifold discrimination against women—is to provide theoretical foundations for feminist politics. Nagl-Docekal believes that philosophy is able to make a contribution to practical politics but that this can occur only if philosophy's previous distortions are corrected through a rigorous feminist analysis. If philosophy is indispensable to feminism, feminism is also indispensable to philosophy.

Like many in the first generation of feminist philosophers, Nagl-Docekal has taken professional risks to get feminist issues recognized as central to philosophy. In *Feminist Philosophy*, she challenges professional philosophers' attempts to dismiss feminist issues, attempts that sometimes focus on rhetorical excesses of feminist authors in order to discredit their substantial concerns. Her aim is to carve out those elements of feminist philosophy that are so well-founded that they can no longer be ignored by philosophers who wish their work to reflect the current state of the discipline.

Feminist Philosophy is a landmark contribution simultaneously to feminist politics and philosophical scholarship. Already becoming a classic in German philosophy, I am proud to introduce it to an Anglophone audience.

Alison M. Jaggar

ACKNOWLEDGMENTS

THE WRITING OF THIS BOOK was supported in many ways by colleagues and friends in the United States and Canada sharing the concern to employ a feminist perspective in academic discourse. My reflections greatly benefited from information on current debates made available by the Society for Women in Philosophy, which I joined as a member many years ago, and by a number of sessions at APA meetings dedicated to feminist issues. First and foremost I am obliged to Seyla Benhabib, Steven Burns, Kurt Rudolf Fischer, Mary Mosher Flesher, Nancy Fraser, Alison M. Jaggar, Lorraine Markotic, Linda Lopez McAlister, Ruth Anna Putnam, Robin May Schott, and Iris Marion Young; I would like to thank them all for their inspiring work, for many stimulating conversations, and for their sustained commitment to cultivate trans-Atlantic relations. This book is dedicated to Ludwig Nagl, who has connected these two worlds in his philosophical work for more than three decades.

INTRODUCTION:
FEMINIST PHILOSOPHY
UNDER POST-FEMINIST
CONDITIONS

SHOULD THIS BOOK BEGIN WITH a definition of feminist philosophy? Presumably this field of scholarship has long been known. In the context of the student movement of the late 1960s, women philosophers—like their fellow combatants in other disciplines—began to confront their field with the problem of the existing hierarchies of the sexes. This beginning was, strictly speaking, a resumption; discrimination against women due to their sex was problematized in the philosophical context much earlier, for instance, by John Stuart Mill and Harriet Taylor Mill, or—to give another example from the seventeenth century—by the Cartesian François Poulain de la Barre. But these were individual investigations that did not found a research tradition. The term *feminist philosophy*, first coined during the new beginning at the turn from the 1960s to the 1970s, serves as an umbrella term for the entire development since then, which presents itself as an increasingly differentiated discourse.[1] This decades-long continuity and a considerable number of publications suggest that feminist philosophy is a well-established field of research. The countless individual studies and journal articles, the periodicals and book series specifically dedicated to this subject have created such a mass of texts that it has become impossible to keep an overview.[2] Quite a few publications that aim at facilitating orientation have come out in recent years, such as bibliographies, compendia, and syntheses.³ Nonetheless it would be too quick to conclude that feminist philosophy is today as recognized as other innovative approaches in contemporary philosophy, such as applied ethics or the debate on multiculturalism and the rights of minorities.⁴

The amazingly persistent reservations have different reasons. If one considers the critique voiced within the philosophical profession, especially in public and private discussions, then it becomes apparent that often the term *feminism* as such is rejected. This form of distancing, which is not limited to male representatives of the discipline, usually results from a restricted understanding of the term: *Feminism* is associated in this case with certain simplifying conceptions of patriarchy and militant practices from the early days of the student movement and women's lib. But shouldn't we expect philosophers to have the ability and willingness to focus on the core of a problem even if the way in which it was presented in its early forms of articulation still lacked differentiation? This core lies in the discrimination of women because of their sex—an asymmetry that in diverse forms still shapes all areas of social life. Of course, some decisive changes have been achieved in the last decades. In many countries existing deficits regarding the formal equal rights of women have been leveled out, measures have been taken to eliminate asymmetries between the sexes in the areas of family and divorce law, or labor law, and legal instruments have been created to provide specific support to women. Nonetheless women still are massively underrepresented in bodies of political decisionmaking, in leading positions in the economy and the academy, and among those commanding high salaries.⁵ Correspondingly, the percentage of women among those who live below the poverty level is still high. The new poverty resulting from recent economic changes—especially the international increase in part-time and low-pay work as well as the accompanying reduction of social rights—is carried to such an extent by women that today one must diagnose a feminization of poverty.⁶ Therefore the thesis that women still face discrimination in many ways is well founded. This thesis is the very core of the term *feminism,* which comprises various nonhomogeneous efforts aiming at overcoming the asymmetries of the sexes. Why, then, should feminism be rejected out of hand? Must not all who think democratically share its central concern? The philosophical argument implied in this question will be elaborated in the last chapter of this book; there we will consider how the feminist claim can be spelled out in terms of moral philosophy. As regards terminology, the expression *feminism* is used in the following as a general concept referring to the core problem of discrimination. This makes it possible to include the considerations of some authors who have rejected the appellation *feminist*. Such self-distancing can usually be traced to the fact that the term *feminist* is understood in a narrow sense and is associated with certain early configurations of thinking and acting. In contrast, a thematic relation to the named core problem is the decisive criterion for this study.

More recently reservations in regard to feminism have also been articulated in the form of the thesis that the present must be evaluated as a post-feminist era. This thesis is shared by people whose opinions in general belong to very different schools of thought. On the one hand, there is the criticism "from the outside." It corresponds with the common diagnosis in commercialized culture, especially in advertising, that feminism is an aberration, which belongs, fortunately, to the past, since women have readopted a feminine, fastidious lifestyle. Obviously such an opinion cannot be taken seriously in regard to its descriptive claim, since it ignores the discrimination and the deteriorating quality of life that many women face at present. Therefore it is important to analyze the strategic function of this perspective. Examined more closely, traditional gender roles are undergoing here a new aestheticization, which is aimed at distracting the public gaze—and that of women themselves—from the discrimination inherent in these clichés. Such reappraisals function in the opposite direction to the efforts to eliminate the asymmetries between the sexes. Therefore the so-called post-feminist era should be seen as what it is: a political-programmatic statement of a conservative thrust rather than a descriptive proposition.

Another variation of post-feminism is characterized by a criticism "from the inside." The point of this critique is that issues of "gender" must be discussed in another manner than when they were first discussed. That such a change has taken place already is evidenced by the fact that concepts like patriarchy or liberation are no longer in use as core categories while the issue of the discursive constitution of the body and the heterosexual matrix, as well as the concept of the recognition of difference (to name only a few examples), have now gained a central position in the international discussion. This development calls for a differentiated response. Obviously a research project can only maintain its currency if it takes on an increasingly subtle shape. Some of the analytical tools used in the beginnings of feminist theory were certainly insufficient, insofar, for instance, as overly simple oppositions such as dominance and oppression were adopted and as the central terms *man* and *woman* were hardly examined in their semantic depths. Furthermore, specific projects of philosophical research cannot be isolated but must be pursued in reference to the various strands of current thinking. For this reason the debate about gender relations up to now has been shaped by a multifaceted confrontation with virtually all currents of contemporary philosophy.[7] Of particular importance proved to be suggestions to appropriate and further develop current theories that focus on the counterintentional consequences of the Enlightenment.[8]

But why should this process of transcending the original models of feminist thinking not be understood as an interior development of the debate? The expression post-feminist evokes the idea of an abandonment, not an increasingly differentiated argumentation. Different motives, it seems, play a role here. The intended abandonment is not primarily motivated by a rejection of the early narrow definition of the term *feminism*. More often, it is insinuated that the entire problem of the hierarchy of the sexes belongs to the past. This view seems informed by the law of the market. What really counts is innovation as such. Philosophical questions are put *ad acta,* not because they can be considered solved, but because they have lost the appeal of the new. This attitude exists in regard to other important social issues too. For women, the consequences are doubly dangerous. If this type of thematic innovation were to prevail, discrimination against women because of their sex would be eliminated from the philosophical agenda at the very moment when this discrimination starts to increase. Thus the second variation of post-feminism, in spite of its altogether different intention, plays along with the first and contributes to a backlash[9] that has been observable for some time. Nancy Fraser warns that "it will not be time to speak of post-feminism until we can legitimately speak of post-patriarchy."[10]

This book refers specifically to this state of the debate. It explores how the basic feminist project has to be reformulated in the context of the current discourses, taking into account recent research on the topic of gender. Attention is also paid to studies pointing out that the disadvantaging of women is not in every case caused by the same mechanism of discrimination,[11] and that it is often intermingled with discrimination on the basis of other conditions such as belonging to a certain ethnic, cultural, or religious community or to a group defined by economic parameters, skin color, or sexual orientation.[12]

The lack of acceptance that feminist philosophy encounters cannot be explained only by skepticism toward feminism in general. In the academic field, connecting philosophy and feminism raises suspicion.[13] These reservations have been differently accentuated. While some critics fear an ideologization of philosophy and thus a loss of its argumentative power, others argue that what they miss is a new methodological approach. In regard to the first criticism, I believe that the concept of philosophy that is appealed to here deserves questioning, since it is apparently defined in a narrow scientistic sense. Such a self-restriction has far-reaching consequences. As soon as the debate on sex asymmetries is denounced as a subversion of the academic dignity of philosophy, this evaluation must also be applied to all other attempts to contribute with philosophical means to the solution of moral and social problems. Under this critique, feminist philosophy would be in the best of company, since the verdict is valid for the entire field of practical philosophy.[14] This point should not be underestimated. Philosophers who do not subscribe to a narrow scientistic understanding of their discipline cannot consistently withdraw themselves from the core problem of feminism. Why, for instance, should a philosophical theory of law investigate all possible forms of injustice, except those that are based on sex discrimination? Starting from this question, the final section of this book will discuss how the issue of justice and gender could be sorted out in terms of contemporary contractarian conceptions.

Responding to the methodological objection, this introduction needs to define the project of feminist philosophy, although the necessary clarifications have been available for a long time.[15] Feminist philosophy does not claim to develop a specific methodological approach in the manner of analytical philosophy or phenomenology. Those who contend that it lacks a new methodological approach are missing the very point of the research program they portray as having failed. The central claim of feminist philosophy is aimed at confronting the entire field with the problem of the hierarchical relations of the sexes. This claim covers not only the full range of systematic subfields (e.g., epistemology, ethics, aesthetics, etc.) but also the different schools of thought by which the canon of the history of philosophy as well as the contemporary debate are determined. Feminist philosophy crosses the specific methodological approaches such as the analytical, the phenomenological, and so on. Its endeavor may be characterized, as was done in the Anglophone world, by "doing philosophy as a feminist."[16] (That the term *feminist* refers to men as well as women is important, since the philosophical debate over injustice is not restricted to those who are personally affected by it. Therefore the—unfortunately common—opinion that the term *feminist philosophy* designates a theory by, about, and for women is a drastic misconception.[17])

The innovative potential of this approach is revealed in the variety of questions that result from the central point of feminist philosophy outlined above. Starting from the facts of discrimination, we must first investigate the extent to which philosophical thinking past and present has contributed to the development and legitimization of the hierarchy of the sexes. As will be discussed more in depth in the part of this book dealing with the theory of science, the aim of such a critical rereading lies not only in exposing explicit misogynist theorems but also in making the androcentric patterns of thinking visible which, because of their inexplicit character, have proven especially fateful. Research in this area has yielded a great number of critical studies on all periods of the history of philosophy from antiquity to the present.[18] One element of the effort to challenge the masculine character of the philosophical tradition is the rediscovery of women philosophers. The cliché that philosophy is men's business has shaped the perception of the discipline to such an extent that the philosophical works of women are hardly mentioned.[19] The main thrust of feminist philosophy is, however, not of a historical-critical nature; it rather focuses on what means philosophy can offer to make discrimination against women visible in its full extent, and how it can help develop alternative conceptions that provide the theoretical underpinning for the elimination of existing asymmetries. Under this perspective, the idea of taking a fresh look at the canon proved fruitful. The manifold feminist theories elaborated over the years have appropriated elements from virtually all currents of contemporary philosophy and have engaged the classics of all periods, starting with Plato and Aristotle.[20] To encompass this wide range of issues and theories, I suggested, when I first proposed a definition, to characterize feminist philosophy as a "philosophizing guided by an interest in the liberation of women."[21]

This study is not an overview of the debates that have been going on so far or the main currents of contemporary discourse. Rather, it attempts a provisional assessment in a systematic fashion. Focusing on a number of core disciplines of philosophy, it explores what has been accomplished through the inroads of feminist research. For this purpose, two modes of proceeding will be combined. First, I shall specify which differentiations have to be made in order to challenge the problem of gender hierarchy in its diverse aspects. Carrying out this argumentative task, I shall—and this is the second element of my approach—critically analyze some theories of particular relevance for today's international feminist discourse. This focus on topicality organizes the inner structure of the book. If this study concentrates on philosophical anthropology (Chapter 1), aesthetics (Chapter 2), theory of science and the critique of reason (Chapter 3), and the philosophy of law (Chapter 4), this is because the most influential conceptions and controversies have evolved in these fields in recent years. Concerning the individual contributions taken up and discussed from this perspective, I have chosen an exemplary method: I closely analyze specific text passages in which opinions are formulated that are broadly shared and therefore keep recurring in the discussion. If I give preference to such a reading *en detail* over a summarizing description, my intention is to allow the reader to follow my critical comments—for instance, on the ideas of Hélène Cixous, Evelyn Fox Keller, Luce Irigaray, or Judith Butler—right away. I do not intend with this procedure to generally evaluate the work of the authors in question but discuss paradigmatic, influential figures of argumentation.[22]

Such a reevaluation of common theses in feminist theory is, I think, also the best way to steer against a development that has surfaced recently. A phase of heated controversies has been followed by a drifting apart of single currents, which tend to be discussed mainly among those who share their main parameters. This has lead to a kind of orthodoxy. Certain theorems are now understood as received opinions that no longer require reasoning. But closer examination reveals that the move to place a certain position beyond discussion is often based not on good reasons but only an interest in warding off other theoretical options. Therefore, one concern of this book is to subvert such dogmatism. In close readings of paradigmatic text passages it will be shown that, for instance, the widespread identification of feminist philosophy with a thinking that proclaims the "death of the subject" or with a constructivist understanding of "the body" poses a problem, since it is not in all aspects well founded by argumentative reasoning but rather deploys rhetorically overdrawn figures of dismissal.[23] This critical rereading is essential also in regard to a favored form of discrediting feminist theory. Rhetorically excessive theses have frequently been used as easy targets by those who wish to fight off the entire project of feminist philosophy. This strategy can be countered only with argumentative means. Therefore it is the main aim of this book to carve out those elements of feminist philosophy that are so well founded that they can no longer be disregarded by philosophers who claim to reflect in their work the current state of their discipline.

1

On the Anthropology of the Sexes

Why there is no natural order of the sexes

THE CORE CONCERN OF FEMINIST CRITICISM is to expose the manifold ways in which men are privileged and to oppose discrimination against women. Consequently, we must first address what we mean when we say *woman* and, by extension, *man*. The meaning connected to each term is essential for all further theorizing. In what sense, then, can we speak about *men* and *women*? Where do we start?

It seems reasonable to first examine the colloquial use of these expressions and the ideas conveyed by them. On the one hand, the terms "woman" and "man" are used to express the obvious bodily differences of each sex. On the other hand, a number of idiomatic expressions refer to social roles, for instance, child rearing as *women's work* or politics as *men's business*. These expressions are based on normative ideas.

Take the expression *women's work*. From a woman's perspective, this means because my body shows female sex characteristics, I am expected to choose my occupation within a certain limited spectrum. Although I might be perfectly capable of working in a certain field, I am often overtly or indirectly excluded because this domain is assumed to be for males only. If I try to break through these barriers, I am socially sanctioned and my behavior is viewed as unfeminine.

Those who defend a sexual differentiation of social roles, talents, and so on, believe—even if not explicitly—that the social structure can be justified by "nature." Just because a man and a woman have different bodies, they cannot share social roles. By portraying the "order of the sexes"[1] as natural, this view suggests that this social structure is incontrovertibly valid. Those defending this understanding use two different forms of justification. The division of labor is described as (1) "given by nature" or (2) "wanted by nature." The first regards the social order as based directly on nature, and the second assumes that it needs to be implemented through norms referring to "Nature's intentions." The latter, for instance, informs the still commonly heard rule that it is a "woman's nature" to run the household or choose a helping occupation, such as nursing. Both forms lead to fundamental problems.

From the beginning, feminist research has exposed the conflation of bodily characteristics and social norms. Numerous studies of the life and thought of European and Western modernity document that (in contrast to the egalitarian ideas of the early Enlightenment)[2] from about the middle of the eighteenth century the image of the ideal couple (the man and the woman) designated different social tasks for each sex, men being assigned to the public domain and women to the domestic. This conception retains its normative significance to the present. This research also demonstrates that the gender model originally tailored to the bourgeoisie patronizes and disadvantages women.[3] Thus, the reference to nature still serves to legitimate patriarchal structures.[4]

Historical reconstructions of this kind attempt to decode current asymmetries between the sexes from the perspective of the bourgeois experience. Moreover, they expose historical contingency: As they demonstrate that the "order of the sexes" that prevails in many ways today is hardly more than two centuries old, and they disprove the idea that this is a natural institution. This result corresponds with investigations of earlier periods of history (i.e., about epochs before the Enlightenment)[5] as well as with ethnological studies of non-European cultures, since they confront the natural argument with a variety of highly diverging gender relations. With regard to the tasks carried out by men and women or the virtues cultivated by them, there is no constant allocation model independent from history.

The notion of the natural character of the reigning order is disproven not only by historical and ethnological research. Analysis of the logic of attempts to justify social norms by referring to nature reinforces their dubiousness. As already mentioned, two widely used forms of argumentation can be characterized as *given by nature* and *wanted by nature*. The first variation leads to biological determinism, as the order of human communities is not basically distinguished from animal cohabitation. The division of labor between the sexes is assumed to have been determined in a way similar to the functions in a beehive. This theory, on closer examination, cannot prove the natural character of social norms, since its conceptual frame offers no place for norms. The term *norm* only makes sense in the context of a theory of freedom—however it may be conceptualized in detail. As I will explain below, norms appeal to people who face a decision. If all human activities are considered natural events, then they can be explained by instinct. Recourse to norms means an inconsistency in this line of argument, since it insinuates that certain human activities cannot be described as animal behavior.

Furthermore, this variant of the natural argument does not do justice to the everyday self-understanding of human beings. On the one hand our body performs automatic reactions (i.e., reactions that we do not cause deliberately). For example, if an object approaches our face at a certain speed, our eyes close; this is a reflex (i.e., involuntary) reaction, not an action. On the other hand, we are constantly

confronted with situations that require us to make a decision. This is
the experience that philosophical theories of freedom examine more
closely. While *freedom* is often interpreted (and misunderstood) as
omnipotence, here it is considered in a restricted frame: The situation in which I am called on to make a decision must not be created
by my doing, and it can present me with alternatives in which I must
choose the lesser evil. My specific perception is decisive for the situation in which I find myself. It depends on my previous experiences
and my educational background, my understanding of the situation,
the options for action I see and my standard for evaluating them. It
refers to the conventions of language and the interpretation of my
time and my social environment. In this sense one must state an unavoidable situatedness of action. However, that we make decisions in
a certain context does not speak against freedom as it is here understood—as fundamentally distinguished from natural performances.
What is crucial is whether it is up to me—in the above specified
meaning—to make a choice. If so, I am called on to act and expect
the solution of the problem that I face not from a pattern of involuntary behavior. (This decisionmaking renders the distinction between
the terms *action* and *behavior* meaningful.)[6] I cannot possibly avoid
the choice, as our everyday experience shows. If I decide in a certain
situation to refuse to make a decision, then I act too, since such a decision can only be dealt with adequately in the field that is discussed
under the term *freedom*.

Some have defended biological determinism by depicting the
concept of freedom as generated by self-deception. An occurrence
that presents itself subjectively as an action can be explained in terms
of human species-specific behavior. This statement, however, does
not take into account that two different perspectives are here in play:
Certain forms of animal and human behavior are examined empirically
from the outside, while the perspective of the first person arises from
the inside. When a person faces two different options (e.g., different
job offers) the decisionmaking cannot be facilitated or evaded by the
consideration that the behavior pattern characteristic to the species

will take its course anyway. Rather, the person is confronted with the question of what is the right thing to do. This call for a decision presents the starting point for a philosophical discussion of freedom. The first-person perspective is sufficient to justify the use of the term *freedom*. The question of whether we can produce a theoretical proof of freedom can therefore be left open in this context. The limits of the empirical method are obvious: A purely observational perspective is incapable of grasping adequately what it means to consider and evaluate the various possibilities of action in a certain situation. Of course, actions are *also* empirically perceptible events. But calling an observable event an action implies that we assume that in this case a decision from the perspective of the first person has been made. Ascribing actions to cerebro-physiological or biochemical processes cannot visualize the reasons for or against the discrete options weighed by the person under consideration. Thus the empirical sciences can neither explain nor refute freedom.

A philosophical theory of freedom must deal with a number of concepts that play a role in my further reflections, including autonomy, morals, ethics, rights, politics, power, and history. The expression *norm* or *social norm* acquires meaning only in this context. Only when people feel called on to decide between different options can norms have relevance as guidelines for their actions. (When *norm* is understood more generally as principle of action, it can refer to Kant's conception of the maxim. According to Kant, unless an action can be referred to a maxim, it cannot be conceived of and justified as a real action based on a deliberate decision.)

Researchers working in comparative behavior have attempted to derive morals phylogenically. Certain animal behavior patterns are characterized as "the inhibition of killing clan members, incest taboos, mating for life, devotional care of the brood, selfless readiness to fight for the protection of the weakest."[7] This behavior is evaluated as evidence for the "instinctive bases of human moral systems."[8] But this method is problematic for several reasons. First, the difference between *action* and *behavior* is not taken seriously. Whoever attributes the mild outcome of a conflict to a "killing inhibition" assumes that there was no deliberate decision and therefore no action based on moral norms. Konrad Lorenz speaks of merely "moral-analogous" behavior with reference to animals.[9] But this expression only reveals the deficiency of theories that locate the basis of human morality in behavior patterns. The logic of analogies has not been sufficiently thought through. One characteristic of the analogy is that it starts with a difference: Phenomena perceived as undoubtedly non-identical are being connected. Lorenz's use of the expression *moral-analogous* suggests that nothing but a comparison is made—between instinctive behavior on the one hand and moral action on the other. But how could a behavior that is considered moral-analogous be the origin of morality in the actual meaning of the term? It is only possible to speak of a phylogenic genesis of morality if the analogy that is drawn in the beginning is denied in the next step.

A further problem (apparent in the description of behavior patterns quoted above) lies in the circularity of the argument: The claim to "derive" morality phylogenically presupposes that morality is projected onto the animal kingdom with the help of anthropomorphizing language. How can animals have a concept of taboo, disqualify polygamous forms of life, or orient themselves toward a norm of selflessness? Certainly an observer can use the same words to describe certain behaviors among human beings and animals. For instance, newborns receive care for a while. But both cases cannot be explained in the same way. A term like *morality* can't be used for animals because norms direct action differently than instinct governs behavior. If I have a moral rule in my mind in a certain situation, it does not automatically orient my decision toward it. Thus people who care for children see good reasons for doing so and act in accordance with them. But they are not governed by an instinct that leaves them no choice but to "care self-sacrificingly for the brood." Again, the term *morality* only makes sense when there is freedom of decision. If norms functioned like instincts, it would be impossible to distinguish between responsible and immoral action, and the concepts of norm and action would be contradictory.

Special attention must be paid to the content of the norms, which the theory of evolution claims to trace back to a biological foundation. Obviously these norms are not notions of correct actions shared by all people. We are confronted here with the strategy of keeping historically contingent concepts of social order beyond debate by attributing to them a natural origin. If there is a foundational correlation, it runs in a contrary direction to the one claimed: The so-called morality of animals is intentionally characterized in a way that corresponds to the defended social order. The questionability of this strategy is immediately clear: There are animal behaviors that cannot be explained in terms of a steady relationship or an incest taboo. Since an arbitrary selection is at work here, the statement of the phylogenic origin of morality must be based on a strong interest in the legitimization of certain social norms. Consequently the philosophical debate on these issues is dismissed and the customary rules adjudicating serious scientific research are grossly violated.[10]

The *wanted by nature* argument leads to comparably great difficulties. Initially the first-person perspective, which is decisive for action, is taken seriously. One of the different options at hand is said to correspond with the intention of nature. This, so the expectation, will bring the agent(s) to conclude that this option is the one that is best justified and is therefore to be carried out. The difficulties of this line of thought become obvious in light of the two dimensions of everyday experience addressed above. Because we have reflexes, it seems legitimate to speak of humans' having "natural" processes. The Aristotelian way of defining nature in opposition to art is relevant in this context, even if the ontological frame in which this distinction is formulated in Aristotle can no longer be defended. It makes sense to call an event "natural" only if it takes place (spoken from the perspective of action) automatically—if it is not due to intentional planning. No norms are required for such processes to take place. A norm

makes sense only in regard to the second dimension of experience—
when we can or must make a decision.

In this second context we need to clarify our own intentions, and
a reference to an intention of nature does not have a compelling
character. Those who assume that it does, risk a performative contradiction. The fact that an *ought* is formulated at all suggests that the
case in question is not left to the discretion of a natural course.[11] I can
orient myself toward natural processes and, for example, retire for the
night as early as the birds do. But in such a case, too, I act in the narrow sense of the word: It is my decision to use the evening behavior
of birds as a model. My retiring for the night does not happen by itself; rather, it comes from my decision to choose this particular option. To sum up, when we are called on to decide and to act
(although only in this regard), it can be said (in a variation of a well-
known formulation from Herder) that human beings have always
been enfranchised from nature.

These distinctions support a feminist rejection of any attempt to
legitimate a division of tasks between the sexes, in the private or the
public sphere, by ascribing them to an intention of nature.[12] Those
who want men and women to organize their relations in a certain
way have already presupposed that their contact is not regulated by
itself but requires deliberation. Yet if their relationship is not fixed by
nature but is a product of freedom (in the meaning defined above),
then it cannot be legitimized by references to nature. Rather, every
proposed relationship configuration must be confronted with the
norms that are applicable to human actions in general, particularly
the principles of morality and justice. Moreover, the concept of a division of labor between the sexes is questionable *toto genere*. If principles of morality and justice, as elaborated in the current philosophical
discourse, are brought to bear on this issue, the concepts of man and
woman must be dismissed as categories of the social order.[13] The historical variety of gender roles addressed above can be accounted for
in these terms: Since the relations between the sexes are not shaped
by unalterable patterns of behavior, they can be formed differently in

individual epochs and cultures—in the context of the power relations, conflicts, religious convictions, political ideals, and so on, that shape the course of history in general.

(In differentiating natural conditions, on the one hand, and referring to them in the context of human action, on the other, I intend to point out an indispensable basis for feminist criticism. Without this distinction, a serious inconsistency will result: The logic of the naturalistic explanation remains effective. As I will argue in the following, this problem exists wherever it is assumed that the traditional hierarchies of the sexes can be overcome simply by questioning the biological differences. In that case there is a danger that a patriarchally conceived naturalism may be replaced merely by another form of naturalism.)

Corporality as an issue of freedom

The relation of the sexes has repeatedly inspired naturalistic argumentation, although objections of the kind presented above have been known for a long time. In the shaping of the relations of the sexes—no matter the time or the culture in which it actually takes place—natural conditions are an issue of freedom. As explained above, the term *freedom* refers to the fact that we are able to take various positions in given situations. Were freedom defined by an action lacking a situational context, an action out of nothingness, then the term would make no sense, at least with reference to human beings. Usually situations are generated by various factors. Basically, two types of conditions can be distinguished (although most cases combine elements of both groups). The situations in which we act derive, on the one hand, from historical developments to which our previous actions belong. On the other hand they are defined by natural conditions. For example, it is up to me to determine the time when I go to sleep. Perhaps I consider spending the night in a bed or a hammock.

Whatever I decide, I always refer to a phenomenon that appears in my body by itself—in the sense that it is not under my control—for example, my need for sleep. This accounts for the cultural history of sleeping. People have dealt with this natural situation in very different ways. Analogously, the cultural history of cooking is based on the fact that we cannot survive long without food. This is also true in regard to refusal, for instance, a politically motivated hunger strike or a religious fast. The logic of the negation actively confronts the natural need for food; the negation would be impossible without this prerequisite. It is, of course, hardly justified to regard our needs as merely given by nature; even our bodily needs change in each historical or cultural context. Although I will return to this issue below, the picture remains basically unchanged. Regardless of how far our formative potential can reach, the basic constellation—that people take a position relative to their corporality—remains untouched.

Returning to the relation of the sexes, an analogous argument can be made. First, we need to note that the term *sexes* designates certain physical differences. It is not limited to humans but refers to any organisms in which two different body forms have emerged, whose cooperation is needed for reproduction.[14] These sexually differentiated bodies form a situation toward which one can take various positions. Human bodies either show predominantly female or male forms or they combine sex characteristics in such a way that a clear assignment is not possible (I will return to this topic). The crucial point is that these conditions constitute an issue of freedom. My physical features do not tie me down to one particular way of life. If my body shows the biological prerequisites for pregnancy and childbirth, this does not establish a preliminary decision. Whether I decide to give birth to a child and then care for this child as she grows up are questions that can only be answered through action:[15] by weighing the possibilities and norms involved in each situation. To be more precise, it is not about just *being able* to take a position; it is unavoidably necessary to make such decisions.

With a view to concrete situations the fact must of course be addressed that women are often pressured, especially in regard to preg-

nancy and birth. Power relations of this kind will be discussed in
other sections of this book. In this chapter we deal with the more
fundamental issue that sexually differentiated bodies necessitate interpretation and formative activity. Recognizing this allows us to examine conflicts on the level of acting—for instance, conflicts arising
when certain groups insist on a monopoly of interpretation and try
to enforce their concept of an order of the sexes by denouncing other
orientations as "deviant" and imposing sanctions. Feminist investigations of patriarchy engage precisely this dimension of freedom.

Because bodily conditions present an issue of freedom, there is
great variation in the cultural or social history of gender relations.[16]
Furthermore, these manifold interpretations and practices deal with
the body not only in its givenness; they also treat it as a medium of
figuration: They inscribe themselves into the body. These inscriptions
are not foreign to ordinary language but are expressed in references
to *features* in which much of the fate and character of a person can be
read. Such a reading can take in the entire body. As a "gendered
body,"[17] it undergoes modeling processes from the earliest stages of
socialization that lead us to literally embody the gender norms of our
culture or social stratum.[18]

The statement that the bodily difference of the sexes is an issue of
freedom has the character of a fundamental clarification. Further differentiation is needed—specifically in regard to the way in which corporality presents itself to us as a given. Our body is given to us in a
different way than all other things. Although our body seems to be
an object of perception like any other, we are not able to see ourselves entirely—in contrast to other things that we can view from all
sides. The possibility of keeping a distance, which is decisive for comprehensive perception, is lacking. Edith Stein, referring to the
thoughts of Husserl, remarks: "Any other object I can approach and
distance myself from again; I can turn to and away from it, which
means it vanishes from my focus."[19] My body, however, is always
here, and I find myself "irremovably tied to it. This being tied, this
belonging to my body, can never constitute itself in outer perception."[20]

Not only is my body a close object of empirical knowledge, but it also performs all my perceptions. The sentient body is not just an instrument for the perception of outer conditions. We are aware simultaneously of our body itself—from the inside. Some sensations refer exclusively to the body, for example, tiredness or hunger. Edith Stein refers to the "body-aware body."[21] (The internal perspective gave rise to the development of two different terms in the German language: While the word *Körper* refers to all "outer" objects of perception, the term *Leib* designates the corporality experienced as mine,[22] meaning an awareness "from the inside.")[23]

The sexual body is both a physical body *(Körper)* and a lived body *(Leib)*. Observation discloses the sexual characteristics of our body, and we have inner sensations that are related to our sexual being. For instance, menstruation and pregnancy are observable but also sensed—sometimes before they are empirically perceived. The historian Barbara Duden focuses on this dimension of sensation. Modern methods of prenatal diagnostics, such as ultrasound, make pregnancy increasingly an object of outer perception, even for pregnant women themselves. Duden's central concern is understanding how pregnancy, in the time before modern medical technology, primarily belonged to inner experience. Referring to numerous historical sources, she demonstrates that this quality was also expressed in women's talk about pregnancy.[24]

Observations of this kind, however, do not give any reason to question the fundamental thesis concerning the relation of the body and freedom. My sensations provide information about my body, but the body is not aware of itself; rather, I have a bodily experience. By using the phrase *my body*, I distinguish between my sensed corporality on the one hand, and knowledge about it on the other. Husserl explains that "having a body" differs from "being a body."[25] In ordinary language people say "I am thirsty" or "my foot hurts."[26] This I-perspective is the prerequisite for my body to be an object of my actions. Yet it is not as if I first learned something about my body in a purely receptive form in order to then deal with it in action. The first-person perspective is already relevant for the perception of my body: I am formatively active in experiencing it. An indication of this is the historicity of the body experience. Duden's studies show that pain is not exclusively a natural and unvarying phenomenon. What I sense also depends on expectations and patterns of interpretation that are common in my culture, as well as conventions of verbaliza-tion.[27] (This also applies to sensations that do not directly refer to our body, like suffering from pain. Hilge Landweer points this out in her investigation of whether men feel differently than women.)[28]

These general observations are also valid in respect to sexual ori-entation. I do not choose the characteristics of my body, but the fact that I find certain sex characteristics in my body does not tie me to a specific kind of sexual relation. Some persons are born with a body that shows female organs and body functions. Yet these individuals have great diversity in their sexual experience. Heterosexual and les-bian relations can be enacted quite differently, and also combined, or negated through a decision for celibacy. It is up to me how I live my body. In this context the historical variety of the sexual life provides ample illustration. Merleau-Ponty expresses this creative potential as follows: "Sexuality is not an autonomous cycle. It has internal links with the whole active and cognitive being, these three sectors of behavior display a common typical structure."[29] The connection be-tween sexuality, cognition, and action suggested here needs further investigation. Merleau-Ponty designs a complex "relationship of re-ciprocal expression."[30] Whether he achieves a consistent theory or only formulates a program for thinking the three components to-gether lies beyond the scope of this discussion.[31]

One way of challenging my line of argument could be to maintain that our biological condition is not limited to its physiological com-ponents, but also includes drives that steer our sexual behavior. Here we face the danger of circular argumentation: That somebody leans toward a certain pattern of sexual behavior—the fact that is explained as caused by drives—is simultaneously presented as the only proof for the existence of the given drive. Judith Butler, who contends that existing conceptions of the sexual drive lack scientific proof, exposes yet another problem. In her view these conceptions are based on a naturalization of norms, which she seeks to demonstrate in psycho-analysis. According to Butler, Freud's theories on drive originated in views on gender typical for Freud's time and social class, which in-clude well-known normative concepts of heterosexual relations be-tween men and women. Freud projected these views, she continues, onto the physical differences between the sexes so that heterosexual orientation appears to be biologically given. This strategy renders the process of projection invisible and therefore mostly unquestionable.[32] As Butler's reconstruction demonstrates, Freud's concept of the sex drive immunizes the ubiquitous social pressure favoring heterosexu-ality against any critique.[33]

Should all assumptions about instinct-oriented sexual preferences of human beings therefore be considered obsolete?[34] This question cannot be answered completely through philosophical means. But there is no immediate need anyway as far as our topic is concerned. Even if sexual drives in men and women could be proven using methods that avoid projection, my basic statement would still not be in question. Such a proof would establish nothing but preconditions, in regard to which different positions can be taken. Even a well-argued drive theory could not show that our sexual biography is decided en-tirely by nature. (Anyone who tried this would become ensnared in the difficulties of biological determinism shown above.) Conceivably, such research results might shed greater clarity on the given condi-tions that we need to deal with in our actions.[35]

It should be clear by now why, in regard to relations between the sexes, naturalistic conceptions endure. The fact that the term *sex* refers first to biological differences tends to be misunderstood as sug-gesting that the form of relations between women and men, espe-cially their sexual relations, is determined or at least normed by nature. My response is that persons take positions regarding natural conditions—including their own body—so that their sexual life does not take a predetermined course. The questionable basis of the term *perversion* is obvious. Insofar as this expression denounces behavior *contra naturam*, it is marked by a performative self-contradiction. The term *perversion* assumes that the norm condemning all sexual relations that are not heterosexual could be derived from the fact that there are bodies with female sex characteristics and bodies with male. But such a way of thinking has to be confronted with its own unreflected implications: The fact *that* a norm is formulated presupposes the insight that the sexual life of human beings is *not* determined by nature but is developed in social interaction.[36] Human sexual relations can be generally called *contra naturam* since they are always (independently of whatever form they take) based on the fact that natural conditions are being dealt with in action. Only as part of the realm of freedom can sexual relations be the object of moral judgment (and legal regulation). The question is not whether a specific form of sexual relations violates the natural order, but how the individuals involved treat each other. Problems like sexual oppression and exploitation as well as conceptions of mutual recognition are topics that arise at this point. In other chapters I discuss whether general principles of morality and justice as they have been elaborated in the current philosophical debate may be utilized for the clarification of these issues. Here I want to point out that a feminist critique of the various forms of discrimination and oppression of women in regard to their sexuality can be consistently argued only with the precondition of a concept of freedom.

Are binary oppositions discriminating speech acts?

In the context of today's debate in feminist theory, the conventional wisdom no longer differentiates between nature and culture or sex and gender.[37] In the following I address some of the reasons that have been given for this.

Jacques Derrida inspired the rejection of any kind of *binary thinking*. When, according to the main point of this view, two terms exclude each other reciprocally, the first term is defined by means of a negative delimitation of the second. This second term is subordinated not only in the formal meaning of the sequence, but because it includes all that must be negated to constitute the first mentioned term. The usual characterization of this structure of thinking ascribes to it an *abjection of the other*. With this kind of portrayal, these reflections, which at first seem to be devoted only to argumentative logic, take on a tone of moral evaluation. Many authors think this aspect makes the analysis of binary thinking a useful instrument for feminist criticism. Indeed, it reveals a pattern of thinking that shapes different areas of life and has caused lasting harm to women. The abilities and achievements ascribed to men are often defined in a way that positively distinguishes them from characteristics that are assigned to women and evaluated as inadequate. For instance, rationality is ascribed to men but irrationality to women.[38]

Despite its critical potential, Derrida's analysis of binary thinking is susceptible to exaggerated argumentation. The moral or political-legal problems that have to be addressed here cannot be generated by logical forms as such.

Regarding the relations between language and morality, we have to keep in mind that the use of moral categories makes sense only in regard to action (see above). Therefore a moral reproach is only appropriate when human actions lead to individuals or groups being harmed or ignored.[39] When individuals or members of groups are not taken seriously as human beings, this calls for a critical judgment with reference to principles of morality. To raise a moral reproach means to say: "One must not treat human beings like this!" The scope for moral judgments is broader than it may seem at first sight, since certain ways of speaking also have the character of action. Speech-act theory, especially, has dealt with this subject. According to Austin's conception, whether speech has the significance of an action can be seen in the consequences for the persons involved. One example of such a performative utterance is marriage vows. The "I do" spoken in a wedding ceremony has a binding character. And certain forms of

speech are actions insofar as they hurt certain people. Thus oral ut-
terances are appropriately the object of moral disapproval—or even
subject to legal measures, for instance, if libel constitutes grounds for
filing a lawsuit.

What is relevant for feminist criticism of binary oppositions is that
if women are described as other than men and therefore deficient,
then this way of speaking has its equivalent in manifold forms of discrimination. There is a correlation between the widespread penchant
for calling women "irrational" and their being underprivileged in education, professional careers, political decisionmaking, and so on.
The term *discrimination,* which literally means differentiation, expresses this relation between pejorative description and contemptuous treatment. (But this is not a simple model of cause and effect. As
MacKinnon, among others, has shown, oral disqualification does not
necessarily come first; often women's differentness is generated in
oppressive relations before it is expressed in language.)[40]

Discrimination always has the character of action—even if "only"
words are its medium:[41] Certain persons or groups are treated con-
temptuously. A certain attitude is taken: The abjection of the other
comes in because those who speak in this sense face the other with an
air of superiority. This can happen in a relatively unreflected form
when mediated in everyday language. But even if jokes about "female logic" are regarded as a common expression of humor in certain
circles, the finding remains valid that the speaker takes a position of
superiority.

If discrimination is based on an attitude of contempt toward certain persons, then its roots do not lie in a logical form but in a kind
of *dealing* with the other. Therefore the logic of argumentation as a
specific topic is to be distinguished from the moral level. Logical figures do not *eo ipso* call for moral or legal judgment. When they are
used to articulate a certain kind of action, then only this practical aspect, not the logical one, needs to be judged. Therefore, when a disjunction of two reciprocally exclusive concepts is carried out, it does
not necessarily disadvantage certain persons or groups.

A critique of language under the viewpoint of political correctness is exaggerated when it seeks the cause for a moral problem in the realm of logic.[42] Before using any logical structure, one must first examine whether or when it is factually appropriate. This also applies to the complete disjunction. Whoever encumbers the latter *toto genere* takes on a burden of proof. Why should it not be meaningful in the context of a theory of the organism to operate with the concept pair alive/dead,[43] for instance? An across-the-board rejection of the binary opposition eventually questions itself. Any distinction that uses a dichotomy, such as good/bad or responsible/irresponsible, must be discarded—but how is it then possible to denounce the abjection of the other? (We are always confronted with phenomena that cannot be sufficiently determined by dichotomy. In the context of philosophical logic, one way to analyze this fact is the concept of dialectics, which has been debated since antiquity. This differentiation notwithstanding, the distinction proposed here—between the logical structure of a statement and the morally relevant attitude expressed by it—retains its relevance.)

Cartesianism: A reproach that needs further precision

Common objections to a distinction between freedom and corporality are not always based on reservations in regard to logical structure. Often such a distinction is rejected because it supposedly leads to Cartesianism. But this would be too rash, at least in regard to the conception advocated here. According to my understanding, the objection criticizes the unacceptable tearing apart that results from Descartes's distinction between *res cogitans* and *res extensa*. Often this critique is connected with an appeal to undermine modernity's characteristic distinction between *subject* and *object* and to develop an alternative philosophical theory that is based on a unity of both terms.[44] I do not find this line of argument convincing. Although I share the opinion that Descartes's conception leads to a number of difficulties, the distancing discussed here in many regards seems incomprehensible.

A plausible theory of cognition cannot be developed from the simple opposition between the cognitive subject and the cognized object. If such an opposition is introduced, then one ignores that the objects, even if they seem simply given to us, are constituted, and therefore the process of this constitution remains unexplored. Moreover, the perceiving and acting *I* experiences a reification. Interpreted as *res cogitans,* it receives impressions and causes effects, which means that it itself is thought as a kind of given thing. Thus the thinking thing is (albeit invisible) located on the same ontological level as the cognized objects. A problem in this interpretation is that the epistemological question leads into infinite regression.

But showing this or other difficulties in Descartes's conception should not lead to a tabooization. Theories that operate with concepts like *I* or *subject* are universally suspected as Cartesianisms in today's debate, so that legitimate philosophical topics are threatened with elimination. I propose to move two aspects back into focus. In order to create a plausible philosophical theory of cognition, it is not enough to conjure a unity that does not allow an opposition of subject and object. Rather, the postulated unity must be spelled out clearly. This rather trivial point is important in regard to the term *construction,* which is as fashionable as it is underdetermined. Since these difficulties will be picked up again in the following,[45] here I note briefly that the term *construct* is often used in the context of the thesis according to which historically contingent discourses—and not the subject's faculties of reason—are decisive for the genesis of our world of objects. But this thesis makes the question of how objects are constituted not superfluous. It merely leads to a shift since now, with reference to discourses or discursive practices (Foucault is often invoked in this context), questions must be posed about their foundational capacity, questions analogous to those which modern philosophy has elaborated in connection with the term *I.* This also applies for the extreme variant that interprets the term *construction* in such a manner that objects are literally produced by discursive practices, which must explain how and through which faculties this production is achieved. More generally, if the question of the conditions of our world and our actions cannot be rejected, then some of the issues, first debated under the titles *I* or *subject*, are still relevant.[46] Picking up these topics does not lead inevitably to the construction of a thinking thing. This is, I think, the important point for the current debate, since some blanket reproaches of Cartesianism are apparently based on such a misunderstanding. Since Descartes, the terms *I* and *subject* have not been defined in an ontological manner by all authors who work with the terms.

These reflections also concern our understanding of human beings as existing bodily. Ideas that assume two separate entities—mind and body—are untenable. Since they inevitably provoke the question how the composition of these two elements is to be thought, such ideas lead into the difficulties shown above in regard to the "thinking thing." Insofar as the Cartesianism reproach addresses the problem of a missing unity, it is legitimate. But that does not clarify the complex philosophical issue. A theory is needed that does justice to the fact that we experience ourselves as a living bodily existence—that we not only live but also have specific knowledge about living (see above). In the context of feminist discourse, an attempt is made to escape an unacceptable dichotomization through a concept that defines the human being exclusively in recourse to the body. But this leads to an alternative that produces a twofold problem. Such a conception either must remain epistemologically naive or must enrich the concept of physical body *(Körper)* to cover the ability to speak of "my lived body" *(mein Leib),* which also delimits the term *physical body (Körper).*[47] The problem becomes evident, for example, in Eve Browning Cole's concept of the embodied self: "An embodied self can displace the only questionably embodied Cartesian ego. . . . To conceive the self as essentially or intrinsically embodied means to acknowledge the centrality of the physical in human psychology and cognition, for one thing. It means opening the door to the possibility of a bodily wisdom, to revaluing the physical human being, in ways that promise both better metaphysical schemes and more ethical models for human interaction."[48]

Moreover, the following differentiation must be made: Epistemological basic issues, including critical analysis of a naive contrast of I and the object of cognition, must be distinguished from considerations that address our self-understanding. I formulated my suggestion of choosing the perspective of the first person as starting point with regard to this topic. The concept of freedom, as I define it, refers to an experience that we cannot escape: We are continuously confronted with situations in which we must make a decision and act. Methodically, this is about how an experience can be explicated, independently of how the prior epistemological questions are solved.

The reproach of Cartesianism is also critical of power. To some authors it makes no difference whether these are questions of epistemology or of practical experiences. They rather contend that such terms as *I, subject,* or *spirit,* as well as a concept of freedom that is defined by a demarcation from nature, are inseparably connected with a claim to power. One indication they see is that these terms are connected with the hierarchy of the sexes. I address this specific issue later on. But in general such an argument is in danger of mixing different levels. The problem pointed out in regard to the critique of binary oppositions recurs when here a *terminological distinction* is (mis)understood as a *morally relevant action.* For example, the way in which we deal with nature can and must be judged according to moral considerations that also include a critique of power. But to make such an evaluation, we must (even if we do not acknowledge this to ourselves) start from a concept of action and a theoretical differentiation between freedom and nature.

The concept of nature requires further investigation. The objections to Cartesianism that are formulated in the context of feminist discourse contain a legitimate issue insofar as the term *res extensa* leads to considerable difficulties. A philosophical theory that interprets everything empirically given along the lines of a mechanical model cannot do justice to the phenomenon of the living organism.[49] This is also true in regard to the sexually differentiated corporality of the human being. The idea that we are differently constructed machines does not address the growth of organs or processes such as conception, pregnancy, and birth in a philosophically adequate manner. Nor does it offer the conceptual prerequisites to investigate the experience of our bodily existence. (This theoretical deficit, by the way, can be articulated even if a satisfactory alternative theory of the *organic* has not been achieved.) But criticism goes too far when it implies that terms like *I* or *freedom* inevitably lead to the complementary conception of an underdetermined nature that is defined as *res extensa*. (For instance, it would be a misunderstanding to identify Kant's limiting conception of the thing-in-itself with the term *res extensa*.)

Sex/Gender:
How a long-running debate could come to a conclusion

In the following I will examine reservations about my understanding of the relation between freedom and sexually differentiated corporality that may come up with special reference to the sex/gender dyad. This pair of terms was initially developed[50] to distinguish the bodily difference between men and women (sex) on one hand and the symbolic and social constructions such as gender roles on the other.[51] Many now consider this distinction erroneous, but not always on the same grounds.

One form of criticism argues that the terminological differentiation conceals a form of biologism. Elaborating its point, this critique first emphasizes that gender implies a dual configuration in referring to the ideal couple—it relies on a social construction in which *man* and *woman* are defined in the manner of ideal types. Then it draws our attention to the fact that sex and gender are usually linked so as to relate all individuals with a female body to the ideal type woman and all individuals with a male body to the ideal type man. This linkage presents the bone of contention: Does it not necessarily presuppose that both ideal images are "in accordance with nature"? How else could it be considered legitimate to assign the two ideals to two kinds of bodies?[52] Consequently problems arise, which are discussed above in regard to a structure wanted by nature.

Expounding the problems of biologisms, no matter how valid, does not do justice to the intentions that have guided the development of the paired terms *sex/gender.* After all, the term *gender* was not introduced by advocates of a naturalistic foundation of social norms but by authors who wanted to examine the genesis of biologisms. The term *gender* constituted the crucial device in clarifying that concepts of social structures represent a different level from natural conditions.[53] Only in demonstrating that ideas of typical masculine and feminine characteristics are normative concepts does it become possible to explain that such ideals cannot be legitimated in reference to a biological difference of the sexes.

The term *gender* should be judged differently depending on whether it is used as an instrument of critical analysis or a normative injunction. As an instrument of analysis, gender provides a significant premise of feminist research. It is the leading category of diverse studies examining how gender relations have been envisioned and practiced in different cultures and during different historical periods. In addition, the term *gender* has been a valuable tool for the feminist critique of the sciences in exposing a problem that is common in all branches of scholarly research:[54] Often unreflected ideas of gender differences influence scholars' research. Claims of objectivity are in many cases not justified but supply an easy cloak for androcentric statements. (I will elaborate this point in Chapter 3.)

Yet the potential of the concept of gender is limited to analysis and criticism. Problems arise wherever concepts of gender-specific behavior claim to be valid today and in the future.[55] Such a claim assumes that a dichotomized pattern is indispensable. This assumption, however, is unfounded. It is the crucial point of a distinction between sex and gender that ideals and norms of behavior are historically contingent concepts that cannot be derived from nature. Thus it is not clear why the biological difference between men and women should be connected to a dichotomy of images at all.[56] Men for a long time have been provided with a multitude of paradigms for the shaping of their identities, and this is increasingly true for women as well. A number of authors have decided to use the plural form *genders* to discuss gender identity.[57] But this form may imply on the one hand that the ideals, despite their variety, divide into two groups applied either to men or to women. In this case the assumption of natural identity differences has not been overcome. On the other hand it is possible to connect the plural with a multiplication of genders—an idea that is held by a number of authors. But what exactly does it mean? Since the term *gender* is no longer connected to corporal differences, its denotation has to be questioned. To illustrate this problem: If the various tasks in the professional world are no longer distributed according to the principle of typical "male jobs" as well as typical "female jobs," gender identity is no longer important to the choice of profession, but rather individual abilities and interests of people who obtain training or employment. This change indicates a separation of work from gender and not a multiplying of gender identities. In this context the term *genders* does not prove appropriate.

The idea of a multiplication of genders has shifted in the current debate. Derrida, for example, as well as a number of authors inspired by his thinking, uses the term *genders* in the context of a theory of sexuality. In this case the term is directed against conventional categories of sexual preference—*heterosexuality* and *homosexuality*. Rejecting this kind of schematization, the argument suggests that each specific sexual relation should be recognized and realized in its own special quality. The idea of multiplication has been developed to encourage all individuals to develop different genders in the course of their sexual biographies.[58] It is certainly legitimate to make us more aware of the fact that each of our sexual relations, just like our relations in general, has a unique and distinctive character. Natural conditions, including our sexually differing bodies, can be dealt with differently in each specific situation. But the term *genders* might be misleading in this context. Even though the term is used in its plural form, *gender* remains a general term that suggests a typology which aims at subsuming individual cases and consequently foils the intended emphasis on diversity. If one characterizes oneself as belonging to different cultures, one avoids a homogeneous representation but nevertheless fits into given contexts. Similarly, the use of the term *genders,* despite avoiding a dual differentiation, seems to be trapped in the tradition of psychoanalytic concepts of bisexuality (which presuppose certain patterns of sexual preference when trying to reveal their combination in individual beings). Certainly the term *genders* serves the intention of outgrowing every typology. Derrida formulated it this way: "When we speak of sexual difference, we must distinguish between opposition and difference. Opposition is two; opposition is man/woman. Difference, on the other hand, can be an indefinite number of sexes."[59] With this multitude, however, the concept of gender becomes devoid of any distinction; in the true sense of the word it becomes meaningless.

Thus use of the term *gender* only in its plural form does not go far enough. This insight invites a further consideration: A number of authors argue in favor of obliterating the term *gender* in terms of the ideals of a free society. Since norms for interpersonal relations cannot be derived from nature, this proposal seems to be based on good reasons. I will show that convincing arguments cannot be provided for a gendered distribution either in regard to moral principles and virtues or in regard to legal regulations of rights and obligations. This statement implies no denial of bodily differences. The point is that we should not be coerced into a dichotomous code of behavior merely because we were born with a male or a female body. In short, seriously thinking through the differentiation of sex and gender would result in a demand to abolish man and woman as social categories.[60]

Now let us examine the second argument against differentiating between sex and gender. In this case it is the term *sex* that is under scrutiny. The argument maintains that everything we call natural is bestowed on us in the form of language. In accordance with the linguistic turn of contemporary philosophy, it is pointed out that natural phenomena are inaccessible to us beyond language. This general conclusion currently dominates the dispute over a corporeal difference of the sexes. In this context, it was first emphasized that the understanding of the structure and function of male and female bodies has changed quite a lot in the course of time. Thomas Laqueur investigated the history of ideas on human sexual organs.[61] According to Laqueur, in traditional European ideas we find two totally different beliefs that succeeded each other, which he called the one-sex model and the two-sex model. Referring to numerous cases, he argues that from ancient times until well on in the modern age, the predominant opinion was that there is only one type of sex organ; the difference between male and female bodies consists in this sex organ being in one case external and in the other turned inside. Laqueur emphasizes that this conviction was retained after scientific methods such as dissection enabled medical scientists to study the human body empirically. During the eighteenth century "a new model of radical dimorphism" was substituted for the one-sex thinking. "The conception of the woman now placed special emphasis on an anatomy and physiology of incomparability."[62] From now on the female body was regarded as absolutely different from the male body in relation to the sexual organs and in all other aspects.[63] According to Laqueur, this change is closely connected to the development of a middle-class social order. The exclusion of woman from the public sphere, resolutely carried through as never before, received scientific legitimization: "Two biological sexes were developed in order to justify the new social roles."[64]

This situatedness of knowledge underwent a constitutional-theoretical interpretation. Nowadays a "soft" interpretation is frequently rejected: Distinguishing between a historically independent "natural difference of the sexes" on the one hand and divergent, historically contingent descriptions of this difference on the other is declined.[65]

Consequently a "strong" interpretation prevails. It contends that because natural phenomena are not accessible to us beyond language, it
is wrong to assume a preset difference of the sexes; the task is rather
to inquire how biological differences are constituted through discursive practices. This line of thought results in the crucial statement
that sex is an "effect of discourse."[66] The differentiation between nature and culture is discarded as the notion of a nature independent
from us is culturally generated. "The 'penis' is always already constituted by the 'phallus,'" as Maihofer gives expression to this
thought.[67]

The conception of a discursive construction of sex (the constitution thesis) can be spelled out differently. Basically there are two options, depending on how the question concerning the possible
reference of language is answered. Both, however, lead to problems.
One option is to attribute to discourses the ability to literally produce. This kind of argument characteristically uses the term *effect* in
the sense of the dyad cause/effect. This applies, for example, to Butler's discussion of how discourses develop into matter.[68] According to
Butler's theory, everything that appears to us as naturally given can
be traced back to a "process of materialization, that stabilizes over
time to produce the effect of boundary, fixity, and surface we call
matter."[69] For Butler, in reference to Foucault (or her particular reading of Foucault), social norms determine this process.[70] She describes
materiality as the "dissimulated effect of power"[71] and therefore
thinks it appropriate to ask, "Through what regulatory norms is sex
itself materialized?"[72] With the formulation of this question, the perspective has changed inexplicitly: The topic that was originally discussed in terms of the contemporary philosophy of language has
become a matter of ontology.[73] The linguistic turn that serves as the
starting point for this kind of argument primarily aims at a critique of
knowledge: We can know nothing about nature as such because we
cannot transcend the limits of language. This thesis addresses two
kinds of boundaries: If we can say nothing about a world that exists
independently from us, we can neither claim nor deny the existence

of such a world. Butler replaces the thesis of our epistemological re-
strictedness with an ontological conception that asserts the nonexis-
tence of a given nature and maintains that seemingly natural
conditions can be traced back to a materialization of discursive practices.[74]

This shift in focus becomes obvious in the ambiguous usage of
the central term *constitute*. The terminological choice suggests at first
a link to the epistemological concepts, known from the history of
philosophy, of an interaction between sensory experience and reason.
Because any reference to something given is ruled out as Cartesian,
however, the term *constitute* loses its specific meaning and eventually
becomes synonymous with *produce*. It does not refer to the way an
empirical reality appears to us, as it used to (e.g., in transcendental
philosophy), but refers directly to the genesis of things. So Butler explicitly insists on sex, like matter in general, being discursively produced.[75] A number of other authors hold a similar concept of
production. Donna Haraway, for example, writes: "Bodies . . . are
not born; they are made. . . . One is not born a woman, Simone de
Beauvoir correctly insisted. It took the political-epistemological terrain of postmodernism to be able to insist on a co-text to de Beauvoir's: one is not born an organism. Organisms are made; they are
constructs of a world-changing kind."[76]

To advocate such a pointed view of social and symbolic construction is to take on a burden of proof. How should we interpret the
idea of discursive practices actually producing materiality or, more
precisely, organisms?[77] What premises are attached to a normative discourse with a potential like that? One cannot avoid being reminded
of ideas of creation: "In the beginning was the Word." This, however, may arouse the suspicion that Foucault's theory of normative
power is interpreted here in terms of a divine omnipotence.[78] In any
case, the proposed conception of materiality seems to depart from
the philosophical terrain of argumentation. In regard to human sexuality, the argument under investigation implies that we start out without any corporeal qualities and decide on our sex based on the

structure of discursive practices.[79] These objections could be countered with a number of passages in Butler's texts that point in another direction. It could be argued, for example, that the process of
constituting sex is often characterized by presupposing a rudimentary
form of pliable flesh.[80] Some of Butler's elaborations give cause for
this reading. In this case a problem of inconsistency arises, but I am
not going to explore this problem here.[81] My core concern is to investigate the viability of the strong version of the constitution
thesis.[82]

At this point, the second variant of viewing the potential of language needs to be analyzed. The model of formation claims that
what appears as nature is always already a product of the cultivating
capability of discursive practices. This idea of formation requires raw
material, and thus the question arises of what this given is made of.
Again we encounter the term *materiality,* but this time it refers to a
prerequisite of the constitution of sex. This usage of the term evokes
the idea of a formless substance that is newly shaped according to
particular discursive practices. According to Elizabeth Grosz, "Flesh,
a raw, formless, bodily materiality, the mythical 'primary material,' is
constituted, through corporeal inscriptions (juridical, medical, puni-
tive, disciplinary), as a distinctive body capable of acting in distinctive
ways."[83] On closer examination, serious problems arise, and I will
consider three of them. First, an infinite regress seems inevitable. The
corporeal materiality itself, which is presupposed, is already mediated
through language. To call it "formless" does not refute this diagnosis. As soon as a term is used at all, the question begins to shift and
one must search for a materiality of the materiality. Second, an unac-
counted-for change of topic emerges. In this case too the analytical
approach to philosophy of language, which was referred to in the beginning, is being exchanged for an ontological perspective by assigning to discursive practices the capacity of actually producing physical
differences between the sexes.

The third difficulty, in my view, leads directly to the heart of the
whole problem. It results from calling the raw material of which

Grosz and other authors speak *flesh*.[84] This choice of terms can be challenged by showing that flesh belongs to a language which assumes that animals (including humans) exist. According to its semantic content, the term *flesh* does not imply the idea of atomism, according to which all that is empirically given is put together from the smallest components. Neither does it refer to a malleable material that, through discursive practices, can be processed into animals and therefore also into human bodies. Flesh exists only in dependence on the existence of animals. Without this background, the word *flesh* makes no sense. One could object that this reflection fails to address the actual issue. One could argue that Grosz intended to make a different point that should be taken seriously despite her terminological problems. According to this understanding, her theory is not so much about the genesis of corporality in general as about the constitution of sex as bodily difference. The discursive processing, in this case, presupposes raw material consisting of living organisms, while the shaping of female and male sexual characteristics occurs only following an inscription of juridical, medical, and other disciplinary norms. But this train of thought does not dispel the problem. Obviously what is claimed to be the result of the constitution has already been presupposed. Living animals, including human organisms, cannot be understood without sexual difference. For flesh to come into existence, there already had to be female and male individuals who ensured the preservation of their species.[85]

In the end Grosz, like Butler, does not consistently stick to her concept of constitution. The discursive practices from which sex differences are said to derive are determined by regulating norms of the juridical, medical, and disciplinary kind. The inconsistency lies in the fact that these norms always presuppose natural givens exactly where they intend to regulate them. (I will return to that.)

Notable too is a striking difference between the thesis of the discursive origin of sex and its limited application. Obviously *in concreto* one speaks only of human beings. But how should sexual difference be thought of in regard to animals and plants? Anybody who supports the constitution thesis appears to be trapped in an argumentative crisis. Strictly speaking, one would also have to claim that bodily differences between hens and cocks are effects of juridical, medical, and other disciplinary norms, but this does not happen, probably because it would not sound plausible. In this context the historical dimension of the problem becomes obvious. Considering that norms indisputably are subject to cultural change, and maintaining the constitution thesis, the idea would be that the biological features of plants, animals, and human beings are newly created, as well as differently described, in each period of time.[86] Some historical periods could even go without this creative process. The helplessness of constructivist thinking in regard to a philosophy of nature here becomes all but clear.[87]

Thus we see that propositions for interpreting sex as discursively generated lead to aporia in regard to a philosophy of language, an epistemology, and a philosophy of nature. But something else has come up as well. The reference to Foucault and the central position of the term *regulating norms* imply that the core motivation of the whole argument lies in the criticism of power. This suggests that both results should be correlated. Likely the aporia just mentioned are caused by the impetus to criticize power in the most radical form possible, especially in regard to control of our sexual behavior. The aim of uncovering all the interconnections of power obviously has led to a quick blow. Consequently, questions that needed specific philosophical analysis were rashly crossed with each other. In contrast to such a strategy, I shall try to disentangle the different levels of inquiry, since I believe that a differentiation of three subject matters is necessary. One should distinguish between, first, the topic of human freedom; second, the question of the constitution of empirical objects; and third, the level of theory of science. Some links exist between these three issues, but these actual relations can only be reconstructed on the basis of the suggested distinction. To distinguish different levels is not equal to claiming they are also *de facto* separate. Moreover, it could be quite hard in particular cases to decide which contribution each level has made. But problems of judgment should not entice anybody to evaluate the project of differentiation as unsuccessful. Whoever concludes hastily, as happens frequently, that there are no different levels involved, gives up the possibility of a careful analysis of complex interrelations.

Power and criticism of power have their genuine place in the sphere of freedom. Regulating norms (whether we experience them as external forces or have internalized them) instruct us to turn our actions in a certain direction. One effect is that our perception of reality will be correspondingly accentuated. In a community marked by racist politics, skin color becomes a conspicuous phenomenon, whereas it is hardly noticeable—almost invisible—where it has not gained social importance. But although regulating norms may influence our perception, they should not be confused with the potential of language or reason to constitute empirical objects. Skin color is not produced in a biologically comprehensible sense through racial discourses but is highlighted by such discourses. We therefore have to distinguish between the level of empirical knowledge on the one hand, and that of an assessment influenced by a particular claim of power on the other. As I am concerned only with emphasizing this fundamental difference, there is no need to elucidate more specific questions. Thus it is not necessary here to reflect on recent developments in the philosophy of language or theory of knowledge, or even to consider more precisely to what extent advocates of the constitution theory adopt and link elements from philosophical traditions that are not compatible. It is not of primary significance here *how* the constitution of empirical objects should be philosophically defined; rather, *that* it is always already achieved before power can be a matter of concern.

Juridical, medical, and disciplinary regulating norms, which are claimed to be the source of what we consider natural facts, presuppose natural conditions. Only in confrontation with an already constituted reality, as well as corresponding options of action, can there be an interest in regulation. Without the question of how to deal with certain facts, there would not be any norms. It cannot be denied that orders and rules may change realities, but this is a secondary aspect. First and foremost it has to be stated that the already constituted reality is a *conditio sine qua non* of norms. For example, even though it seems true that demands for a specific kind of posture and walking, with which children are confronted from early childhood on in regard to their sex, lead to a kind of "ingestion" of these norms, the existence of children—of their corporality and their capability of controlling their movements—is still required for such regulations to be developed at all.

The aim of power critiques suffers no restriction through this kind of differentiation. On the contrary, only now can it be deployed in an argumentatively plausible form. As long as norms are ascribed the function of object constitution, criticism of power implies the demand to actually create things in a new way. According to this logic, racist politics can be countered only with an alternative description of the human body that *denies* differences in skin color. Only if the point of norms exists in their judgment of actions (and not in their producing an empirical reality) can a criticism of racism be formulated that does not employ a vulnerable counterconcept. Now it can be demanded that skin color should *not be relevant* anymore in regard to the social position or citizenship of a person. The same could be said in reference to the biological difference of the sexes. We are not forced to deny bodily differences between men and women in order to reject sexist politics. Rather, it should be clarified that belonging to a certain sex must not influence decisions regarding education, income, civil rights, and so on.

The current widespread haziness about this point invites a recurrence of naturalistic concepts. The constitution thesis seems based on a false naturalistic conclusion. Both versions of this thesis seem to hold that the idea of a given corporeal difference between men and women introduces inescapable norms, including the enforced heterosexuality criticized by Butler.[88] When we assume this, the line of argumentation becomes comprehensible. Now we can realize why it

seems important to show that (and how) regulating norms have always already defined natural conditions. It also becomes clear how
the widely shared conviction emerged that disciplinary norms regarding our sexual behavior can be thrown off—and consequently free
spaces can be created[89]—only if the bodily differences between
women and men are denied. (Of course, problems are not resolved
because their place of origin can be named.)

The empirical sciences also presuppose a given world. Hempel's
concept[90]—even with the legitimate criticism that has been directed
against the program of unified science—can still claim validity as it
formulates the thesis that all empirical research is initiated in the context of everyday bearings. For example, we observe that water freezes
and want to know how it happened, or we develop an interest in
plants and animals that serve us as food and want to know more
about their growing conditions. This kind of questioning belongs to
everyday language that mediates a given world to us. More precisely,
empirical science presupposes not just the constitution of objects but
also the sphere of freedom. As numerous studies on the relationship
of theory and practice have shown, the initial questions of scholarly
inquiry, be it the natural sciences, the social sciences, or the humanities, are always formulated in contexts where people as agents try to
specify their options.[91]

With this background, we can sort out the results of Laqueur's research. His two models of understanding sex have often been assigned a constitutive character. In contrast to this interpretation, we
should bear in mind that what is true for science in general is also
true for a theory of comparability and difference of female and male
bodies. It commences with the fact that we are directly confronted
with the differences of the sexes in our everyday lives and therefore
search for a more precise understanding of them. Furthermore, this
difference remains; the everyday empirical world cannot simply be replaced through progressive research. If, as Laqueur asserts, the one-
sex model predominated for a long time, it cannot be concluded, as
is repeatedly done in the current debate, that Europeans living some

centuries ago did not know about a bodily difference of the sexes. That there always has been some idea of corporeal differences and their function is proved by the fact that a new generation of humans was always born. Moreover, how did terms like *woman* and *man* develop without such an idea? (Laqueur's bold terminology is misleading. Even the one-sex model contains a clear differentiation, since female sex organs are seen as the inversion of male organs, not as identical to them.)

Nonetheless, the realms of science and everyday language are not wholly separate. Questions that represent the starting point of science aim at providing a different picture for everyday orientation. Sometimes this leads to striking results—medical theories undoubtedly influence how we observe human bodies, even how we experience our own body. But it does not follow that scientific language can or will supplant everyday perspectives entirely. Doctors still depend on patients' statements about their condition. In general, despite the influence of the sciences on our view of the world, we move on different levels. We assume that scientists develop theories about contexts of which we also have knowledge apart from the sciences.

Our knowledge *that* we are mortal lies on a different level from scientific conclusions about the indications of death, time of death, and so on. This difference does not dissolve just because we orient our actions, when someone dies, on such scientific conclusions. The same can be said in regard to sexual difference. Our knowledge of men and women lies on a level other than anatomical, physiological, or biochemical theories. Strictly speaking, the history of science and ideas addresses this difference more or less explicitly when it studies "the development of ideas about . . . (death, sexes, etc.)." "About . . ." implies the assumption of a given phenomenon that has in the course of time been differently defined.[92]

The reservations I just voiced are not directed against the core intention of the constitution theory. If it seeks to reveal that our corporality has always been connected to symbolic constructions and social norms, it promotes a legitimate cause that leads to interesting questions. My objections are focused on specific proposals for the achievement of that intention and not the intention as such. In my view, we are only able to investigate the constructive design of our corporality on the basis of the disentanglement of philosophical queries. Only by not overstretching this topic into a *prima philosophia* can it be dealt with in a manner that will escape being attacked as a category mistake. Human bodies, including our own, are never purely natural, while *natural* here means an already constituted world. There are always two elements involved. Like the sun, moon, and stars, our bodies are phenomena that we subsume under the term *nature* because we did not create them as we do technical items or works of art; yet from the very beginning our corporality is subject to interpretation and styling. There are early interventions; for example, we are trained to sleep at night, eat during the day, and use the potty. Our biorhythms are superseded by forms of upbringing. These processes were studied by Hegel, who saw continual repetition becoming habit that eventually turns into the foundation for a "shaping and creation of corporality." In this context Hegel formulated the idea, often employed today, of second nature.[93]

Since such development takes place from birth or even before, it could rightfully be said that we do not know our natural body. This insight, however, is not an adequate reason to dissolve the nature/culture dyad. Distinguishing between both terms does not presuppose two spheres that are separated from each other. A glance at the etymology makes this clear. If culture originally meant farming, the term aimed from the very beginning to express the concept of working on nature.[94] The point in distinguishing nature and culture is to differentiate the roots of certain phenomena in contrast to attempts at monocausal explanations. To abandon this distinction is to find ease in oversimplification, but it prevents a reconstruction of more complex conditions. Without this distinction, we would hardly be able, for instance, to do theoretical justice to experiences that indicate a resistance in our body to cultural norms—experiences of the "body that has so to speak become independent," according to Plessner.[95] Even everyday experiences, like failing to fall asleep, cannot be analyzed in the detailed manner that Merleau-Ponty,[96] among others, has presented.[97]

Two different components are involved in the sex of our body. First, we find that our body exhibits or develops certain sex characteristics, which we take as natural conditions (in the above specified sense of being mediated through everyday language), just as we confirm sexual differences in animals and plants. The widely held view that only two types of sex exist must be discharged. Scientific research has established a catalog of criteria to ascertain the sexual difference in human bodies. The catalog consists of distinguishable features that include the internal and external sex organs, as well as chromosomes and hormones. The application of this set of criteria has revealed that hardly any individual possesses all the features that characterize either a female or a male. Most people, however, have a significant accumulation of the features of one sex, although a considerable number display a combination that does not allow their attribution to either the female or the male sex.[98] These findings imply no need to deny *that* our body shows a particular sexual condition; they rather illustrate that natural facts are much more complex than generally assumed.

The second component is of a historical character. All cultures and historical periods have developed norms that regulate actions in regard to bodily differences. Usually the norms are put into action as soon as the child is sexually classified at birth and the consequences correspond to what has already been ascertained. It is not enough to speak of training in certain kinds of behavior; actually, it is more the fashioning of the bodies themselves (a process that I will examine below). Gender norms usually have repressive effects. Typically, when a society adheres to two complementary gender images, it seeks to present biological facts in a doctrinaire fashion as strictly dichotomous.[99] In particular cases this leads to the exercise of force with severe consequences. If newborn babies are always assigned to one of the two sexes, those who cannot be clearly subsumed under the schematic for the above mentioned reasons understand the specific condition of their body, when they learn of it, as negatively connoted.[100] (This is only one of a number of examples, since the adoption of dichotomous ideals also causes experiences of repression for numerous other groups of people.)[101]

When we observe individual people and define them as men or as women, it is not only biological sex characteristics that give them a male or female appearance. The corporeal manifestations of all individuals are marked by the ideal images that were decisive during their socialization.[102] That corporality is to some extent fashioned is shown by the fact that some processes which may at first seem purely natural are actually historically variable. The age of sexual maturity, for instance, has continually changed during European history.[103] Such shaping is part of the specific condition of human corporality and cannot be evaded. If gender-specific norms are rejected in the future, for example, this idea would also have an impact on our behavior, and would find corporeal expression.

Even though such inscriptions inevitably occur, they do not legitimize a rash suspension of all differentiations. By fashioning our bodies, we presuppose them to be something given. To illustrate this once again by an example: The human face is not just part of an organism but displays an expression that reveals something about a person's social experiences and therefore is subject to change. Yet our experiences can be expressed only because we possess a face in the biological sense. Why then should we avoid differentiating these two components by employing the pair of terms *sex/gender*? Shouldn't we rather plead for a specific use of this terminology?[104] The sex/gender dyad offers a suitable instrument to demonstrate that social norms must be distinguished from bodily conditions, even though they may be literally incorporated. I insist on the fruitfulness of this distinction because the current debate is marked by some striking theoretical insufficiencies in this regard. Since feminist authors today are almost required to do without the differentiation proposed here, theories oscillate between two forms of reductionism. Body and discourse are alternately used as the leading categories of monocausal explanations. Another version of this problem occurs when a unity of nature and culture is assumed (see, for example, Alison M. Jaggar[105] and Elizabeth Grosz[106]).

Avant la lettre, Simone de Beauvoir already employed the distinction of *sex* and *gender*. Her often quoted statement—"One is not born a woman, but, rather, becomes one"[107]—cannot be understood as denying the biological characteristics of the female body. De Beauvoir rather elucidates the traditional normative interpretation of such facts and the severe consequences for women on whom these norms have been imposed from childhood.

2

ART AND FEMININITY

Art is gendered

WHY HAS THERE NEVER BEEN A FEMALE Michelangelo or a female Mozart? Feminist theoreticians are often confronted with questions such as these, without being expected to answer seriously. The form of the question suggests the validity of the statement that women have a deficient cultural capacity.[1] Supporters of this statement do not always refer to Freud's scientific wording, nor to later modifications of his theory.[2] They seldom refer to earlier authors who held similar opinions before the development of psychoanalysis in a tradition that goes back centuries.[3] This view has become a commonplace hardly worthy of an explanation.

In response to this problem, in the late 1960s and early 1970s a feminist aesthetics project emerged.[4] Since then a polyvalent debate has developed that can best be analyzed by unfolding the often interlacing approaches that have developed.[5] In the following discussion I take up a few central themes and make no claim to completeness. I will show that it is reasonable to distinguish a broader definition of the term from the question of how or whether one can speak in a narrower philosophical sense of feminist aesthetics.

One argumentation level consists in questioning common clichés through intellectual and social history. The statement that women lack artistic talent creates a false impression. Because it is presented as an assessment of facts, its normative character remains invisible. One who assumes that art history presents an asymmetry between the sexes and goes on to investigate the possible causes encounters a cliché: The idea that only men were capable of true genius. For centuries, as numerous historical studies show, this idea has been the basis for a discriminatory treatment of women in education as well as the way their productions were perceived. Today the "deconstruction of the cult of the genius"[6] is broadly accepted. Nature, in the sense of talent, is not considered the sole precondition for artistic creativity. Social context is also considered: To what extent do opportunities exist for acquiring manual competencies and learning to engage already existing forms of artistic expression? It is significant that women have found it almost impossible—at least in European history—to be accepted by master artists or art academies.[7] Since women's access to working artists has thus been restricted, how could it be surprising that the quantity and quality of production reflects an imbalance between the sexes?[8] The consequences of the traditional exclusion of women extend into the present. The conditions of admission to institutions of artistic education have changed in many countries in accordance with the principle of formal equality; nonetheless, experience suggests that women artists still receive less support than their male colleagues.[9]

This asymmetry is further amplified in the reception of works of art. In our time the cliché mentioned above still affects the perception and evaluation of artistic works. The case of the *Portrait du Mlle. Charlotte du Val d'Ognes* is exemplary. As long as this painting was ascribed to Jacques-Louis David, critics gave it the highest recognition. This changed suddenly when it became known that not David but Constance Marie Charpentier painted the picture.[10] Another variant of this problem is the differing application of general categories, for instance, applied art. While works in media that are usually more accessible for women, such as pottery or embroidery, are often excluded through this labeling from the field of genuine art, this does not happen to architecture, a traditionally male domain, although this too is applied art.[11] The disqualifying attitude is often evident even where it is not formulated explicitly, for instance, in the art market. Female artists are still less present in exhibitions and galleries than male artists, and their works generally bring lower prices. This asymmetrical reception ultimately found its way into the history of art. Women who, despite all obstacles, achieved much in painting and music, often were—and are—neglected; many renowned art guides do not include their names.[12] Therefore the question of where women painters and composers are to be found should not be addressed to feminist theoreticians but to those who represent art and music history.

The diagnosis that art is gendered is therefore legitimate.[13] If the term *feminist aesthetics* is understood in a broader sense, then its definition is based on this diagnosis. The term embraces a broad spectrum of questions and analyses that investigate the "operation of gender throughout the Western art world"[14] and develop alternatives.[15]

Engaging methods of intellectual and social history also results in a quest to recover women artists of the past and rewrite the so-called general history of the arts. This kind of research is part of the project of women's and gender history that has developed since the 1970s and focuses, in all aspects of history, on the experience of women or gender relations.[16] (The ongoing investigations of the history of women philosophers also belong to this project.) The leading motivation of the quest was put into words by Walter Benjamin, who in criticizing the practice of historiography pleads for "winning the past from conformity which is about to overwhelm it."[17] This approach to art history has produced a great number of academic studies and has initiated exhibitions and performances of works of once forgotten women artists.

A further project examines the representation of women and the relation between the sexes in literature and the fine arts as well as in operas, songs, and films.[18] These studies generally agree that these

representations have predominantly been shaped by masculine imagi-
nations. (The term *masculine* in current usage refers to the patterns
of thought and action typical for men in the Western tradition, but it
does not connote an assumption of biological determinism. It would
be inadmissible to insinuate that male artists inevitably mediate masculine conceptions.) The world of imagination that has no place for
the artistic creativity of women is often evident in the productions
themselves, as well as art education and the art market. Feminist research has made it clear that this should not be underestimated. Foucault's considerations on the power of discourse help us see the
inadequacy of the notion of art as largely dependent on the zeitgeist
and the artist as simply a child of his times—a notion that is often
presented in an exculpatory manner. The representation of women[19]
in accordance with patriarchal ideas not only reflects social reality but
supports gender politics that give the cliché its social effectiveness.[20]
(This normative aspect is especially obvious in Western literature of
the eighteenth and early nineteenth centuries. The bourgeois family
model at the center of numerous literary works of the era was not
consistent with social reality but had recently developed in opposition to it, especially feudal forms of social life.)[21]

The critique of the masculine imagination in art is also articulated
in the medium of art itself. Women artists, for instance, restage traditional images of women, presenting them as clichés.[22] The work of
photographer Cindy Sherman has received worldwide recognition.
Other women artists try to depict experiences connected with their
bodies and the conventional world of women from the internal perspective. Paintings by Frida Kahlo are internationally known examples of this. Another form of confrontation explores alternatives to
the patriarchal images of man and woman. If it is true that art has
participated in gender politics, this social potential can also be used
with subversive intentions. The term *androgyny* regains significance
in this context, while postmodernism supports a broad deconstruction of the heterosexual matrix.[23]

Sometimes productions of this kind are viewed as the only form adequate to realize artistically the theoretical program of a feminist aesthetic. But in regard to the broad version of the term that I propose, this restriction would have regrettable consequences. Critically confronting femininity clichés in art goes far enough only if the envisaged alternative challenges the given discrimination in its full breadth. If we demand that women with artistic ambitions have the same chances as their male colleagues, this implies giving women the freedom to choose their topics and the means to express themselves. When women predominantly get attention for tackling the gender problem in some way or another, this means that again differences are made by sex. There is the danger that genuine art will again be defined in opposition to the work of women. The demand that art by women which does not focus on gender also be taken seriously is one of the core concerns of a feminist aesthetic—one that is congruent with the self-understanding of many women artists.[24]

Those who like to raise questions such as the one cited at the beginning of the chapter might try to circumvent these asymmetries and exclusionary mechanisms entirely, arguing as follows: Even if all these varieties of discrimination can be verified historically, what does it prove? The fact of discrimination alone is insufficient evidence that women are equally capable of artistic creativity as men. Could there not be differences between the sexes that are not based on historically contingent conditions but are constant? Thus the statement of deficiencies in women's cultural competency is brought again to the fore. Psychoanalytical theory has undertaken the most ambitious attempt to provide a scientific foundation for this thesis. Therefore we turn to this area of feminist aesthetics, in which I confine myself to the writings of Freud.[25]

Sigmund Freud and the woman artist

Given the usual boundaries between disciplines, a book on feminist philosophy need not deal with psychoanalytical concepts. But this would be shortsighted for two reasons. First, in today's philosophical debate—under the influence of postmodernism and deconstruction—theories of psychoanalytical provenance are continually encountered; second, in view of the often uncritical mixing of language games, it seems especially important to reflect on the differences between the methods that are used.

Authors who raise feminist objections to psychoanalysis refer not only to Freud but to a number of different theories that have been elaborated following his research. The more general treatments tend to suffer from a lack of sharpness in distinctions. Freud has been criticized for claims he never made by authors "violently rejecting a Freud who is not Freud," as Juliet Mitchell observes.[26] This problem can be avoided by concentrating on Freud. In the following discussion I critically analyze some of Freud's texts, but not with the intention of questioning the entire project of psychoanalysis. When Freud followed the genesis of early childhood desire—and when he made the neurosis-generating condition of the bourgeois family a subject of science—he performed a theoretical change of direction that also proved a decisive prerequisite for feminist-motivated research.

What theoretical achievements does psychoanalysis seek with a view toward treating patients? In the opening passages of *Lectures on the Introduction to Psychoanalysis*[27] Freud explains that he is interested in a specific concept of the soul. Freud sees "the psychic" (his words) as a separate realm, so to speak, located between the body and consciousness. In arguing for this double distinction, Freud emphasizes that psychoanalysis must stay clear of any prerequisite foreign to it— anatomical, chemical, or physiological.[28] Taking Freud at his word, certain common objections seem unwarranted. Although a number of critics have argued (in regard to the significance Freud assigned to sexual difference in the sense of bodily sex characteristics) that psychoanalytical theory implies a biological determinism, this objection contradicts Freud's explicit intention. This critique can be maintained only if it shows that Freud, in spite of his clear statement, nevertheless interprets the "anatomical, chemical, or physiological" conditions as fundamental.

The distinction between the the psychic and consciousness brings the conception of the subconscious to the fore. Psychoanalysis "maintains that there is . . . unconscious thinking and unconscious wishing."[29] It tries to explain the formation of this thinking and wishing in the course of infantile sexual development (discussed below). Let us first consider the relation of the subconscious to conscious thinking and wishing. At this point Freud turns his attention to human cultural achievements with the statement that "sexual impulses have contributed invaluably to the highest cultural, artistic, and social achievements of the human mind."[30] In Freud's elucidation of this thought the term sublimation plays a decisive role. Not only the genesis but also the continuation of "cultural work" depends on the fact that "energy is turned aside from its sexual goal and diverted towards other ends, no longer sexual and socially more valuable."[31] At first the question of how this relationship is to be understood remains open. Although strong formulations suggest that processes of sublimation (and therefore the sex drive) form the basis of culture, Freud calls them only "contributions not to be underestimated." It remains to be clarified what the other "contributions" are and how they are connected. (I will return to this topic.)

In regard to women, Freud concludes that they have "less capacity for sublimating their instincts than men."[32] That means that they are less capable of participating in cultural achievements. Freud states explicitly that women have "little sense of justice"[33] and he agrees with the common opinion that "women have made few contributions to the discoveries and inventions in the history of civilization."[34] He asks whether techniques of braiding and weaving should be excluded from this verdict in a way that does not challenge the general statement. Freud expresses the belief that these techniques could have their unconscious origin in feminine shame—in the intention to conceal "genital deficiency."[35] He adds that women can be credited with the modest achievement of imitation: "Nature herself would seem to have given the model which this achievement imitates by causing the growth at maturity of the pubic hair that conceals the genitals. The step that remained to be taken lay in making the threads adhere to one another, while on the body they stick into the skin and are only matted together."[36] One can hardly fail to link these considerations with the disqualification—still common today—of artistic production using weaving or quilting. That we have to discuss Sigmund Freud and the woman artist should be clear by this point. The following reflections move beyond this problem to focus on Freud's opinions of "woman's nature" in general.[37]

Freud identified the cause of woman's sublimation deficiency as the fact that "the development of the little girl into a normal woman is the more difficult and complicated since it embraces two tasks for which there is no counterpart in the development of the man."[38] The girl has to change "erotogenic zone and love object" while both are kept "by the more fortunate man."[39] Before Freud begins to explain this difference more closely in his lecture 34, "Femininity," he repeats the empirical claim of psychoanalysis: "It brings forward nothing but observed facts, almost without any speculative additions."[40] I emphasize this since I will try to show that there are many good reasons to question this claim.

In the development of the libido in early childhood there is, according to Freud, no substantial difference between boy and girl. This is especially true in regard to the phallic stage: "With their entry into the phallic phase the differences between the sexes are completely eclipsed by their agreements."[41] Freud focuses on the fact that children of this age masturbate. But how does he describe the similarity? "We are now obliged to recognize," he notes, "that the little girl is a little man."[42] This formulation is of consequence for Freud's whole theory. It is based on his opinion that the clitoris is a "penis-equivalent."[43] With this view, he starts to deviate from a purely descriptive procedure. Beginning with his characterization of the girl's body, his attempt to do the empirical facts justice with a specific terminology gives way to indirect descriptions through the medium of the comparison. The body of the boy becomes the yardstick—in a rather unmetaphorical sense—to which the body of the girl is compared. The statement of equivalence quickly turns into a description of deficits. This line of thought also shapes Freud's remarks on child masturbation. While the focus here is on the internal perspective of children—their experience of being able to satisfy lust—Freud abandons it in favor of an outer perspective in which the male model dominates. The little girl appears as a "little man" and only under this precondition can Freud speak of a "phallic phase" both sexes go through. "It brings forward nothing but observed facts, almost without any speculative additions." This claim can hardly be considered fulfilled. What can be observed and stated as a fact is that the little girl knows how "to get pleasure by the excitation of her clitoris," but not that she behaves in a "masculine way" while doing so.[44] Freud's belief in the empirical validity of his conclusion has consequences that should not be underestimated: A scientific appearance is generated for a speculation in which parts of women's infantile sexual experiences are viewed as unfeminine, via a kind of retrospective expropriation.

These difficulties also concern Freud's central point that the girl, unlike the boy, has to change her erogenous zones. But why is a change necessary? Would it not be possible to speak of an additional dimension? If the excitement of the clitoris is apostrophized as "male," then it has to be excluded when a "feminine" sexuality is defined. In this sense Freud refers to the "truly feminine vagina."[45] But this polarization is not mandatory. We must distinguish between the generative function of certain organs on the one hand, and sexual sensations on the other. If the vagina is assigned an exclusive meaning in Freud's argument, then we may suspect that both levels remain fairly unseparated and the sexuality of the woman is investigated with a focus on procreation. Such a conception agrees with the identification of the terms *woman* and *mother*, which marks the traditional gender image that was characteristic of the social stratum to which Freud belonged. The man was viewed as sexually

active, and the woman as passive. This is not only about different behavior but also about a distinction along the lines acting/not-acting.
When the woman is seen as passive, the question of her sexual experience remains marginalized. (Under a normative perspective, this attitude often had repressive features, for instance, influencing
educational practices that, at least in the English-speaking world, are
called Victorian.) Freud views this active/passive schema critically,
but he only modifies it while retaining the core. For instance, "There
is only one libido . . . if, following the conventional equation of activity and masculinity, we are inclined to describe it as masculine, we
must not forget that it also covers trends with a passive aim. Nevertheless, the juxtaposition 'feminine libido' is without any justification."[46] Freud speaks finally of a "wave of passivity . . . which opens
the way to the turn towards femininity."[47]

In regard to Freud's methodology, the following problem presents itself: Reading Freud results in an initial impression that he first
focuses on the infantile development of the libido and explains its
phases in an empirical manner and then formulates, on this basis,
statements about adult women and men. On closer scrutiny, however, the process is actually reversed. The conventional image of different gender characteristics already shapes the view of children—and
for this reason features of independence and activity that do not fit
the feminine ideal are described as male.

The "wave of passivity" also accounts for women's lack of cultural
ability. How does Freud explain this? Here the oedipal phase is para-
mount since Freud located the separation of the two sexes in that period of development, deriving from the phallic phase. According to
his argument, it is of central importance that the "relation of the
Oedipus complex to the castration complex"[48] in boys and girls tends
in a contrary direction. The development of the boy begins oedi-
pally—he desires his mother. Thereby he becomes the rival of the father and fears his punishment, castration. "Under the impression of
the danger of losing his penis, the Oedipus complex is abandoned,
suppressed, . . . and a severe super-ego is set up as its heir."[49] With

girls, Freud believes, the castration complex is the beginning of development. When the girl discovers that "her mother is castrated,"[50] she turns away from her and forms the oedipal relationship with the father. She can take refuge in it as in a haven: "In the absence of fear of castration the chief motive is lacking which leads boys to surmount the Oedipus complex. . . . In these circumstances the formation of the super-ego must suffer; it cannot attain the strength and independence which give it its cultural significance."[51]

These considerations lead to problems in regard to their method and their internal logic (elaborated here only as they are relevant). As long as Freud argues generally that cultural achievements always demand a renunciation of the sex drive, his explanations are plausible. Equally plausible is the thought that the capacity for drive renunciation must be acquired in early childhood development and that the painful experience of alienation from the mother causes this learning process. But serious problems result from Freud's belief that this development takes place differently in each sex.

As shown above, Freud sees the origin of the development of difference in the contrasting experience of the castration complex in girls and boys. In this context he formulates his concept of penis envy. The point of departure is an empirical observation: Little girls who start to notice physical difference sometimes remark that they want to "have something like it [penis] too."[52] Assuming this to be a proven fact, let us concentrate on Freud's description: "The castration complex of girls is . . . started by the sight of the genitals of the other sex. They at once notice the difference and, it must be admitted, its significance too. They feel seriously wronged . . . and fall a victim to 'envy for the penis,' which will leave ineradicable traces on their development and the formation of their character."[53] Where does the significance lie, which the little girl at once understands and which causes such a strong feeling of envy? According to Freud, two reactions of shock deserve attention here. On the one hand, he notes that the girl "loses her enjoyment in her phallic sexuality."[54] This assessment, however, is hardly comprehensible. Since it is not stated that the girl experiences lust through the "sight of the genitals of the other sex," it is not clear why the girl should, based on this perception, cease to satisfy herself with the help of her clitoris. Freud has changed his perspective and turned away from the girl's internal point of view. His own terminology—phallic phase—might have tempted him to take a perspective from the outside comparable to that which motivates boys from time to time to engage in measuring competitions and to use the language of boasting and teasing.

Freud seems to understand the second form of shock reaction as the more substantial one. As soon as the girl recognizes that not only she but also her mother is castrated, she drops her as a love object. "This means, therefore, that as a result of the discovery of women's lack of penis they are debased in value for girls just as they are for boys and later perhaps for men."[55] The problem here is to imagine how the little girl should go from the perception of lacking a penis to the idea of castration. These two statements are not the same. The lack of a penis describes physical difference, but the term *castration* implies an entire story. Since this term also connotes punishment, the narrative core can be summarized as follows: Once upon a time my mother had a penis. But my mother did not follow the rules of behavior that were imposed on her and her penis was cut off as a punishment. Consequently, now I do not have a penis, either.[56] If one holds to the details Freud gives, then the father fits into the story as the dominating figure who makes the laws and carries out the punishment.[57] But how does the little girl come up with such a story in order to explain the observation that her body has no penis?

This question immediately leads to another one: How does Freud come up with the idea of assigning the girl such an interpretation of her physical qualities? Since he offers the castration complex as an explanation for the girl's detachment from her mother, for him the logic of this story must be somehow obvious. I believe that the key for understanding his line of thought lies in the above quote that through the "discovery of women's lack of penis they are debased in value for girls just as they are for boys and later perhaps for men."

Freud refers here to the observation that the woman can appear devalued to the man. But how should this lack of esteem be derived from the anatomical fact of penislessness? When Freud moves the heterosexual relationship—and especially its procreative aspect—into the center of his theoretical interest, he cannot seriously regard the "little difference" as a legitimate reason for disparaging women. Therefore the quoted sentence has to be read in the reverse direction, so to speak. In the beginning, then, comes the observation that women are little respected by their husbands and children. Taken by itself, this statement is fully legitimate. The fact of subordination can also be formulated differently: Those whose bodies do not feature a penis are often relegated to an underprivileged position and subjected to a lack of respect. This depiction is not a causal explanation but presents a historically contingent connection of penislessness and disregard whose genesis falls into the field of historical research (which has already brought to light a number of details).

The conception of penis envy features the same methodological inconsistency explained above: While Freud seems to examine the comparative perceptions of the little girl, his own experiences with the hierarchy of the sexes have priority; they guide his interpretation of the girl's utterance to want "to have something like it, too." Also relevant is children's social perception. Since they experience from early on who has power in the family, it can be assumed that they develop an understanding of the hierarchy of the sexes in their families. Before they can even articulate it, they make the connection between belonging to the female sex and having an underprivileged status. Therefore it can be concluded that for little girls who are about to determine their position in the network of family relationships, it is experiences with the social relevance of sex that form the primary category of interpretation—as is also true for Freud himself. It is not the "sight of the genitals of the other sex" as such that gives them a self-understanding of the stigma of disadvantage.

But maybe this was precisely the point that Freud intended to make when he spoke of the significance little girls assign to the penis?

This question could be raised by those who read Freud as a critic of bourgeois society. According to them, his investigations aim to identify the decrepitude of society and enable change. Read this way, penis envy makes visible the damages that the girl experiences from traditional forms of socialization. A threefold differentiation needs to be made in regard to such an interpretation. First, Freud's texts, particularly the detailed case studies, create an image of the upper social stratum of fin de siècle Vienna and therefore offer material for a critical theory of this society (with consequences reaching to the present). Second, Freud's intentions have to be examined independently from the first point: Did he aim to change society or reintegrate the patients as much as possible into the given structures? Third, and to the point, was the method Freud chose appropriate for outlines of alternative social models?

To clarify the last question we need to examine the relevance assigned to the body. Penis envy in Freud's view results from the comparative observations of the girl. It is not given by corporality, like a drive, but rather derives from a certain form of perception or interpretation. To this extent it is legitimate to state that Freud's considerations do not start with biological determinism. But at the same time there is an aspect of inescapability. As Freud describes it, the girl has no other choice. This subsequently applies to the other developmental steps of the oedipal phase not only for the girl but for the boy. The biological fact that the mother has the same sex as the girl but not the same as the boy seems to be decisive for the complete dynamics of the relationships in the family triangle. Freud, who first declared his intention to keep psychoanalysis free from "any prerequisite foreign to it, be it of an anatomical, chemical or physiological nature" (see above), formulates in this context a strong postulate: "The anatomical (sex) distinction must express itself in psychical consequences."[58] Here a greater argumentative context becomes visible: (1) The starting point is the ideas and structures of sexual hierarchy, which Freud acknowledges as conditions of his world. (2) These ideas are in turn projected onto little girls who notice that they do not have a penis. Thus penislessness and being devalued are linked, and this linkage forms the core of the female variant of the castration complex. (3) The subordination of women appears as a consequence of the anatomical difference, and its historically contingent character is concealed. (4) Freud's theory suggests the conclusion that over-turning bourgeois society would not change the order of the sexes and therefore fulfills a legitimizing function. (5) This is finally ex-pressed in Freud's disparaging remarks about the feminist criticism of his time.[59]

From here the statement of women's deficient cultural capacity can be broken down. Freud's psychoanalytic theory cannot provide a scientific foundation of the thesis. One rather finds a *petitio principii*—the reduced cultural potential of the woman, which according to the claim is explained from the infantile development of the libido, stands de facto already at the beginning of the argumenta-tion (points 1–2). The crucial thought is that in girls the formation of a superego and therefore the ability for drive sublimation are handicapped. The social environment in which this thought is formulated can be characterized as follows: Under the conditions of bourgeois socialization, the girl can build a successful relation to her father only if she subordinates herself. She must accept the concep-tion according to which the man is the head of the family and the guardian of his wife—a conception elaborated in the philosophy of law of the Enlightenment that also determined the legal reality Freud had in mind. For the girl this subordination is decisive not only for her relation to her father, but for her life to come. The woman moves from the guardianship of the father directly to that of the husband.[60] The girl is required early on to give up essential dimensions of her autonomy. The popular idea that disputes women's intellectual and artistic independence is a case in point. When Freud is read with this gender image in mind, his statement that "the formation of the super-ego suffers from these circumstances" can seem accurate. It is plausible that this "creation of a superior agency within the ego" (as Freud characterizes the formation of the superego)[61] is hardly compatible with a far-reaching surrender of self-determination. Difficulties arise, however, from the fact that Freud sees the origins of these limitations in the dynamics of penis envy. In this manner the bourgeois construction of gender relations, in which there is, among other things, no place for women artists, is projected back into the libidinous logic of the little girl who judges her body to be unsatisfactory.

The decisive move comes from Freud's interpreting clitoral masturbation as male. When the girl lets go of this activity and adopts passivity, the "masculine" activity is repressed altogether. If Freud dismisses the formulation "feminine libido" as absurd, then he rejects in the same breath the thought of female creativity. The projective element of his thinking remains unreflected, however.[62] The connection between the concepts of genius and masculinity can now be understood along the lines that the anatomical sex difference must have psychic results. This means that the bourgeois social construction no longer appears as historically contingent; the constellation of the sexes that is outlined in this construction is presented in such a manner that it seems to be based on empirically evident physical difference and therefore appears to be inevitable (points 3–4).

Freud does not deny that there are culturally active individuals of the female sex, but he situates them in a strange interworld. According to his conception girls have two possibilities: If they enter the oedipal relation to the father "like a haven" and choose the path of normal[63] heterosexual relations, then the price is an unsatisfactory development of the superego and the subsequent cultural meaninglessness. If they do not turn entirely to the father and can connect in sublimated form with the activity of their phallic phase, they have the ability to engage in intellectual and artistic pursuits, but they are no longer regarded as women. They are, according to Freud, "rather male than female."[64] The woman artist (like the woman philosopher or the intellectual from other cultural fields) has no place in society. She does not belong to "normal women," but neither is she a whole man. (Space does not permit us to examine to what extent in Freud's theory the woman artist and the lesbian are characterized analogously.)[65]

Here an astonishing phenomenon becomes apparent. While nothing seems more obvious than the need to problematize such a (non)placing of the woman artist or the intellectual from a feminist perspective (and to work out the bourgeois conception of femininity is its background), this aspect of Freud's theory has enjoyed broad acceptance in feminist theory. Many feminist authors assume that intellectuality is a male characteristic. I show the grave consequences of this reception history[66] in other places in this book, but simply note a basic distinction here. Under conventional circumstances a woman can become an artist only if she does not enter the feminine sphere (i.e., become a homemaker). But why should withdrawal from this social construction be equated with masculinization? If women reclaim a space for themselves that so far has been occupied by men, this does not mean that they develop a masculine identity; they rather try to free this space from its gendered connotation. As long as the woman artist or intellectual is interpreted as masculine, this is an indirect consent to the idea in which the woman is defined through the sequence of terms vagina-passivity-lack of cultural ability.

Freud advised caution. In the final paragraph of the thirty-third lecture he advises his fictitious audience: "But do not forget that we have described the woman only insofar as her nature is determined by sexual functions. This influence is far-reaching, but we have to keep in mind that the individual woman might be beyond that also a human being."[67] Should feminist theory not take this advice too? Freud's approach is hardly appropriate to examine this "human being beyond that" more closely; it might prove to be impeding in that respect. I have the following problem in mind: The fact that "the psychic"—which Freud assumes to be of decisive influence on conscious thinking and willing—is tied to the anatomical difference of the sexes has the consequence that all areas of human life eventually are subjected to a dual grid. That Freud places feminine braiding and weaving next to male art is a case in point. A suggestion formulated in a later context to differentiate in regard to moral judgment between a masculine and a feminine form can be understood as a part of the reception history of Freud's thought.[68] While I elaborate a number of the resulting problems later, I emphasize two consequential aspects here. The first is that problems concerning everybody are obscured by the polarizing point of view. This happens, for example, when political or juridical conceptions of equality are rejected out of hand with the argument that they would cause a leveling of differences. A number of feminist authors broadly agree with those who defend the traditional conception of gender difference in understanding equality only in terms of an adjustment of women to men. The second aspect is directly related. With the dual grid the assumption operates that the differences among individuals are less important than the shared "nature of women" (or of men). With regard to the current critiques of essentialism these problems will have to be elaborated further.

Next I will examine attempts to challenge the connection between art and masculinity by delineating a specifically feminine form of creativity.

Writing with white ink

Feminist objections were formulated immediately after the Freudian view of women was published. In his later texts, Freud referred to these critics. For instance, in 1932 he reported in the *New Introductory Lectures on Psychoanalysis*: "For the ladies, whenever some comparison seemed to turn out unfavourable to their sex, were able to utter a suspicion that we, the male analysts, had been unable to overcome certain deeply-rooted prejudices against what was feminine, and that this was being paid for in the partiality of our researches."[69] Since Freud could not invalidate this suspicion,[70] the criticism continued, guided by a twofold motivation. On the one hand the patriarchal direction of Freud's thought was demonstrated with increasing clarity; on the other hand, critics examined whether the libidinous biography of the woman would not have to be narrated differently.

Taking up the latter objective, feminist authors referred to other schools of psychoanalysis. For the more general, not exclusively psychoanalytically oriented feminist theory, the link to object relations theory (of which I will speak in a later chapter) on the one hand, and Lacan on the other, became specifically relevant. The term *French feminism,*[71] which (at least in English-speaking discourse) has become common, refers to the works of authors such as Hélène Cixous, Catherine Clément, Luce Irigaray, and Julia Kristeva,[72] who work with Lacan as well as the Derridean reading of Lacan.[73] I now turn to this kind of theory formation. I will focus on its claim to provide an alternative view of the relation between femininity and artistic creativity.

The critical impulse is easy to comprehend. Contrary to Freud, who justifies his statement of the deficient cultural ability of women by acknowledging only a male libido, it seems logical to assume a feminine libido and assign to it specific cultural competencies of women.[74] The project of an *écriture féminine* has its roots in this intention. Hélène Cixous contributed the most to bringing this topic to central significance in France in the 1970s.[75] Notwithstanding her reservations toward Lacan (which I address later), Cixous follows the basic steps of his thinking, adopting the concept of symbolic order, or rather the connection between psychoanalysis and language theory that characterizes this conception. Cixous assumes that all structures in our culture—from grammar and patterns of social order (starting with the family) to the aesthetic ideas expressed in artistic production—are shaped phallically. She refers to the distinction between penis and phallus as Lacan formulated it, especially in his analysis of the mirror stage. According to Lacan, language acquisition begins when the dyadic unity of the child with its mother, which is distinctive for the pre-oedipal phase, is destroyed by the appearance of the father. At first the child enjoyed an imaginary joint identity with the mother. Now the child learns, because of the family's triangular structure, to say "I am," as distinguished from "you are" or "he is." Order is mediated through language and the individual is assigned to its position. This is also a story of loss: "The speaking subject who says 'I am' in reality says 'I am the one who has lost something—and the experienced loss is the loss of the imaginary identity with the mother and the world' . . . To speak as a subject is therefore the same as to express the existence of a repressed desire."[76] Since the drastic experience of language acquisition starts with the appearance of the father, the symbolic order is also characterized in a way that it implements the law of the father. In this context the term *phallus* is assigned its function—to signal this connection of the order with the father: "To enter the symbolic order means to accept the phallus as a substitute for the law of the father. Every human culture and all social life is dominated by the symbolic order and thus by the phallus as a sign of lack."[77] This is valid for both sexes: For boys and men too culture is a sign of lack. In Lacan's theory phallus is not the same as penis because its primary function is not to name a specific attribute of the man but to refer metaphorically to the law that is binding on everyone.

Cixous takes up this theory, as do other French feminists such as Irigaray, with an important change. She believes it is not "every" human culture and "all" social life whose libidinous past Lacan breaks down, but the Western tradition, which has been shaped in the course of history and therefore must be understood as change-able. With this reinterpretation, Lacan's theory can be connected to feminist cultural criticism. If the symbolic order, as described by Lacan, assigns to all individuals their social position, then women's being assigned positions marked by oppression and speechlessness must be addressed. For authors like Cixous, the task is to investigate why the girl in the course of her infantile development gets into this subordination and falls silent. This critical analysis aims at pointing out alternative options to this positioning. Yet a simple addendum to Lacan's theory proves impossible; Cixous decides rather in favor of a differentiated rereading. On the one hand, she takes from Lacan the instruments that expose the mechanisms through which the girl is si-lenced by culture; on the other she raises the reproach that Lacan has not analyzed the privilege of the man firmly enough and therefore has contributed to the stabilization of it. Thus arises the need to redefine the phallus concept. This term signifies not only the symbolic order in general but also the monopoly established through it in which only men have a say. The term *phallus* thus moves as a metaphorical concept closer to the term *penis* (compared to Lacan's original terminology) and becomes a cipher in feminist criticism for the patriarchally structured culture.

In this context, the authors of French feminism often level the reproach of phallogocentrism derived from Derridean thought. (Derrida saw in Plato's concept of the logos the perfect example of Western metaphysics; this is how he came, in the course of his radical withdrawal from this tradition of thought inspired by Heidegger, to critically talk of logocentrism. In psychoanalytical theory, according to him, metaphysical ideas can still be encountered; while rejecting those, Derrida formulates the concept of phallocentrism[78] that refers to Lacan.) From the viewpoint of this criticism, Lacan's theory no longer seems to be as far from Freud as it claims. With some irony, Cixous writes of Lacan's conception: "It reproduces the masculine view, of which it is one of the effects. Here we encounter the inevitable man-with-the-rock, standing erect in his old Freudian realm, in the way that, to take the figure back to the point where linguistics is conceptualizing it 'anew,' Lacan preserves it in the sanctuary of the phallos (Ø) 'sheltered' from castration's lack! Their 'symbolic' exists, it holds power."[79] (We will later see that Cixous, like some other authors who take a comparable position, has not followed this critical conclusion consequentially enough.)

In her outline for an alternative interpretation of the infantile development of the girl, Cixous describes the beginning of the oedipal phase—as it usually happens in Western culture—as a time when the girl is forced to deny herself. If the girl develops shame, this happens, Cixous believes, not because she understands her penislessness as a lack and tries to hide it. On the contrary, she feels forced to understand her own spontaneity and strength as inappropriate and gives

them up. "Where is the . . . woman," asks Cixous, "who . . . led into
self-disdain by the great arm of parental-conjugal phallogocentrism,
hasn't been ashamed of her strength?"[80] The term *castration* now appears in a different light. If the beginning of the oedipal phase is
marked by a crisis, for Cixous this is not caused by the girl's discovery
of having always belonged to the "weak sex," but by the fact that she
sees her libidinous and creative self threatened by death. It is not the
girl herself who represses activity, but her phallogocentrically shaped
environment. The process of infantile development here is more dy-
namic than in the classics of psychoanalysis. Cixous can assign a potential of resistance to the girl. The demanded mortification is, she
assumes, a rule that is not performed completely. In spite of threatened sanctions and internalized sensations of being frightened by
their own desire,[81] girls are usually able to resist the pressure to a certain extent. Suppressed but not destroyed, "they've saved their skin,
their energies."[82] The term *castration* in the end proves inappropriate
in both variants. Whether castration is connected to the mother, as in
Freud, or comes from the law of the father, as in Lacan, it means a
denial of the libidinous energy of the girl. "Which castration do you
prefer?" Cixous asks ironically. "Whose degrading do you like better,
the father's or the mother's?"[83]

Here the project of an *écriture féminine* starts. Cixous pleads for a
writing that expresses the buried feminine libido: "Woman must
write herself."[84] This does not simply mean that women should write.
Entirely in line with Lacan, Cixous is of the opinion that almost all
the texts written by women authors so far have been determined by
the phallic order. "Nearly the entire history of writing is confounded
with the history of reason. . . . It has been one with the phallocentric
tradition."[85] As exceptions, Cixous mentions only the texts by Colette and Marguerite Duras, which she calls examples of "feminine
sexed texts," or "sexts."[86] Where is the source for this other form of
expression? Cixous sees it in the pre-oedipal unity of child and
mother, and she again follows Lacan in taking up his concept of the
imaginary, which precedes the symbolic order, to suggest a new use

of this concept. The imaginary is formed through feminine creativity into an anti-Logos weapon. While the phallus stands for the rationally shaped symbolic order, it is now confronted with the figure of the mother, as the personification of a nonverbal relationship developed in the medium of corporality and the sound of the voice. Cixous requests that an *écriture féminine* ensures with specific means that this figure is listened to. "In women's speech, as in their writing, that element which never stops resonating . . . is the song: first music from the first voice of love which is alive in every woman. . . . A woman is never far from 'mother.' . . . There is always within her at least a little of that good mother's milk. She writes in white ink."[87] The aim of such writing is not to strengthen feminine self-confidence to arm women for the struggle of the sexes. Rather, this struggle, which always follows the model of mutual castration ("the struggle for mastery which can end only in at least one death") should be overcome entirely. For Cixous, the image of the mother mediates an alternative relationship model in which giving oneself away and opening up to heterogeneity are characteristic features.[88]

This line of thought leads into a number of problems. The central concept, feminine libido, remains blurred. This is caused by a shift of perspectives that Cixous carries out covertly. At first she follows Lacan's conception of the imaginary, which depends on the depiction of the earliest phase of infantile development from the child's internal perspective. If Lacan speaks of imaginary unity with the mother, then the idea is to describe what the child experiences before it learns to say "I am." In the pre-oedipal phase girls and boys do not exhibit differences and consequently it is hardly possible to develop a conception of a specific feminine libido by referring to this imaginary unity. Cixous in fact suddenly changes perspective and speaks from the viewpoint of the mother who breast-feeds the child, hums it to sleep, and so on. But in this context Lacan's concept of the imaginary no longer seems appropriate. In spite of her caring, the mother does not experience her relationship with her baby as a physical unity beyond any differentiation between I am/you are. Even for the most motherly woman, her life—the horizon of her relationships—is not exclusively defined by her baby (even if it might seem so from the viewpoint of time economy). She has not lost her capacity for different language games—beyond the "first voice of love"—and remains connected with other people through a network of relations, for instance, with older children who may loudly express jealousy toward the newcomer. If the relationship between mother and small children is depicted in a way that assumes an imaginary identity of the mother with her baby, then the level of reflection and norms threaten to disappear from the picture. The danger concerns, for example, the caring communication between adults in regard to the health of the baby or the pedagogical claim that accompanies the observation of the child from the beginning. A sense of responsibility that devalues one's own needs in favor of the child cannot be accounted for, nor how much this is shaped by the traditional division of labor between the sexes.[89]

To defend a conception that reduces motherliness in such a drastic fashion approaches, even if unintentionally, a naturalistic concept of the rearing of the next generation.[90] Why should the mother's preverbal communication with her baby be considered the only genuine form of expression by the woman? In the experience of the baby, indeed, the physically and vocally mediated care from the mother is the only decisive sensation. In short, the problem here is that the feminine libido is determined through the perspective of the baby. In the end, this theory comes close to the reductionist perspective already observed in Freud according to which the sexuality of woman is defined through the figure of the mother.

These difficulties also affect the conception of the *écriture féminine*. It can be said that (depending on the specific interpretation of this project) either writing or femininity becomes questionable. How can one imagine a "writing with white ink?" First, this idea is not about a simple reproduction of the voice of motherly caring (which would not be a writing in the sense of artistic production) but comprises a creative process as well. Cixous's remarks that the idea of feminine writing has seldom been realized makes this clear. Yet if what matters is artistic development, then the question has to be posed whether this can be performed in a way that could be called specifically feminine. A literature that intends to mediate something never heard before has to choose means of expression that can be read by others; otherwise, it would not be writing.[91] But the circle of readers—also for Cixous—cannot be split up into groups whose reception ability is defined or restricted by their belonging to a certain sex. In terms of the referentiality of artistic production to reception, literature always transcends the limits of gender-typical experiences— even if it tries to express just those experiences. Furthermore, Cixous assigns to *écriture féminine* a task that cannot be restricted to women. If this kind of art expresses an alternative form of relationship that is borne of the infantile experience of being accepted by the mother, then it cannot be thought of as excluding men due to their sex. The dominant element of art thus defined is the shared early childhood experience of girls and boys, not the mother's subconscious. As an example of feminine writing, Cixous lists Jean Genet next to Colette and Marguerite Duras. Here the adjective *feminine* has lost its original meaning and no longer refers specifically to the libidinous energy of women. The implications of this changed usage of the term remain to be investigated.

This ambiguity is caused, I think, by the fact that Cixous operates with five paired terms. She seems to believe that each expresses the same difference, although closer scrutiny reveals that in each case different fields of reference are addressed. The pairs are (1) symbolic order/imaginary fusion, (2) law of the father (phallus)/voice of the mother, (3) masculine hegemony/feminine recognition of the heterogeneous, (4) male libido/female libido, (5) rationality/poetic mode of expression. (These dyads and their overlapping aspects play an important role not only in Cixous's theory but also in the broad field of current debates. We will encounter them again in varied thematic contexts. For this reason the following considerations, although they also deal with basic issues, ultimately remain oriented to the topic of the aesthetic.)

At this point it becomes crucial that Cixous does not go far enough in her criticism of Lacan. It is, of course, legitimate when she addresses the problem of male dominance. Our linguistic and cultural conventions constantly convey masculine conceptions of order. But it would be rash to deduce from this fact that language and culture as such were shaped by masculinity. Here two different topics are involved. On the one hand, we need a precise analysis of hegemonic patterns (the many studies from the fields of history, sociology, literary criticism, and so on have relevance in this respect). On the other hand, the capacity for language and culture as basic human capabilities has to be discussed in an examination that refrains from the dimension of content and focuses on the question of preconditions. A specific argument would be needed to ascribe a masculine form to this basic level. Cixous does not keep these two topics apart because she partially holds on to Lacan's ideas. Her objection against Lacan is, as already noted, only that the term *phallus* is a sign for the privilege of the man. The central thought—referring the symbolic order to the law of the father—remains untouched. The consequence is a kind of domino effect. Because Cixous starts from the equation symbolic order = phallus = masculine hegemony, her critique of the language monopoly of men in Western culture is directed at the same time against our capacity for language and culture in general.

I believe the concept of the symbolic order needs to be reconsidered. If we accept the assertion that the language acquisition of the child leads to the loss of the original closeness to the mother, this does not warrant the conclusion that language imposes the law of the father. If language acquisition implies the differentiation of I am/you are/he-she-it is, this does not necessitate the dominance of the father. On closer examination, Lacan's theory is marked by a circular structure of thought similar to that found in Freud. While the powerful father may appear to stand behind all culture and language, the symbolic order only seems to be phallic since the hierarchy of the sexes of the bourgeois family has been projected on it. But this kind of projection means that again women's competence for participa-

tion in human cultural achievements is negated.[92] Therefore the most
urgent task of a feminist criticism is to reject the joining of the symbolic order and phallus concepts. This can be shown by a thought experiment. If we avoid disconnecting these terms, all that remains is
the effort to provide women with an anti-Logos weapon. This
means, as has been rightfully pointed out, to advise women to turn
away from dealing with issues of the social and political order.[93]
Cixous's reservations concerning the demands for equality articulated by the women's liberation movement—and her related distancing from the term *feminism*—are entirely along these lines.[94] But
such a way of thinking is threatened by unintended consequences.
Although its prime concern is to address male dominance, it eventually performs itself an expropriation of the woman.[95]

For the woman artist, the concept of writing with white ink leaves
only the following option: Either she claims to produce art outside of
the symbolic order, and thus is pressured to create something that is
entirely different from art as we have known it, or she refuses to be
pushed outside and must be prepared for the reproach that her writing is actually masculine.[96] (Other culture-producing women are frequently confronted with these alternatives by their opponents. A
feminist theory of art that insists on alterity therefore joins a dubious
alliance.) Cixous dismisses the writing of most women authors as
phallic. For her the literary work of writers such as Virginia Woolf or
Simone de Beauvoir falls into this category. The problem that arises
here is that although Cixous intends to free the woman for art (and
with the help of art), her conception, on the other hand, clearly reduces women's options in this regard.

It's not entirely absurd when sharp-tongued female critics express
fear of "an idea of a women's art which, of all possibilities, comes
from the for millennia overstrained natural abilities of the female: A
uterus art of gargling amniotic fluid, of guttural lullabies, of the ex-
tremely kind-hearted knitting patterns."[97] Numerous authors emphasize that the term *feminist aesthetics* is not to be equated with a
theory of *feminine art*.[98]

Here the fourth of the mentioned pairs of terms—male libido/female libido—comes into play. The problem just outlined results from a structural difficulty already mentioned. Since psychoanalysis operates with a man/woman typology, it remains tied—in all its applications, be it to art or other areas—to this dyadic grid.[99] Here the point is not whether libido is ascribed only to men or in a specific form to each sex (and a competent decision on this cannot be reached through purely philosophical means). Regarding the problems of alterity, it seems reasonable to heed the caution uttered by Freud concerning the question to what extent cultural achievements can be referred back to sexual drives.[100] Male as well as female authors articulate their individual experiences, including their early sexual development, in their texts. But this cannot serve as evidence for a theory distinguishing feminine and masculine writing. (Such a distinction neglects, as has been pointed out, the creative aspect of art and its hermeneutic character of mediation.)[101]

Cixous's theory contains yet another idea that is not directed at an immediate combination of art form belonging to a sex; *écriture féminine* is also possible for men. Here the fifth pair of terms—rationality/poetic expression—becomes relevant. Tacitly the assignments have changed. The dividing line no longer separates forms of language derived from the libidinous economy of men and women. Differing styles of thought and expression are open to men as alternative options because boys too experience in their infantile development a form of relationship that differs essentially from the masculine world shaped by demands of dominance and competition. Poets especially draw from this source. (Obviously the five paired terms that we can distinguish when we read Cixous's texts each concern another difference. The concepts of symbolic order, phallus, masculine hegemony, male libido, and rationality have different fields of reference.) Here Cixous's considerations carry on the long tradition of representing the artist—or the creative man in general—as feminine.

If this use of *feminine* causes discomfort, this can happen for different—virtually opposite—reasons. First, it might seem obvious to depict the problem like this: Qualities traditionally ascribed to women, such as sentimentality, sensuality, and procreativity, will now be appropriated by men; consequently women will find themselves robbed of their last remaining prerogatives. The process of expropriation sharpens: First the woman is denied her participation in language and culture, then she loses the specific terrain that was allotted to her as well.[102] But it would be a fallacy to conclude that the feminist alternative lies in a defense and revaluation of the purported special competencies of women, since this strategy would reproduce a traditional gender design.

Therefore the criticism must be formulated differently. Why should abilities and virtues that can be recognized in men and women as human qualities be apostrophized masculine or feminine? On the one hand, the identification of the symbolic order with the law of the father is not convincing; on the other, the interpretation of the imaginary as feminine is dubious. Another de-connection is necessary here. While it can be left undisputed that different styles of expression have developed (poetry speaks another language than the business world or the sciences), the gendered connotation of this difference must be questioned. Why should women and men not have or acquire abilities in both fields? In Cixous there is an asymmetry that remains unfounded. While she firmly welcomes Jean Genet's transcending of the masculine style, she forcefully rejects attempts at complementary development—like feminist efforts to exceed the limits of the femininity cliché. Here we again encounter the problem that in Cixous's theory the distancing from traditional images of the sexes is not sufficiently radical.

Some might reject this criticism by remarking that terms such as *phallic* and *maternal* or *feminine* have exclusively symbolic meaning in the Lacanian tradition and may not refer to real women and men. What does it mean when the adjective *feminine* is also applied to men? This adjective no longer refers to women in the biological sense, but only to certain characteristics. Nonetheless, these characteristics, by being called feminine, are connected with women; otherwise this expression would make no sense. A metaphor evokes a certain image to illuminate certain facts with the help of an association. "My love, a rose," is an example often used in rhetorical literature.[103] One who does not know the meaning of the word *rose* is not further informed about *love*. Therefore stressing that an expression is merely symbolic is unhelpful. To call the poet "feminine" evokes traditional clichéd ideas whose rejection is one of the main concerns of feminist criticism.

I leave it to my readers to judge to what extent the basic questions raised here in regard to Cixous can be transferred to other authors. I would like to add a word on Kristeva, however, since her considerations are often too rashly seen as being in entire agreement with those just discussed. Kristeva also operates with an opposition, differentiating between the symbolic and the semiotic. But this does not equal any of the five paired terms we find in Cixous's texts. Rather, both of Kristeva's concepts are constructed differently than the mentioned disjunctions.[104] Kristeva considerably expands the term *symbolic*. She describes the child's entrance into the symbolic order as not only a loss but also a freeing step that leads the way out of the emotional ambivalence of the pre-oedipal phase.[105] She seems to concur with Lacan when she states that language and culture are centered around the phallus. But in her view this claim is valid only as it refers to the characteristic features of European-Western tradition.[106] This restriction enables her to develop a more complex theory of the symbolic. In this theory she also brings to bear her specific approach to psychoanalysis, which is shaped by her semiological investigations.[107] Kristeva cannot agree to refer the symbolic *toto genere* to the law of the father.[108] For her, language is a medium that allows us to articulate and digest prelingual experiences—herein lies its liberating aspect.[109] Avant-garde poetry thus moves into the center of attention. It is able, she believes, to bring "into the symbolic processes which in the case of psychosis remain encapsulated in the pre-symbolic."[110] While Kristeva criticizes the phallic order, she does not demand a total distancing from the symbolic.[111] She is interested in a redesign of it, as the example of literature shows. The revolution in poetic language (also the title of Kristeva's main work) happens in a way that the poetic text supports and at the same time undermines the traditional system of assigning meaning. To fulfill its mediating function, poetry has to employ understandable forms of expression, while unveiling an unfamiliar meaning that has initially remained hidden.[112] Kristeva proceeds in the same differentiating manner in regard to the semiotic, although her thoughts seem at first familiar as they thematize the unity of the child with its mother. Kristeva speaks of a "rhythmic space" as the place of the presymbolic "undifferentiated articulation."[113] To address this space with a specific expression, she borrows from Plato's *Timaios* the term *chora*.[114] More clearly than other authors, Kristeva keeps the mother's and the child's perspectives apart.[115] From this follows, among other things, that in her concept of the semiotic the fact is taken into account more consequently that early experiences are shared by girls and boys.

Through her careful procedure Kristeva avoids polarization in a double sense. On the one hand, she stays clear of simple sexual connotations. The symbolic is not assigned only to the male,[116] nor the semiotic only to the female. On the other hand, in her theory of language she does not introduce a simple disjunction. Where the pair of terms symbolic/semiotic refers to different modes of expression, they are not conceived as mutually excluding each other. According to Kristeva these two modes are present at the same time in any form of speech, although in differing proportions. We never hear merely the content of the utterance, she emphasizes, but also always the sound of the voice that announces something entirely different.[117] This means that the symbolic is connected indissolubly with the semiotic.[118] The claim that poetry sensitizes us for that subliminal dimension[119] does not mean that Kristeva demands the development of a separate outside—as implied in the idea of an "anti-logos weapon." Her concern is not to confront the linguistic order evolving around the phallus with a countermodel; rather, she intends "a completion in the sense of completing the symbolic order."[120]

In spite of the complex design of her theory, Kristeva gets into trouble when she characterizes the semiotic as motherly.[121] The problematic status of her theory becomes obvious as soon as we take a closer look her description of the intended completion of the symbolic order. Kristeva invites us to listen more attentively to the semiotic modality of expression. But then she apostrophizes the semiotic as motherly, and the traditional clichés of the gender characters again come into play. Kristeva stresses that the language of love can also be articulated with a male voice,[122] but this voice is nonetheless associated with women. Therefore the problem investigated above with regard to metaphors recurs. This can be seen in passages of Kristeva's text where the distinction between the mother's perspective and the child's perspective starts to blur, as in Cixous. The paradigm for the semiotic is no longer the pre-oedipal experience of safety in the chora but the caring attitude of the mother. When Kristeva highlights the invocation of Mary *(Eia Mater, fons amoris)* in her interpretation of Pergolesi's Stabat Mater, she brings the traditional view of women into play.[123]

Kristeva is seduced by this association of the semiotic with the mother and finally gets caught in a polarization of the sexes. This comes to mind especially where she turns directly to women. Addressing the question of how women can break through their marginalization and bring themselves into the symbolic order, Kristeva argues for choosing motherhood as a model.[124] She firmly opposes the opinion that there is a single feminine character. Referring to Lacan's often quoted statement, she writes, "La femme ce n'est jamais ça,"[125] to emphasize that nobody represents the feminine but that there are as "many 'femininities' as women."[126] (Consequently she explicitly turns against an *écriture féminine*.)[127] Yet her reference to the diversity of women falls within the variations of femininity or the motherly that are all distinguished from the masculine—however this is thought and subdivided.[128] Thus the dual grid that has been constitutive for psychoanalytical thought since Freud remains in force with Kristeva.[129] Consequently, she gets into the contradiction of rejecting on the one hand any idea of an essence of the feminine, but on the other of assuming an irreconcilable break between the sexes, which can only be claimed if a basic difference is pointed out.[130] Her aim is "surely not some understanding or other on the part of 'sexual partners.'" Rather, the task she has in mind is "to lead to an acknowledgement of what is irreducible, of the irreconcilable interest of both sexes in asserting their differences, in the quest of each one—and of women, after all—for an appropriate fulfillment."[131] Based on these considerations, Kristeva rejects positions in the feminist movement that defend egalitarian programs.[132]

From the texts discussed thus far, we can conclude that it belongs to the main tasks of feminist criticism to question traditional gender dichotomies. A feminist aesthetic that bases itself on conceptions of feminine writing or feminine language invites many objections. This assessment has gained wide acceptance today; sometimes the considerations of French feminism are credited with only a strategic meaning: "While the idea of a categorical woman's art may be philosophically dubious, it was a valuable creative principle for the historical Feminist Art movement . . . right or wrong, it was an enabling myth."[133] Even those who attach more than strategic value to an *écriture féminine* commonly hold that the subject must be formulated differently today. It now seems to be required to speak, as Cornelia Klinger does, of "a feminist aesthetics after the turning away from a concept of femininity."[134] From my viewpoint the question follows how or whether a philosophical aesthetic is possible that is based on a genuinely feminist request. Here we come to the concept of a feminist aesthetics in a more narrow sense.

Feminist aesthetics

Critical-historical analysis provides a useful starting point for aesthetics, as it does for feminist philosophy in general. To what extent are the aesthetic theories developed in the history of philosophy an expression of masculine thought? Numerous studies have tried to prove an impact of prejudice. Their criticism focuses on the classical aesthetics of the eighteenth century and conceptions formulated in the context of the avant-garde art of the twentieth century.[135]

Feminist critics have discussed several aspects of classical aesthetics, particularly the proximity to subject philosophy. It has been objected that this aesthetics is in a "compromising proximity to many, if not all components of masculine Western thought, which today from a feminist perspective (but not only from a feminist perspective) seem suspicious."[136] This objection is directed against concepts of the artist (highlighting the term *genius*) as well as reflections on the reception of art as formulated in the theory of aesthetic judgment. Moreover, a masculine design is attributed to the classical aesthetic categories themselves. Where the distinction between the beautiful and the sublime is discussed, interest is focused on not only masculine connotations of the sublime but also the claim to refer the entire distinction back to patriarchal concepts.

Criticism can be substantiated in two ways: through detecting hermeneutically a "subtext of specifically modern gender relations"[137] and by pointing to the fact that (e.g., in Kant) the categories of the beautiful and the sublime are explicitly and elaborately connected with the distinct character of the sexes. In his *Observations on the Feeling of the Beautiful and the Sublime,*[138] Kant distinguishes between two forms of moral behavior—the sublime type oriented toward principles and the beautiful type guided by emotions—and assigns them to the two sexes: "The virtue of a woman is a beautiful virtue. That of the male sex should be a noble virtue."[139] Several pages earlier, Kant offered this pointed formulation: "It is not to be understood by this that woman lacks noble qualities, or that the male sex must do without beauty completely. On the contrary, one expects that a person of either sex brings both together, in such a way that all the other merits of a woman should unite solely to enhance the character of the beautiful, which is the proper reference point; and on the other hand, among the masculine qualities the sublime clearly stands out as the criterion of this kind. All judgments of the two sexes must refer to these criteria, those that praise as well as those that blame; all education and instruction must have theses before its eyes."[140] In remarks like these, which he wrote under the direct influence of Rousseau's *Emile,* Kant had the bourgeois design of genders in mind.[141] It may therefore seem obvious to draw the following conclusion: If the aesthetic terms of the beautiful and the sublime are of such relevance for the patriarchal construction of gender relations, then these concepts have to be rejected entirely from a perspective of feminist aesthetics.

But closer scrutiny suggests that this conclusion is not mandatory. At first Kant makes the beautiful/sublime distinction independently of the question of the character of the sexes. His central idea is to show that our emotional reactions are based less on the "nature of the external things that arouse them as upon each person's own disposition to be moved by these to pleasure or pain."[142] In regard to the broad variety of human emotions, Kant makes a first differentiation when he confronts the rougher forms of immediate sensual pleasure and displeasure with "a feeling of a more delicate sort," which "presupposes a sensitivity of the soul . . . which makes the soul fitted for virtuous impulses."[143] He focuses on this more refined feeling, and as he tries to structure his observations, he distinguishes in the field of pleasure the sensations of the beautiful and the sublime, and further subdivides the latter category. Only after these distinctions are drawn does Kant illustrate how certain things become the cause that activates the emotions of the beautiful or the sublime. He shows that we can experience such a stimulus from the most different sources in nature as well as art. For example, while Kant notes that "night is sublime, day is beautiful,"[144] he also states that in tragedy the feeling for the sublime is stimulated, and in comedy the feeling for the beautiful. Kant finally examines how human beings can cause such emotions in one another. He takes various factors into account, such as different abilities ("understanding is sublime, wit is beautiful")[145] and scholarly achievements ("Works of understanding and ingenuity, so far as their objects also contain something for feeling, likewise take some part in the differences now being considered. Mathematical representation of the infinite magnitude of the universe, the meditations of metaphysics upon eternity, Providence, and the immortality of our souls contain a certain sublimity and dignity").[146] In this context difference in moral behavior moves into focus, although at first the sexes are not mentioned. True virtue guided by principles appeals to the feeling of the sublime, whereas behavior carried by sympathy and helpfulness appeals to that of the beautiful. In the third section of his text, he deals with "The Distinction of the Beautiful and the Sublime in the Interrelations of the Two Sexes"[147] (and finally attempts to illuminate the differences of national characters with the help of his two categories).

Kant uses the pair of terms beautiful/sublime in a general way that can apply to our emotional reactions to diverse things and serve as a clarifying classification. In this context the task of feminist criticism presents itself as follows: The bone of contention is that Kant suggests a characterization of the sexes at all and thereby follows a patriarchal pattern of thought. Problems arise not only when Kant states that the typical feminine/masculine demeanor elicits emotional reactions according to the dyad beautiful/sublime, but start when he constructs gender ideals as such. Significantly, the two forms of virtue that Kant distinguishes are not presented as equal. The beautiful virtue is weak,[148] since it depends, Kant holds, on the quickly changing mood of sympathy, and represents a kind of preliminary stage before a fully unfolded morality. Strictly speaking, it cannot even be "included within the virtuous disposition."[149] Kant's typology of the character of the sexes states that women can go far in kindheartedness, but they are not able to act according to moral principles or develop "genuine virtue."[150] Kant writes, "Nothing of duty, nothing of compulsion, nothing of obligation! . . . I hardly believe that the fair sex is capable of principles."[151] The core of the problem lies in the contemptuous representation that ascribes to women a lower capacity for virtue than men, and not in the fact that in this context the dyad beautiful/sublime is applied. Feminist criticism should keep these levels of argumentation apart. The (intolerable) thought of a moral ranking of the sexes is not dependent on the two categories of aesthetic feeling. It must be rejected in itself and this has, of course, happened already. On the other hand, the differentiation beautiful/sublime can be formulated without reference to speculation on the character of the sexes. But it leads to questionable results if it is used for the aesthetic categorization of people in their moral behavior. Feminist criticism therefore should firmly reject an aestheticizing concept of gendered morality. Such a distancing does not require the complete dismissal of the categories of the beautiful and the sublime. Although the dyad was in fact used, with serious consequences, this is not a sufficient reason to conclude that this pair of terms is in general not fit to characterize our emotional reactions. For the moment it may remain open whether—to use Kant's examples— our susceptibility for natural phenomena such as day and night or genres such as comedy and tragedy can be analyzed by distinctions like beautiful/sublime.

Some critics may assume that Kant always had in mind the interrelations of the two sexes—also where he presents the beautiful and the sublime in a general form. Indeed, certain indications provided by textual analysis support this statement,[152] as well as the fact that the *Observations* were written shortly after Kant read Rousseau's *Emile*.[153] But this changes nothing. Kant's views on the bourgeois design of gender relations may have the status of a context of discovery; thus it remains open whether the terminological differentiation gained by this—and then separated from the original context—can be substantial enough for the development of an aesthetic theory.[154]

To summarize, feminist criticism has to reject attempts to combine aesthetic categories and ideas of gendered virtues. But if terms like *beautiful* and *sublime* are read as insinuating a patriarchal character per se, then this combination is not seen as a problem but remains in force. It may well be that classical theory proves insufficient in general, as is often assumed today; but a detailed analysis of the specific aesthetic conceptions in question is necessary to defend this claim.

Feminist critics of classical theory have often turned against terms like *aesthetic judgment* and *genius,* or the theses of disinterested delight and truth in art. But in this context too care must be taken. On the one hand, it must be shown how these terms traditionally connote bourgeois ideals of masculinity. On the other hand, from a feminist point of view, the problem lies in this very connection. Challenging these terms as such requires examining the theoretical claim they imply in greater detail. (I will come back to this point below.)

Let us now turn to the feminist debate over twentieth-century aesthetics. Many authors at first assumed a shared concern.[155] The withdrawal from traditional aesthetic ideas characteristic for the avant-garde appeared to meet the feminist agenda. Points of convergence seemed to occur in the rejection of a universal validity of aesthetic judgments, the "deconstruction of the cult of the genius,"[156] the abolition of conventional separations (e.g., between art and life or between pure and applied art), the dismissal of the statement viewing art as an expression of absolute truth and the related emphasis on the historical situatedness of the artist. Common opinion holds that all these forms of distancing can be interpreted as a rejection of masculine ideas. More recently, however, differing ideas have moved to the fore. One point of disagreement is the fact that the term *sublime* in the context of abstract art reached a new significance. Barnett Newman, for instance, characterizes the reduction of the image to a pure form or to line and color with reference to Kant's distinction: "The failure of European art to achieve the sublime is due to (the) blind desire to exist inside the reality of sensation (the object world . . .). In other words, modern art, caught without a sublime content, was incapable of creating a new sublime image. . . . some of us . . . are finding the answer, by completely denying that art has any connection with the problem of beauty."[157] This opinion received a philosophical formulation in Lyotard's postmodern philosophy.[158]

Today a number of feminist authors see a problem in this claim to a conceptual continuity. They note that those elements of the classical theory have been retained that show a masculine character, notwithstanding the grand gesture of the break with tradition which marks the art and aesthetic theory of the avant-garde in all its forms.[159] From this perspective it may seem logical to break even more radically with aesthetic ideology and call for an entirely new approach.

But are we really forced to draw this conclusion? A closer look at the issue of a break with tradition as it presents itself in philosophy reveals that in our discussion of theories we do not face the alternative of either complete appropriation or complete rejection. There are always more options, since the concepts in question allow a variety of interpretations. Here I refer to a methodological suggestion by Seyla Benhabib and differentiate between a strong and a weak interpretation of the classical aesthetic.[160] If the theories developed in the eighteenth century on aesthetic judgment and genius (as well as later developments of these theories) are understood along the lines of a strong thesis, then a questioning is commendable. The various objections against this strong thesis suggested that it is hardly possible today to defend an unrestricted aesthetic universalism, and this is true in regard to the artists as well as the reception of art. A claim to express absolute truth, or to judge aesthetic qualities bindingly once and for all, can only be raised at the price of not doing justice to the status of the debate. The topics of situatedness and historical contingency have been exposed too plausibly to permit a return to the strong terms. (It remains to be questioned whether the classical art theories indeed have supported the strong thesis, as many assume today. It should be examined, for instance, to what extent we are justified in rejecting the concept of judgment in a global criticism of universalist conceptions of rationality. Kant distinguished the term explicitly from reason and rationality by pointing out that only subjective validity can be assigned to the reflecting judgment.)[161]

When such strong theses are no longer defended, problems reappear that were originally intended to be solved with their help.

Obviously, with the rejection of certain answers the questions that they tried to deal with do not automatically disappear. Thus a weak interpretation of the classical conceptions could be introduced. The accent would be not so much on the theories themselves, but on the underlying task of reconstructing in a philosophical terminology what is meant when we talk in ordinary language about art. From this perspective, the conception of aesthetic judgment refers to a vague sensation that we know from everyday experiences. While in regard to food the principle *De gustibus non est disputandum* seems appropriate, it appears not entirely adequate in regard to aesthetic perception. A weak interpretation of the term *aesthetic judgment* would have the task of encircling, so to speak, this topic. Even if we are not able to explicate universally valid criteria of judgment, we must take seriously that in aesthetic questions we assume that inter-subjective communication is possible. What are the implications of this? Joseph Margolis makes a number of suggestions. First, he em-phasizes that we cannot deny "that artworks and texts are capable of infinitely many interpretations." The work of art has no fixed con-tent: "*What* is interpretable in a text is affected and altered by the very history of its ongoing interpretation."[162] However, this is only one side, he argues; at the same time it must be noted that where a new approach to a piece of art is sought, at least an "operative sense of objectivity"[163] is presupposed. Margolis emphasizes that these two statements do not contradict each other.

A similar point can be made regarding the truth claim of art; in this case too an encircling of the topic seems appropriate. On the one hand, we cannot assume of any of our expressions that it is absolutely true; on the other, a philosophical analysis of art can hardly do with-out any reference to truth. The creation of form—in whatever medium—implies a search for an optimal solution. Even where the artistic intention aims at ambiguity, limited foci, or fleeting moments, a search for the most appropriate mode is performed that corre-sponds to the weak concept of truth suggested here. Similarly, it can be said about an *objet trouvé* (which has not gone through explicit artistic formation) that its observer, through the resituation of an everyday object, is confronted with a truth.

A reading of classical aesthetics that avoids overly strong theses can open up new approaches to its elements. It is possible that Kant's idea of an "indifferent delight" remains valid today. This concept is obviously not aimed (as a common objection insinuates) at disqualifying the utility value of things. Kant rather examines what it means if we think of something as beautiful, and what is the specific aspect of this aesthetic judgment in comparison to other judgments of taste. He points out that we are able to see the same object from the viewpoint of usability or from that of aesthetic value. We can, according to the first option, look at an apple to see whether it might be sour or sweet, juicy or mealy. With regard to an approach in which we are guided by the intention of usage, Kant introduces the term *interest* to distinguish it terminologically from other cases in which we are not guided by such an intention. We can also find an apple beautiful (and it can be the same apple that we have just called sweet and juicy), but we reach this conclusion through another way of looking at it. The prerequisite for this is that we now do not ask for usability; only through this shift of focus is our gaze freed to consider the form. That is exactly what the term *disinterested delight* is supposed to express. It has nothing to do with the disqualification of apple eaters and other gourmets, but with the distinction between different modes of perception.

But does substituting weak interpretations for strong ones solve the central problem from a feminist perspective? Here it could be argued, along the lines of reservations about the contemporary reactualization of the notion sublime, that the masculine connotations of classical aesthetic terms are retained in the proposed reinterpretation. But how can such an objection be confirmed? To interpret disinterested delight as a patriarchal conception presupposes that first the two modes of perception distinguished by Kant are linked up with traditional sex roles. The view guided by interest, aiming at the satisfaction of needs, would be called feminine. But it is not obvious why such an interpretation should be plausible. The problem is well-known: This kind of feminist criticism establishes precisely the linkage of philosophical terms and gender clichés that it initially set out to challenge.[164] It is no coincidence, however, that this pattern of thought appears again and again. The cause is the projection of the dual grid constitutive for psychoanalytical thinking onto very different topics. The bourgeois model of gender difference inherent in this grid forms the unquestioned background of this criticism and is no any longer its target. (If the proximity of the classical aesthetic conceptions to the term *subject* draws complaint, similar problems arise. But the question of to what extent the subject can be interpreted as a masculine conception will be investigated in the next chapter.)

Whoever chooses aesthetics as a topic of research has to have an idea what this concept means in comparison to others. This holds true for feminist reflections on aesthetic issues. They too imply an understanding of what defines the area that is critically examined. Feminist theory therefore faces the same questions that were the starting point for classical aesthetics. It must explain what it means to look at certain phenomena—whether they exist in nature or were produced by human beings—under an aesthetic perspective. Here the significance of a weak interpretation becomes evident: It is not so much interested in a precise account of the history of philosophy, but in the possibility that some differentiations of classical provenance can still be relevant. Feminist criticism seems to have been based—although not explicitly—on such distinctions all along. I have already mentioned that the textile creations of women are frequently disqualified as applied art, while certain productions in the field of (male-dominated) architecture are assigned the status of genuine art. If this distinction—rightfully—is rejected, then this rejection implies something like the following argumentation: The fact that textiles can be used practically is no obstacle to perceiving them from an aesthetic perspective. Like houses, they can also be looked at in regard to their formal design. The differing esteem for textiles and architecture cannot be explained by a structural difference; it has rather its origin in

the contemptuous treatment of women. Whoever speaks in this case
of discrimination against women artists must take the position that
works by women as well as works by men can be objects of disinterested delight. (One must further distinguish between works that are
made for practical usage, on the one hand, and those that follow only
creative interests, on the other. Also in this regard a gendered connotation of either side must be strictly rejected. In this context classical
distinctions could again prove useful.)[165]

In view of the current relevance of elements of classical conceptions, what should be the specific nature of a feminist aesthetic? Let
us first consider which expectations could be tied up with this notion.
The terminology suggests a comparison with analogous formulations—analytical aesthetics, phenomenological aesthetics. But to
think of feminist aesthetics in this sense leads to serious problems.
Since adjectives like *analytical* or *phenomenological* refer to a specific
philosophical method, the term *feminist* would also describe a special
methodology—one method placed side by side with the others. But
in this manner the specific kind of challenge posed by feminist questions would be subverted. All philosophical schools are confronted
by feminist discourse with the problem of the hierarchy of the sexes
(as shown in the introduction to this book). With respect to aesthetics, this means that the actual object of a criticism from a feminist
perspective is not the specific approach as such (e.g., the analytical or
phenomenological approach to aesthetics). The criticism rather addresses the question of whether (or how) the method in question has
been or is put to the service of patriarchal intentions. This focus is
decisive for the goal of feminist criticism: an aesthetic theory freed
from the burden of masculine patterns of thought. (One element of
such a theory is the demand that creative productions in which feminist concerns are expressed must be taken seriously in the same way
as other artworks.) The realization of this goal requires no sweeping
blow or blanket condemnation, but can use already existing distinctions. Many studies have reinterpreted concepts from the history of
philosophical aesthetics from a feminist perspective.[166]

This research notwithstanding, the demand for a new aesthetics is repeatedly articulated as if a feminist aesthetics were analogous to an analytical or phenomenological aesthetics. Therefore, the problems arising from this view need to be examined more closely. To be able to develop such an aesthetic, a specific feminist concept of art or the aesthetic aspects of natural phenomena is necessary. This implies the idea that the achievements of human creativity, and the aesthetic aspects of natural phenomena, are differently viewed for those who are motivated by feminist concerns than for those who are not. Here we encounter a well-known pattern of thought: The term *feminist* has replaced the term *feminine* in the theories discussed above. Therefore analogous problems arise. If it cannot be shown why belonging to the female sex should be connected with a specific kind of creativity, it is also not clear why critical thinking in line with a certain political engagement—like feminism—should lead to specific aesthetic categories. Such a claim cannot survive close scrutiny. We are rather confronted with an alternative that forces us to give priority to either a feminist or an aesthetic focus, as I will now explain briefly. One option is the idea that artistic productions must be judged according to whether or not they serve feminist aims. This implies that no specific valency is assigned to the aesthetic but creative potential is subordinated to political norms. The dubiousness of this approach is well-known from the debates over official art in the totalitarian regimes of the twentieth century. Therefore a number of authors plead for taking the irreducible character of the aesthetic seriously in the feminist context.[167] In order to characterize the problem generated by attempts to circumvent the differentiation of art and politics more precisely, one could use (in reference to Janet Wolff, who draws a comparison to the "naturalistic fallacy)[168] the political fallacy concept.

But if (this is the other side of the alternative) we regard art as an independent dimension, then we need to assume a specific kind of judgment that does not allow a subordination under categories alien to art. Strictly speaking, it is inadmissible to speak of a feminist aesthetic. But this should not be misinterpreted: To see art as a special sphere does not mean that it has nothing to do with political aims. (Kant's concept of disinterested delight is often misunderstood in this sense.) If art guides us toward a new way of seeing, it can also alter our view of political conditions. But the political impulse in this case is a result—and not the condition—of the creative activity. (The political relevance of art is also subject to the infinite process of interpretation mentioned above.) From a feminist perspective, one question arises that must be asked in each case anew: What are the implications of the altered perceptions initiated by art for the relationship of the sexes?

First, objections must be raised if sexist forms of thinking and acting are derived from art. In this context, a rereading of Kant's considerations on the relation of politics and morality might be rewarding. I refer here to Kant's understanding of politics as an independent sphere that has morality as a "limiting condition."[169] Analogously (the acceptance of the independence of art notwithstanding), a limiting condition must be formulated from a feminist perspective. Second, we have to ask to what degree the political impulses initiated by art can generate a feminist potential. Rita Felski proposes, rightfully, that Adorno's analysis of the differences and connections between art and politics should receive more attention in feminist theory.[170] She primarily refers to Adorno's concept of negative aesthetics, according to which brittle, formal, autonomous art can be a site of resistance against social conventions.[171] However, no new mandatory coherence between the feminist project and certain currents of art can be constructed from here, as is convincingly shown by Felski.[172] In regard to the question about feminist aesthetics in a narrow sense, it would be a misunderstanding to interpret this term as advocating a feminist art. The central aim is rather to formulate an aesthetic theory that is liberated from the burden of masculine patterns of thought and therefore opens up space for an art with feminist potential.

3

REASON: A CONCEPT
WITH CONNOTATIONS
OF MASCULINITY

One problem, many questions

THE CONCEPT OF REASON IS CONNOTED as masculine in everyday understanding and thus it becomes the starting point for a feminist critique of reason. The ideal image of gender difference in Western culture assigns reason to men and emotion to women. Abstract thinking, objective judgment, detached behavior, and an orientation toward general principles are seen as characteristics of the man, while subjectivity, spontaneous reactions, and an orientation toward the concrete, individual case are regarded as typically feminine. For women this means, on the one hand, that their capacity for reason is in doubt (as expressed in common jokes about women's logic) and, on the other hand, that the cultivation of their rational faculties is rejected as unfeminine—a rejection evident in pejorative terms such as *bluestocking*. Georg Simmel diagnosed the masculinization of reason thus: "The artistic demands . . . the justice of practical judgment and the objectivity of theoretical recognition . . . all these categories are, as it were, according to their form and their claim commonly human, but in their actual historical formation masculine. If we call such ideas, presented as absolute for the time being, objective as such, the equation: objective = masculine is valid in the historical development of our species."[1] The widely shared view summarized by Simmel implies a hierarchical pattern. Since reason and emotion are commonly perceived in a relation of subordination, the abilities assigned to the man are understood as superior to those of the woman. This means that the concept of reason, in its common understanding, carries with it a claim of patriarchal power.

The feminist critique of reason therefore investigates the roots of this connection between reason and masculinity and develops alternative ways of thinking. Widely divergent approaches to this task have been suggested, ranging from calls to reformulate the concept of reason to outright rejection of it; the feminist critique of reason does not form an internally consistent body of argumentation.[2] One cause of this heterogeneity is that individual authors have different definitions of reason. In the following discussion I elucidate this diversity. Selecting some paradigmatic texts, I show that the problem of masculinization has been attributed to different concepts, or at least different aspects, of reason. An unresolved conflict will become visible between the articulated critique of reason on the one hand, and the ways in which the feminist critique appeals to reason, albeit inexplicitly, on the other.

Rationality and gender blindness in the sciences

In the Western world science is commonly understood as the epitomal achievement of reason, and thus the feminist critique of reason focused on it first. The debate in which this issue was elaborated saw

a shift of emphasis. Sandra Harding characterizes this change succinctly: "From the woman question in science to the science question
in feminism."[3]

In the beginning, it was necessary to establish the fact that
mainstream scholarship was marked by a masculine bias. A great
number of individual case studies proves this is true for all branches
of the humanities as well as the sciences. Opinions typical for men
(more accurately, for men of the social strata to which scholars generally belong) often shape research.[4] This problem appears in a variety of forms. Although in some cases we are confronted with
explicitly misogynist statements, less obviously patriarchal thinking
also exists. Since the latter predominates—and is easily overlooked
because of its disguised appearance—it is of particular concern for
feminist analysis. A paradigm case is the phenomenon of androcentrism. Certain statements are presented with the claim of universality although they are de facto only valid for men. For instance, in
the pharmaceutical field, new medicines are frequently tested exclusively on male subjects for effects and side effects but then are used
therapeutically without sexual specification. An example from historical scholarship is also informative. In 1907 a law was passed in
Austria that allowed adult men of all social classes to vote. This was
called "universal franchise," although women were excluded. When
women were finally granted equal rights in 1918, this regulation
was treated linguistically as a special provision. The universal franchise notion was not, as might have been expected, expanded;
rather, the formulation 'Women's right to vote' was used. This split
terminology—universal franchise/women's right to vote—has not
been questioned by historians and remained in schoolbooks until
the 1980s. The erroneous use of the term *universal* has been challenged only by feminist historians.

Because the marginalization of women was detected in practically
all fields of research, the project of women's studies appeared at first
to be the appropriate response from a feminist perspective. The
chosen term reveals the aim: securing women the attention from

scholarship that is due them. This demand was Carol Gilligan's motivation when she started to orient her psychological investigations toward the project of describing the moral development of girls independently, not in the categories developed for male children.[5] With research programs of this kind in mind, Sandra Harding discusses the first phase of the debate under the heading "The Woman Question in Science." The call for distinct research on women is still legitimate, and much remains to be examined in this regard. Nonetheless, there were good reasons for the feminist challenge to scholarship to move beyond this project. First, research projects that focused exclusively on women soon proved too limited. Social and political scientists have emphasized that a number of genuinely feminist topics (e.g., patriarchal power structures or emotional relationships) make it necessary for scholars to deal with both sexes.[6] Consequently women's studies has been complemented or replaced by gender studies in virtually all academic disciplines. (From today's perspective, this development led to another problem, however. Gender studies—especially from a constructivist approach—have concentrated on questions of identity to an extent that threatens to displace the problem of discrimination against women.)

Another reason for moving beyond the project of women's studies in a narrow sense was the need to investigate the origins of the androcentric character of many mainstream theories. A lack of consideration for women or a distorted representation of women can be attributed to either the scholar or the research methodology. In this sense, Donna Haraway distinguishes two forms of criticism: The first understands androcentrism as bad science, while the other assigns it to normal science.[7] Objections that follow the first line of argumentation regard the problem as primarily individual and accuse the scholars in question of proceeding unseriously and performing "bad science." This criticism leads to a demand to follow the rules of academic work more consistently. Yet this kind of argumentation does not grasp the full depth of the issue. It is only one form of the problem that misogynist statements are presented frequently as the result of research—with "evidence" that the same author would reject in another context as simply unscholarly. In such cases it is legitimate to criticize an unserious procedure. But where patriarchal thinking influences scholarship in an inexplicit way, the reproach of bad science does not fit. It can hardly be claimed that all historians who ever stated that universal franchise was introduced in Austria in 1907 abused scholarship for the propagation of misogynist ideas. Many of them do not seem to comprehend the discriminatory implications of their usage of the word *universal*. Their view of the history of the Austrian law can be best characterized as gender blind.[8] Such cases of androcentrism cannot be traced simply to an individual departing from the norms of academic work. A different line of interpretation is needed here: If a statement can only qualify as scholarly if it is well-founded and made accessible to an intersubjective examination[9] and if the term *universal franchise* (in the restrictive meaning) was used for almost a century without causing criticism, then one must conclude that the methods developed in the mainstream for examining statements proved to be insufficient. At this point, a feminist critique directed against normal science is called for.

Traditional methods of research obviously lack sufficient mechanisms for warding off masculine bias. References to the "malestream" of science are warranted. Therefore a more precise feminist critique must investigate which components of the common understanding of scholarship are responsible for the propensity toward gender blindness. This question carries with it a significant shift of focus as the prime topic of critical analysis is no longer the specific methods and results of individual disciplines but the different theories of science. At the turn from the 1970s to the 1980s this move led to the project of a feminist epistemology.[10] Lorraine Code's essay "Is the Sex of the Knower Epistemologically Significant?"[11] is paradigmatic for this development. (The concept of feminist epistemology has provoked intense objections.[12] Different interpretations play a role here: Where the concept refers to a specifically feminist or feminine logic of investigation, grave problems result, analogous to those encountered in connection with feminist aesthetics. These problems do not arise, however, where the concept of feminist epistemology refers to a specific mode of questioning—where it expresses the critical intention to confront the received theory of science with the facts of androcentrism that can no longer be denied.)

This turn to the science question in feminism[13] took place in the context of a more general theoretical development. Objections to the concept of unified science were raised from different positions of contemporary philosophy. The critique of objectivity and specific components of that conception was especially relevant.[14] Feminist authors appropriated, for example, objections emphasizing that the strict separation of the context of discovery from the context of justification, as it was suggested by scholars defending the concept of unified science, is untenable. The term *context of discovery* can be used in different ways. For example, it can refer to arbitrary associations that actually have nothing to do with my research topic but "give me a new idea." It is certainly legitimate to maintain that the external cause for a new idea can be distinguished from the actual process of research. The entire project of a strict distinction between both contexts gets its plausibility from this point. But the situation becomes more complex where the term *context of discovery* refers to the questions of everyday life from which scholarly work begins. Some authors maintaining a unified science concept have emphasized that the point of departure for scientific research lies in everyday problems that people face and find themselves unable to solve, which are handed over to science as an explanandum (the subject to be investigated). A closer look at this connection of life world and science reveals, however, that the clear separation of the two contexts that these authors advocate proves impossible. When the explanandum is formulated, preliminary decisions are made that affect the research work. Aspects of a phenomenon that are not taken into account in the formulation of a particular issue remain excluded from research. For example, the common understanding that the course of history is determined by "great men" meant that investigation of the lives of "little people" was often neglected. In this manner, the manifold achievements of women in the past have not been noted.

The ways in which experiments are arranged, data are interpreted, and research findings are presented tend to be influenced by views from the everyday life of the scholar—including masculine bias. In light of this, a strict separation of the context of discovery and the context of justification proves counterproductive. According to the unified science concept, a theory is scientifically warranted if it is based on the logical operations that form the acknowledged set of rules for establishing an explanans—if it is based on the logic of science. But this idea implies a reductionist understanding of legitimization. As it focuses exclusively on the internal processes of research, it fails to follow—and to provide instruments for a critical control of—the actual operations of thinking in their entire course, which begins with the questions formulated in the context of everyday life. This reduced focus allows ideas from the everyday world to leave their mark on scientific work. This leads to the paradox, as Harding has shown, that the rigid positivist concept of objectivity opens the way for an impairment of objectivity.[15] Views that seem so obvious in everyday life that their biased character remains undetected are likely to become shaping assumptions of research.

These observations call for a critical look at the received opinion that modern science is value-free. If ideas from everyday life can influence a science based on the positivist paradigm, and if all areas of society in Western culture are patriarchally structured, then here are the causes of the masculine influence on mainstream scholarship. Elisabeth List uses the term *micropolitics* to characterize this connection. She states: "Androcentric ideologies reproduce themselves in the scholarly discourse in an area that was believed to be free of politics: on the level of the description, naming and classification of phenomena which a naïve empiricism is inclined to equate too quickly with the factual."[16] Unreflective traditional scholarship helps preserve a patriarchal order of the sexes. This micropolitical character of science is not limited to its androcentric aspects; other common prejudices also influence academic work. Numerous studies have revealed that patterns of thinking such as ethnocentrism, Eurocentrism, racism, and class prejudice can regularly be encountered as background assumptions in scholarly work, often intertwined with androcentrism. [17]

As feminist criticism of positivist theories of science developed its instruments, it drew on already existing objections. It has picked up so many elements from the more recent epistemological debate that they cannot be listed here entirely. I will discuss four examples of alliances between feminist criticism and different schools of thought. From this perspective, I first address suggestions for a feminist adaptation of Marxist criticisms of science. Just as Marxism understands knowledge as a social construct in the service of the ruling classes, the androcentric focus of scholarship was linked—following this model—to the patriarchal claim to power.[18] Second, Foucault's reformulation of Nietzsche's conception of genealogy was seen as a starting point for a more radical discussion of the power background of the sciences. In this context, Foucault's plea for a pluralism of methods and his idea of local knowledge were also employed for developing a feminist epistemology.[19] Third, deconstructivist methods were used to further unfold the topic of fragmented knowledge. Specifically the metaphorical aspect of language and the bodily origins of thinking were moved to the center of attention.[20] Fourth, feminist criticism of the concept of unified science also appropriated theories from the area of analytical philosophy; Quine's concept of a naturalized epistemology gained particular importance. Although Quine himself did not suggest this, his thesis that the actual processes of research need to be regarded from a holistic point of view has informed the project to investigate the influence of prejudice, including masculine bias, on the sciences.[21] Since linking itself in this manner to various contemporary schools of thought, feminist epistemology has also exposed itself to objections raised against the theories it utilized. Some instances of this will be discussed later. However, in recent debates, the thesis contending the "situatedness of knowledge" has proved to be well founded.[22]

What alternative should replace positivist conceptions of science? If mainstream research proves patriarchally shaped, how does feminist theory position itself? Should it reject the science project in its entirety, or can it define itself as a different type of scholarship—and if so, how? In this search for a viable alternative to research marked by androcentrism, several options are available, of which I will now elaborate three.

First, a number of authors have argued that academic scholarship is unavoidably shaped by masculine ideas and thus the entire science project must be abandoned. This conclusion rests, however, on a specific and, as I intend to show, overdrawn interpretation of situatedness. According to these authors, all research is guided by the interests of the privileged to maintain their power; academic discourse serves only to disguise the basic ideological character of science. (This way of linking knowledge and power is often formulated in reference to Foucault. One may ask whether such a reception does justice to Foucault, but this question cannot be taken up here.)[23] A strategy of blanket suspicion gets caught up in a performative self-contradiction: Those who try this extensive unmasking exempt themselves from it; they discuss the linkage of knowledge and power in a manner that they do not see as being itself guided by power interests. Similarly, the critique of androcentrism is founded on the (frequently silent) assumption that the micropolitical aspect of science can be made visible from a minority position not tainted by masculine bias. This implies that an adequate analysis of androcentrism can be performed only by critics who themselves enter into a scholarly discourse. For instance, how should works of music history that include no women composers be rejected, if not with the help of sources that prove there were in fact achievements of women in the field of composition?[24] Feminist criticism should not lose its footing by unrestrictedly questioning scientific rationality.[25] But this does not mean accepting a positivist concept of science after all. Rather, studies devoted to uncovering androcentrisms are already informed by another conception of scholarship (if indirectly) in which the idea of scientific rationality no longer has masculine connotations. (This alternative conception will be discussed later.)

The ongoing debate over knowledge and power invites two clarifying remarks. The first concerns the political dimension of scholarship. An objection to certain scientific theories, even if well argued, may not be acknowledged by the academic establishment because those who raise the objection are denied full recognition as members of the community of investigators. Clearly scientific-political measures are necessary. For instance, regulations for the equal treatment and support of women must be provided to make a scholarly education and academic career as available to them as it is to their male colleagues. (In many countries legal instruments of that kind have been created, but as of today the idea of equality is nowhere realized.) On the other hand, there is no need to answer disregard from the academic establishment with a complete rejection of science. We are well able to differentiate between a well-founded argument that we present, on the one hand, and its insufficiently argued rejection, due to status thinking, on the other.

My second remark concerns the concept of reason. It points out the difference between the blurry everyday use of the term *reason* and its actual meaning. On the colloquial level, it is common to describe certain views or suggestions as reasonable. It is equally common to characterize an opinion that one does not share as unreasonable. But this negative evaluation—unreasonable—should not be misunderstood as a rejection of reason. We must differentiate between the content of our opinions, which we can judge differently, on the one hand, and our ability to make such a judgment, traditionally described with the expression *reason,* on the other. Both modes of evaluation—reasonable/unreasonable—originate from the same process. Reason is appealed to as an examining authority; only the results are different. In one case it is assumed that the opinion in question will stand up to an examination by reason, in the other case that it will not. That we distinguish between the content of our thinking and our ability to judge can be seen in the fact that we assume in others and ourselves the capacity to learn. A statement that we initially believe to be reasonable can appear unreasonable after further scrutiny. Changing our opinion does not mean that we retrospectively dispute our ability to judge. On the contrary, we must presuppose this ability because otherwise the reversal could not be regarded as a change of *my* opinion. To those we describe as unreasonable in a certain matter, we at the same time assign the ability to change their mind. Otherwise it would make no sense to argue with others.

This is also relevant in regard to feminist criticism of science. Challenging androcentric statements that are broadly accepted as scientific, and therefore reasonable, does not represent the rejection of reason. If the difference between the content of thought and the capacity for thinking is not kept in mind, this leads to a sweeping suspicion of reason, which implies that feminist criticism can no longer account for its own mode of arguing. (An analogous danger arises, as Käthe Trettin has shown, in the feminist debate over logic.)[26] In short, any discussion of androcentric patterns of thinking requires, as a necessary precondition, a capacity for reasonable reflection. Thus Martha Nussbaum concludes that the feminist critique of reason contradicts itself if it is not able to do justice to its own argumentative prerequisites.[27]

But how, exactly, does our ability to judge work? Here the philosophical debate about reason begins. It analyzes the human ability to which we appeal so confidently in everyday life, and also tries to set out its limits. Feminist theory must therefore refer to philosophical discourse to account for its own argumentative claims, and not only in the critique of science. But there is no single, valid philosophical concept of reason that we can simply appropriate. The more recent developments in this field suggest that we engage in what I term *encirclement*. Any strong concept of reason must be challenged, since some structures of thought that were seen as independent of history and culture in classical conceptions of reason were in fact not independent. Nonetheless, the history of philosophy provides us with sophisticated investigations of reason that can contribute decisively to the contemporary search for a "weak" concept.

Regarding the criticism of science, the second type of response to androcentrism demands acknowledgement of "women's ways of knowing."[28] This demand has been presented in different ways. First, in view of the biological differences of the sexes, some people believe that men and women differ also in the way they think. Such an opinion is implausible for two reasons.[29] Let us assume a woman zoologist discovers a species of animal unknown to date in the Amazon region and a male colleague quotes her documentation. Is it appropriate to state that the feminine kind of knowledge becomes masculine in the process of quoting? Or does the male author adopt, through this quotation, a feminine way of thinking? Both interpretations contradict their starting thesis. They both state a transition in which the supposed border between the sexes is negated. It could also be claimed that the male author quotes his female colleague without actually understanding what she means. But here we encounter the second reason that stands against the assumption of a difference in thinking caused by biological sex: the problem of infinite regression. How can the misinterpretation assigned to the male author ever be proven? A third person would be needed who compares the quotation in his book with the thesis of the researcher in the Amazon. To be able to draw a comparison, this person could not belong to the female or the male sex. Even if this were possible, a further person would have to question the sexual starting position of the third person, and so forth.

The appeal to women's ways of knowing can also be interpreted with reference to gender. Due to the conventional division of labor between the sexes, women and men tend to develop different competencies in dealing with reality and they have specific experiences. These differences have a substantial impact on the field of scholarship, since they shape specific approaches. Researchers such as Jane Goodall and Dian Fossey made pioneering discoveries in the study of primates by developing a sensitive form of approaching chimpanzees and gorillas, which apparently can be connected with feminine behavior that is characteristic for traditional Western culture. But this line of argumentation may also lead to difficulties; everything depends on how it is elaborated in detail. One possibility is to assume that all knowledge is finally based on the different social locations of the sexes and therefore corresponds with one gender type. This assumption follows the same logic as the attribution of knowledge to the biological sex difference, and therefore gets caught up in an analogous aporia. Furthermore, as Waltraud Ernst has shown, it implies a problematic social determinism.[30]

A slightly varied version is the feminist standpoint theory as formulated since the 1970s by, for example, Dorothy Smith,[31] Hilary Rose,[32] and Nancy Hartsock.[33] This theory is inspired by the Marxist project of a revolution of knowledge on the basis of the class standpoint of the proletariat. It assumes that women, since they were pressed into the disadvantaged position in the gender hierarchy, have a sharper eye for reality and therefore are able to achieve better research results. Against this argument it has been rightfully stated that the fact of being discriminated against is, taken by itself, no guarantee of a critical reflection by the persons affected by that asymmetry. Many women whose oppression and/or marginalization has been clearly demonstrated by feminist criticism still do not evaluate their situation as problematic and reject feminist considerations. If no automatic linkage exists between factual discrimination and critical consciousness, then it is also true in regard to research that the underprivileged positioning of women does not *eo ipso* warrant expectations of (in comparison to mainstream research) more appropriate or merely different modes of investigation.[34] Sandra Harding formulates a further objection, pointing to the risk of essentialism. She emphasizes that *the* place of women does not exist; women can be found in the most divergent life situations and therefore have different experiences. (Harding's main point is that there is no need to insist on a viewpoint shared by *women as such* in order to challenge masculine thinking, but to make a *feminist* focus the basis of research. Harding calls for a reformulation of the standpoint theory in this sense.[35] This will be discussed later.)

These objections do not imply fundamental doubts concerning the thesis that gender has a decisive impact on scholarship; they only show that there is a need for further elaboration. The problem termed *essentialism,* for instance, requires a specification: Concerns about essentialist patterns of thought are raised rightfully where it is insinuated that women (or men) unavoidably share certain experiences due to their sex. But such concerns do not invalidate the observation that human beings tend to communicate the experiences they have in the context of their social location (their membership in cultural, ethnic and/or religious groups, their position in the social strata, and so on) with others who live under similar circumstances and to construct shared opinions in this communication process. With this in mind, the danger of an exaggerated antiessentialism in regard to women can be addressed. On the one hand, the idea of a feminine experience shared by all women has to be rejected, since women have very different opinions and aims in the most varied positions in society. But the consequence is not that any assumption of common experiences must be denied. Among those whose circumstances are defined by a patriarchally shaped feminine context of life, certain competencies and attitudes are so widely shared that they can be seen as characteristic for this group. If we acknowledge that scientific questions and theories are shaped predominantly by the perspective of a certain segment of society—by the point of view that is typical for the "adult white man of the middle class in a Western society"[36]—and if we call for an opening of research to other points of view, then it seems consistent to include in this demand those perspectives developed by women under the discussed conditions.[37] To avoid misunderstandings, the term *women's ways of knowing* should not be employed when we raise this demand, since this would suggest a homogeneous feminine approach.

At this point a further danger needs to be noted. If the previous statement were understood as promoting an unrestricted pluralism, the ideal would be for the many, specifically located groups of human beings to develop their special form of scholarship (on the basis of their specific view of reality), including the diverse groups of women, as they differ with regard to ethnicity, language, skin color, religion, sexual orientation, and so on. Some constructivist-inspired arguments in the present debate could be interpreted in this way. First, however, one has to distinguish the level of political utopia from the level of epistemology. With regard to politics, the aim of maintaining and promoting pluralism is legitimate, even inalienable. As recent debates over minority rights and multiculturalism have made clear, it is a political priority to protect and support a plurality of cultures, subcultures, life forms, and so on. (The aim of pluralism is, of course, not the only requirement for a plausible utopian idea. A basic legal framework negotiated among all individuals involved is also needed. For instance, precautions must be taken against groups that attempt to harm or expel others. A utopia of heterogeneity cannot do without agreements in regard to human rights and the fundamental rights of citizens.) For the epistemological field, in contrast, the aim has to be defined differently. Proclaiming plurality in the manner of political utopia would encourage epistemological relativism.[38] The concept of knowledge would become obsolete; if all opinions were awarded the same status, then knowledge could not be distinguished from my opinion. Downgrading all claims of knowledge to simple opinions would have grave consequences, as illustrated by the feminist critique of science: Uncovering androcentrisms would have no greater aim than to make known the opinion of a certain group and place it side by side with the opinions of misogynist groups. But this would abandon the claim of challenging an inappropriate theory and would lead, as Alison Jaggar has noted poignantly, to a situation where feminist criticism would be valid only for feminists.[39]

Concepts such as knowledge, science, and research are based on the principle that theories must be well founded and accessible to an intersubjective examination. A thesis can be considered valid only if it has been checked, as far as possible, by the available methods and confronted with an extensive series of objections. Alternative approaches to the object in question do not remain unconsidered but are, on the contrary, specifically acknowledged. The process of argumentation takes place in the community of investigators in an undistorted form. Thus plurality in an epistemological context has value as a precondition for research, not as an aim. Therefore diverse approaches and opinions (arising in different social contexts, as discussed above) are not, from an epistemological perspective, the final word but are always individual statements that must be related to each other and put to test in the community of investigators.[40]

The methods developed by Goodall and Fossey for a close interaction with primates gained prominence because they could be made accessible and shown to be successful to experts with an entirely different social background. When I speak of individual statements and the ideal of undistorted communication in the community of investigators, this can be related to the current concept of democratic science. How is this conception to be spelled out in detail? It would be epistemologically questionable to understand the term *democratic* from the viewpoint of voting procedures or majority decisions. Rather, the theoretical content of the term—the idea of democracy— has to be taken into account in a comprehensive way. In a pluralist society, how can the rules that regulate communal life be established in a just manner?

The idea of democracy is fully apprehended only if the diversity of opinions is taken as a starting point for a deliberative communication process, not a hermetic juxtaposition that only allows majority decisions. Processes of opinion formation and decisionmaking lead to just regulations only when the voices of all persons affected are made audible and taken seriously, on equal terms. This is a decisive principle also in epistemology: All the diverse approaches and views that have developed in specific social backgrounds must get an opportunity to be expressed and must receive equal attention. Obviously this principle is crucial for scholarship to avoid one-sidedness (e.g., androcentrism and gender blindness).[41]

The third alternative to androcentrism lies in reformulating the term *objectivity* in a way that it can no longer veil masculine thinking.

Some prerequisites for a clarification have already been provided here. First, there is no way back to the idea that it is the aim of scholarship to discover truths that are valid once and for all. In the face of the strong evidence for the situatedness of research, any attempt to renew the concept of objectivity in the rigid sense of a scientistic program would fail. The issue, again, has to be "encircled." The question is how to define the claim of science if, on the one hand, the inevitable contextuality is taken into account and, on the other, an epistemological relativism is to be avoided. This question cannot be discussed here with due reference to the complex current epistemological discourse; only some basics will be outlined that are relevant to the problem of androcentrism. (Recall that the thesis of situatedness of science addresses two different aspects. First, it points out that research starts with questions resulting from problems we encounter in everyday life. This is true not only for scientific investigations that are directly oriented toward application, such as in the medical disciplines. With regard to disciplines whose objects seem to be far removed from practical problems, we also assume their reference to present issues. We express this understanding, for instance, when we claim to take an interest in their investigations. Examined more closely, this relation to interest is a *conditio sine qua non* for research. Therefore, the feminist theory of science may well utilize the typology developed in the 1970s in the positivism debate that specifies different knowledge guiding interests. The second aspect of the issue of situatedness is usually at the forefront, largely due to the dominance of constructivist conceptions in the current debate. The point is that the framework of categories which determines the approach to research questions—in whatever discipline—is not independent from history and culture.)

The conception of a democratic science, according to the interpretation I just proposed, aims for an environment in which all scholars get a fair chance—and are expected—to explain and defend their specific approaches to the research topic in question. The goal here is limited; it is no longer to establish theories that are valid for all times.

A revised concept of objectivity takes shape. It formulates the task of entering a process of thorough weighing, beginning from the different perspectives that can currently be brought to bear on research topics, in search of the most plausible theories (from today's perspective). These considerations are not new, but they provide the theoretical foundation for a feminist challenge to the mainstream sciences.[42] They allow us to account for what is already happening in scholarly practice, for instance, when historians suggest models for the appropriate inclusion of women in historiography with the help of detailed source studies.

If the concept of objectivity is repositioned in this manner, the distinction between context of discovery and context of justification gains relevance. This distinction has not become *toto genere* obsolete but needs a revised understanding.[43] The scientistic interpretation that views the two contexts as clearly separable cannot be maintained. Remember that a theory cannot be falsified by uncovering its origin in a certain historical, cultural, or social context. In this sense Harding notes succinctly: "Newton's mechanics 'works' although it is the product of a specific modern and western mechanistic system."[44] This implies that scientific theories can only be refuted through proper examinations. The claim to carefully investigate cannot be dismissed with the argument that it is merely our perspective that we employ. The individual perspective is not a simple given but is accessible to, as well as in need of, discursive reasoning. Canceling the distinction between the two contexts would have disastrous consequences, not least from a feminist perspective, as Ruth Anna Putnam made clear. Putnam illustrates this with reference to the current discussion of concepts of justice derived from classical contract theory. The fact that the classic concepts were developed in a patriarchally shaped tradition is no good reason to reject, for instance, Rawls's theory. Rather, the contractarian approach has to be examined for its argumentative content and can be modified to cover the specific goals of feminist politics. When feminist critique suggests evaluating and rejecting theories only in reference to the context of discovery, it deprives itself of a decisive instrument for analyzing discrimination and demanding justice for women: "The origin of the principles of justice in a tradition dominated by white, Christian, bourgeois men does not matter, what matters is how well it enables the rest of us to press our claims successfully, without either stepping on each other's toes or simply changing places with our erstwhile oppressors."[45]

To reformulate objectivity in this manner is not a retreat from an originally hard request. Since the situatedness of thinking formerly ignored is now reflected, objectivity has been increased. Along these lines Sandra Harding characterizes her version of standpoint theory (see above) with the term *strong objectivity*.[46] How can the realization of this claim be accomplished? What kind of evidence will move the community of investigators to accept a theory as well founded (from today's point of view)? The operation called reasoning cannot be restricted to the levels of empirical experience and logic. In the historical disciplines, for example, theories need to be tested under four different perspectives, as I explained in a previous study.[47] In particular, the normative implications of historical research must be discussed. If scholars bring to bear their individual perspectives (shaped by their social and cultural environment) and if the academic community discusses them, as suggested in the concept of democratic science, then questions of a political, legal, and moral nature will also have to be debated. What has been stated concerning the scientistic conception of objectivity in general applies to the idea of value-free research as well: It is not only unredeemable but counterproductive. Yet this fact should not be received with resignation. Examined more closely, the aim of establishing value-free theories is not desirable. If one considers the interest background of the sciences (i.e., the first aspect of situatedness discussed above) it becomes clear that research topics do not emerge from our need for information alone but also derive from our present problems of practical orientation. We expect the results of research to allow us to derive arguments in regard to current conflicts and upcoming practical decisions.[48] Searching for value-free theories means ignoring an essential task of research.[49] We have to acknowledge that normative disagreement forms a regular element of scientific discourse and that a comprehensive theory of science must take this fact into account.

A discussion of the normative aspect of research is of elementary significance for feminist criticism of the sciences. It can provide important theoretical preconditions to justify projects of feminist-motivated research. Studies with feminist interests sometimes are reproached for repeating the same mistake—androcentrically biased narratives are replaced by historical constructions based on feminist views that ideologize research. The expression mistake reveals an orientation toward the scientistic paradigm. If we recognize that the idea of value-free scholarship is not redeemable and that its validation is not desirable, then we see that controversies evolving around normative language concerning, for instance, the social position of women, gender relations, and so on, are a genuine element of historical research.

At this point, the proposed reformulation of objectivity might again be questioned. Can we enter a rational argumentation concerning the diverse given normative convictions in search of the norm(s) best justified? If this is not an option—as is assumed, for instance, by decionist concepts—then there is only the relativist position, which suggests that the claim to science is illusory. Here again encirclement might help. Exaggerated expectations must be cautioned: As before in regard to questions of content with respect to problems of a political, legal, or moral nature, too, the idea of statements valid once and for all must be dismissed. Nonetheless, we weigh in an argumentative manner the diverse sets of norms that confront us. For instance, it is not true that opponents of a (post)colonialist politics cannot come up with good reasons for their claims. A developed discourse on human dignity, fundamental rights, international justice, and so on is already providing a sound basis for deliberation. These considerations have prospered to such an extent that the burden of proof has shifted (from a theoretical viewpoint): Those who believe oppression and exploitation to be justified have to defend their opinion in reference to the argumentative standard already reached. The thesis of Ruth Anna Putnam mentioned before is also relevant in this context. Putnam pleads not to dismiss the conception of justice developed in the tradition of the Enlightenment because she sees it as the best theory available (from today's point of view). Starting from here she argues that there is no considerable difference (in regard to the formal structure of the procedure) between an argumentative examination of scientific theories and of political ideas: "In science we need to identify the laws or theory relevant to solving the problem at hand; we work with the best theory we already have, though in the course of solving our problem we may also change the theory. Likewise, in dealing with a political problem we work with the best theory we already have, and in the course of applying the theory to concrete problems, we learn how it must be modified."[50] That normative questions are not beyond the reach of argumentative clarification also applies to the political, legal, or moral judgments that are an unavoidable, inalienable element of scientific research. The normative implications of the term *objectivity* do not generally devalidate it but must be taken into account; only under this condition can the thesis be defended that we are able to found theories comprehensively (from today's perspective).

Sandra Harding's concept of a strong objectivity proves in this respect to be insufficiently consistent, since it implies an unresolved contradiction. In her criticism of scientism Harding pleads for making visible the political background of research and formulates an evaluation: Not all political positions have the same right to initiate research programs; rather, those that aim at liberation from oppression should be favored. Here she refers to an engagement against discrimination with regard to class, race, gender, and sexual orientation. From this perspective, research conducted from a feminist standpoint could claim priority over scholarship employing a masculine point of view. This judgment requires reasoning, but Harding does not go into it; on the contrary, she questions all argumentative procedures in the normative realm. Harding states first that "insisting on formality and abstraction in the form of 'impersonal' rules and procedures could itself be a historically developed and distorting social behavior."[51] She then explains that such behavior is typical for men and reaches the conclusion that the "logic of the 'context of justification'" presents a "hypermasculine distortion."[52] With this statement Harding goes beyond a pointed discussion of scientistic narrowness. In assigning "formality and abstraction" in general to masculine behavior, she rejects any appeal to universally valid principles of justice or morality like those on which human rights are based. Thus Harding subverts the possibility of a justification of normative statements, although this very possibility must be assumed if the concept of strong objectivity is to be consistent.

Harding refers to findings from developmental psychology, specifically object-relations theory. Let us assume to be true that men are more disposed to abstract thinking than are women because of the gender-differentiated socialization common in Western culture. From this diagnosis it cannot be derived that abstraction is disqualified for feminist thought. It is not abstraction as such that has to be questioned, but the traditional division of labor that assigns abstraction to men. (Clearly we also need to ask whether the view that traditionally socialized women are not able to think abstractly is a myth.) Of course it can prove necessary to criticize the level of abstraction of certain theories. For example, claims to establish a uniform logic of research, equally binding for the different disciplines, have led to very general concepts of explanation, which are of limited value for the analysis of the patterns of thought actually employed in the individual disciplines.[53] Referring to this problem, Harding's criticism of a positivist definition of the logic of justification can find consent. But we also need to keep in mind that the core of the problem is that the concept of unified science fails to achieve its objective, not that it has a masculine character. In this context the term *masculine* has a certain inflationary tendency. The precision that is made possible by distinguishing between the terms *male* and *masculine* often remains unused—also by Harding. The phrase *masculine thought* is frequently used in such a broad sense that the distinction between patriarchal ideas, on the one hand, and theoretical competencies, which are (in Western culture) predominately attributed to men, on the other, gets blurred. As a result of this de-differentiation, feminist criticism too is marked by a lack of clarity. Often it is not taken into account that different thrusts of criticism are necessary: in the first case, the hierarchical relation; in the second, the division of labor between the sexes has to be targeted. Where this distinction is not made, an overdrawn criticism of patriarchy results. In this case the distancing from sexist ways of thinking challenges at the same time the competencies allegedly unattainable for women that they could claim for themselves. This leads to an unjustified self-restriction of women and to a familiar problem. A feminist argumentation that rejects competencies cultivated predominately by men with no other reason but this has uncritically internalized traditional clichés of the character of the female sex.

To conclude, processes of research should be altered in such a way that they are no longer shaped by masculine ideas but are oriented toward equal consideration of both sexes. Good reasons can be put forward against patriarchal claims of dominance, and the idea of fair treatment for both sexes can be justified in reference to principles that Ruth Anna Putnam has called "the best theories we already have." If this assumption is suspected of being masculine and thus rejected, the aim of reshaping scholarship must be dropped too. Nothing is left but to accept an invincible heterogeneity; thus the specific normative ideas developed by diverse social groups cannot become the objects of debates scrutinizing their validity. And the possibility of arguing against androcentrism in scholarship is forfeited. A standpoint theory starting from here could understand feminist research only as one possibility among others; looked at more closely, it would have to give up the claim of scientificity. Obviously the issue of an argumentative examination of normative judgments is indispensable, especially in the interest of the theoretical foundation of feminist research. A detailed elaboration of this issue leads beyond the theory of science. The question of to what extent normative judgments can be justified refers to another philosophical context that is traditionally connected with the concept of reason—the debate on practical reason.[54]

Is science founded on aggressive masculinity?

The feminist critique of science does not stop at an immanent analysis of scientism and the gender blindness emerging from it. Some authors claim that the methodological approach to reality originates in the male psyche. Scientific rationality, in this perspective, expresses the masculine pattern of dominance. For a discussion of this approach, let us first focus on the ideas of Evelyn Fox Keller, which many consider fundamental.

According to Keller, a justification for a psychologizing interpretation can be drawn from theoretical texts by the founder of modern science, Francis Bacon. It seems paradigmatic to Keller that Bacon, while describing the relation of science to nature, uses a gendered analogy. According to Bacon, she points out, nature should be subjected to research and the technology derived from it just as the wife is subject to her husband. Keller quotes from Bacon's work "Temporis Partus Masculus" (The Male Birth of Time), in which an older scientist speaks of marriage to his son: "My dear, dear boy, what I plan for you is to unite you with things themselves in a chaste, holy and legal wedlock."[55] Keller illuminates the inner structure of this unity through another passage in the same text: "I am come in very truth leading to you Nature with all her children to bind her to your service and make her your slave."[56] How does Keller, working with the quoted passages, reach her extensive psychologizing interpretation? She reads Bacon's texts concerning the theory of science (even where there is no explicit reference to an image of gender hierarchy) in light of these patriarchal metaphors. As she investigates how Bacon describes in detail the relationship of science and technology with nature, she claims to reconstruct a text on gender relations. Bacon's thesis that the relation between scientist, nature, and God is marked by tension corresponds, according to Keller, with the family triangle. In her view, Bacon depicts the different stages of scientific research in a way that parallels the early developmental phases of male children. Object-relations theory provides the categories fundamental to this understanding (see below). Where Bacon describes the scientist in the primary stage of his work as receptive and submissive, for Keller those female parts of the psyche are addressed, which have to be repressed so that a masculine identity can develop. Accordingly, she sees Bacon's depiction of the further steps taken by the researcher as corresponding with the "transformation of mind to male from female."[57] She maintains that "the aggressive male stance of Bacon's scientist" finally emerges from this transformation.[58]

A hermeneutic approach of this kind is always welcome as stimulating reading. Nonetheless we need to analyze Keller's method and to address the problems it generates. Let us first take a fresh look at Bacon's argument. On the one hand, he maintains that the relation of science and technology to nature is one of domination; on the other hand, he claims that this relation of domination can be described in a metaphorical manner by referring to conjugal relations. Unfortunately Keller does not clearly distinguish these two elements of his thinking. As a result, her critique fails to specify the core problem. From a feminist perspective, it is crucial to focus on the second element and address how Bacon perceives the husband's position in order to expose and reject the wife's subordination. This criticism implies the demand that gender relations no longer serve as a model for hierarchical structures. A reading of Bacon's comparison of the scientist to the husband that is inspired by a genuine feminist concern involves a shift of focus. Such a reading differs from Keller's approach in that the objection to Bacon now relates to only one of the two sides of the comparison he draws. It concerns Bacon's view of relations between husbands and wives, but not, at the same time, his conception of science and technology's relationship to nature.

The thesis of the domination of human beings over nature can be formulated without reference to conjugal relations. If this thesis itself needs critical discussion (e.g., in view of today's environmental crisis), then this is a specific problem. We cannot condemn the human domination of nature simply by underscoring that the subordination of women is unacceptable. The demand for women's liberation does not *eo ipso* necessitate rejecting structures of subordination in any other area. Though Keller's claim to discern explicitly patriarchal thoughts in Bacon's work is justified, her critique loses plausibility when she considers the detected patriarchal traits a sufficient reason for charging Bacon's entire conception of the sciences with masculine bias. That Keller fails to confront Bacon's mode of proceeding in detail (specifically his use of comparisons) leads to an unintended agreement.[59] The wholesale objection she raises presupposes that she tacitly adopts this very alignment of scientific rationality with masculinity instead of articulating a repudiation.

This way of problematizing Keller's point of view may be disputed. Bacon's comparison of the scientist to the husband may be taken as only one explicit manifestation of a far broader context. According to this view, the opinion that the true claim of science is the domination of nature (programmatically formulated by Bacon and maintained to this day) does per se correspond with the masculine attitude, even where it is not expressed in a gendered metaphoric. Keller seeks additional support for this view in object-relations theory. Since this kind of a psychoanalytical interpretation of science is common, I will discuss it in greater detail.

Nancy Chodorow's book *The Reproduction of Mothering: Psychoanalysis and the Sociology of Gender* has been used as the conceptual framework for the thesis maintaining the masculine character of scientific rationality.[60] Chodorow investigates how the ability to perceive reality is developed and at what point early developmental differences between girls and boys can be detected. In the beginning, the child is unable to distinguish between the inner and the outer world. The external environment, which for most children in this early stage consists of the mother, is experienced by the child as an extension of itself. Only gradually does the child learn to distinguish self from nonself. Like psychoanalysts before her, Chodorow notes that as the mother comes to appear as an independent being, the child becomes aware of its own autonomous existence. From this experience ambivalent feelings emerge: on the one hand, a longing for a rein-stallation of the original unity; on the other, the pleasure of experi-encing independence. The complex process of development that is thereby set into motion ultimately leads to the child's acknowledg-ment of a world external to, and independent from, itself. The child then sees itself confronted with objects, and a self-consciousness begins to develop that is established first in opposition to the mother. But the child still has not reached the mature stage. Maturity is a matter of learning that separateness can be overcome without a return to an earlier stage: "Out of this recognition and acceptance of one's own aloneness in the world, it becomes possible to tran-scend one's own isolation, to truly love another."[61]

For all these processes, Chodorow assumes a general validity: Boys and girls both must learn to distinguish between the self and the other. That differences nonetheless begin to take shape is explained by the fact that boys have to go through a double disidentification from the mother,[62] first to establish a self-identity and then to consol-idate a masculine gender identity. Boys therefore tend toward an ex-cessive detachment, resulting in distancing behavior, autonomy, and objectivism—characteristics generally perceived as typically mascu-line. The development of girls proceeds differently. Since they do not experience such a distinct disidentification, they can, according to Chodorow, remain to a certain extent in an ongoing identification with their mothers, which hinders the development of a sense of sep-aration. Accordingly, connectedness, dependency, and subjectivity are usually taken to be typically feminine characteristics.

Feminist theory has brought this idea of a gender-differentiated early development of children to bear in the interpretation of scien-tific rationality. For Evelyn Fox Keller, a continuity exists between a boy's aggressive separation and a science defined by confrontation between subject and object.[63] "A science that advertises itself by the promise of a cool and objective remove from the object of study selects for those individuals for whom such a promise provides emotional comfort."[64] According to her, the same applies to the power aspect of science; consequently, "the dream of domination over Nature, shared by so many scientists, echoes the dream that the stereotypic son hopes to realize by identifying with the authority of his father."[65] This is the very point of Keller's understanding of science. She characterizes the deficiency of science in the following way: "But such dreams are by their very nature self-limiting. They prevent the son from ever getting to know the real mother. And so, it could be argued, they similarly obstruct the scientist's efforts to know the 'real' Nature."

My objections to Keller's critique do not concern object-relations theory as such. In my view, its conceptual core, as well as its findings with regard to the development of gender difference, provide valuable analytic tools (although in what follows I must do without a more thorough investigation). With regard to the family structure characteristic for Western culture, the thesis that the socialization of male and female children proceeds differently seems just as plausible as the theory that these different trajectories each tend to lead toward gender-specific deficiency in maturity. The problem that needs to be addressed here lies in the way Keller expresses her observation that boys at times distance themselves so aggressively that they are not able to perceive the mother as a person. In this context, she uses the word *object* in a broad sense to refer not only to the world of things but also the mother. I will show that Keller was misled by subsuming woman under the concept of object. Keller's criticism of excessive separation, however, is justified. It must be demanded, especially from a feminist point of view, that the relations among human beings take shape in a manner that does not degrade women to object status. (When this demand is discussed in theoretical terms, usually a concept of mutual recognition is foregrounded; Keller, however, speaks of love, to which I shall return later.) A problem arises as Keller rejects not only the object status of women but object status as a rule. She can conceive of women's liberation only in terms of dissolving the confrontation of subject and object in general. The problem is that Keller does not dispute the equation of woman with the world of objects but instead adopts this equation as a premise herself.

Keller's understanding of scientific rationality is burdened with this problem, as seen in the way she seeks to prove the masculine character of modern science. As illustrated above, she argues that nature is oppressed in two ways: as the object of knowledge and of domination through technological means. Supposing this description of nature's oppression is correct, the decisive question remains unanswered: Why should this statement be taken to imply necessarily that modern science is based on a subordination of woman? An indication for a *masculine* claim of supremacy can be seen in this double subordination only on the condition that woman has already been identified with nature. Yet this equation is by no means compelling. On the contrary, it has to be challenged, especially from a feminist perspective.

This problematic implication of Keller's argument has hardly been addressed, perhaps because some of the motives behind her critique of science are plausible and agree with the general objections to positivism formulated in the recent debate. An epistemology that operates with a naive opposition between subject and object must be rejected. Further, scientism must be challenged on the ground that it induces into the humanities a view of the human being that supports a socio-technological, strategic type of action. What is problematic here is not that science has connotations of masculinity; rather, the specific concepts of subject/object relationship and of scientism call for a more sophisticated theory. Both of these issues have already led to complex debates. Keller's work, however, tends to oversimplify. A couple of examples must suffice here. Where Keller denounces domination in general, a number of distinctions are necessary, for example, between the justifiably criticized disenfranchisement of human

beings on the one hand, and a utilization of natural resources necessary for human survival on the other. In regard to the world's current
environmental crisis, a wholesale dismissal of thoughts about human
control over nature is not advisable. Rather, it is necessary to distinguish between utilization that leaves nature's potential for regenera-
tion intact and irreversible destruction of natural resources.
Furthermore, Keller's premises do not give her the means to do justice to the differences between the sciences and the humanities.
Based on her subsumption of woman to nature, she claims that the
scientist's attitude should be inspired by the model of empathy—
love—between subjects. Thus she endorses the view of June Goodfield, who writes, "If you really want to understand a tumor, then
you have to become one."[66] Goodfield maintains that for the practice
of scientific research, "the best analogy is always love."[67] Whether the
term *love* is suitable as a category in the theory of science is dubious,
but it could still be interpreted in terms of a hermeneutic conception
of the humanities. But Keller uses this term in an unspecific manner,
so that it also refers to the sciences. This makes her suggestions for a
renewal of the natural sciences sound almost animistic.[68]

My objections to Keller are not intended to deny that, on the
whole, scientific rationality and reason in general have connotations
of masculinity. Rather, my concern is that these phenomena are not
always analyzed in a plausible way by Keller and must find a more
precise explanation.

The criticism of Western Logos

Another variation of the feminist critique of reason, which enjoys
wide appeal, takes on not only scientific rationality but occidental
culture's way of thinking as a whole, which is characterized by the
concept of Logos. This most encompassing form of feminist critique
is fueled by the belief that logos is permeated by a masculine attitude.
Once again psychoanalysis provides the conceptual foundations of

the critique, the work of Lacan featuring prominently. There is a close connection with the concepts advocating an *écriture féminine* discussed in the previous chapter.

The writings of Luce Irigaray are characteristic of this kind of feminist critique. She directs our attention to the fact that Freud does not develop a concept of female sexuality but refers to women only in terms of what they lack, as the theory of penis envy shows. Drawing on psychoanalytical categories to interpret this, Irigaray concludes that Freud's concept of sexuality is based on an anal fantasy. She refers to the way Freud explicitly maintains that the little girl has to be seen as a small man, and highlights that the woman appears in his work in general as a deficient man.[69] "Female sexuality has always been conceptualized on the basis of masculine parameters . . . woman's erogenous zones never amount to anything but a clitoris-sex that is not comparable to the noble phallic organ, or a hole-envelope . . . a non-sex, or a masculine organ turned back upon itself, self-embracing."[70] Irigaray goes on to note, "About woman and her pleasure, this view of the sexual relation has nothing to say." This remark indirectly expresses the actual aim of her critical reflections.

Irigaray's objection to Freud is not that he distorts reality. Rather, she is convinced that Freud's formulations are the explicit expression of how woman is perceived in Western culture in general, and that this perception also determines the real living conditions and experiences of women. As a result, Irigaray formulates the demand to overcome the negative dependency on the masculine and facilitate the genuine unfolding and expression of the feminine. "As Freud admits, the beginnings of the sexual life of the little girl are so 'obscure,' so 'faded with time,' that one would have to dig down very deep indeed to discover, beneath the traces of this civilization, this history, the vestiges of a more archaic civilization that might give some clues as to what woman's sexuality is all about."[71]

Ending the male monopoly over the power to define is a precondition for such a rediscovery. Here Irigaray's critique of reason comes into play. That the woman is only spoken of *per negationem* is, in her

view, not specific to the discourse of sexuality, but is a consequence of
the fundamentally masculine character of occidental thought. In this
context, Irigaray introduces the term *Logos,* drawing on Derrida's diagnosis of the phallocentric character of Western tradition.[72] She states
that thinking modeled on the guiding image of the phallus will aim
for the "one of form," for proper name and literal meaning. And she
sees "the logic that dominates the West since the Greeks" as being
concentrated on "this kind of unity." Characteristically Western culture tends "to count everything, to number everything by units, to in-
ventory everything as individualities."[73] Irigaray identifies three
principles that guide this unity-oriented thinking: "*identity with*, expressed by property and quantity; *non-contradiction*, with ambiguity,
ambivalence, polyvalence minimized; *binary oppositions*: nature/rea-
son, subject/object, matter/energy, inertia/movement."[74]

Irigaray then sketches a counterimage, the suppressed language
that corresponds to female sexuality. This language is not oriented
toward unity or un-ambiguity. Woman is, for Irigaray, "indefinitely
other in herself. That is doubtless why she is said to be whimsical, incomprehensible, agitated, capricious." Woman's discourse consists of
"contradictory words, somewhat mad from the standpoint of reason,
inaudible for whoever listens to them with ready-made grids, with a
fully elaborated code in hand. . . . It is useless, then, to trap women
in the exact definition of what they mean, to make them repeat
(themselves) so that it will be clear; they are already elsewhere than in
that discursive machinery where you expected to surprise them. . . .
And if you ask them insistently what they are thinking about, they
can only reply: Nothing. Everything."[75] Just as the language of unity
is interpreted as phallic, Irigaray refers ambiguity to the female body:
"Woman 'touches herself' all the time, and moreover no one can for-
bid her to do so, for her genitals are formed of two lips in continuous
contact. Thus, within herself, she is already two—but not divisible
into one(s)—that caress each other."[76] Further specifying the language of woman, Irigaray notes, "One would have to listen with
another ear, as if hearing *an 'other meaning' always in the process of*

weaving itself, of embracing itself with words, but also of getting rid of words in order not to become fixed, congealed in them. For if 'she' says something, it is not, it is already no longer, identical with what she means . . . moreover; rather it is contiguous. *It touches (upon).*"[77]

The attempt to follow the course of Irigaray's thought encounters a number of difficulties. One problem is that her concept of Logos encompasses three disparate elements. First, many of Irigaray's characterizations of Logos lead to the conclusion that modern science is what she has in mind or, more accurately, the claim to exclusivity frequently associated with it. This claim warrants critique. Those who define reason exclusively in terms of scientific rationality must be confronted with the fact that a mode of thinking that uses quantifying methods and is oriented only to the principle of the excluded middle shows clear limits. While this concept of rationality indisputably captures our ability to gain empirical knowledge, it does not cover all the ways of thinking we employ in our everyday lives. Typically we do not consider our judgments concerning issues of justice, morality, and aesthetics to be irrational, although these judgments cannot be adequately analyzed by the narrow concept of scientific rationality. But the manner in which Irigaray problematizes scientism— attesting its phallocentrism—still needs to be examined.

Second, Irigaray presupposes that her critique of Logos can be applied to European philosophy. However, this view is based on a serious distortion. The history of European philosophy, taken as a whole, cannot be characterized as oriented to the concept of rationality espoused by empirical science. A central concern of European philosophy, on the contrary, has been to criticize rationality's claim to exclusivity. Moreover, Irigaray does not acknowledge that the concept of reason, in the history of philosophy, has found a broader definition that also encompasses judgment in the fields of praxis and aesthetics. The problem here lies not only in Irigaray's reductionist reception of the history of philosophy, but above all in the theoretical repercussions arising from it. Irigaray operates with an opposition of scientific rationality and irrationality, and is thus led into the paradoxical

situation of allowing the concept of reason she uses to be defined by
the very position she rejects. Her thinking is burdened by the fact
that she does not pick up on attempts at a broader definition of reason made earlier in the history of philosophy. This problem remains
to be addressed later.

Beyond this, Irigaray applies her critique of Logos to language
and thus creates the third disparate element in her conception of
Logos. She clearly has in mind Saussure's observation that every definition of a subject by a predicate cancels out other options of meaning. Irigaray interprets this canceling out as an indication of the
phallocratic character of the sentence, and she demands the "overthrow of the syntax."[78] In this she is reminiscent of Cixous, who considers not only the dominating conventions of speech but also
language itself to rise from a masculine thrust. This view fails to acknowledge that grammar cannot be altered at will; such alteration
would be at the cost of comprehensibility, and language itself would
be abandoned. Irigaray here slides into a performative self-contradiction: Her call to overthrow syntax can only be put forward by not
being abided. Further, the alternative language Irigaray has in mind
amounts to something unthinkable. Without fixity of meaning—
without any distinction between one word and another—language is
impossible. Even the ambivalence or rather multivalence to which
Irigaray aspires presupposes some fixity; otherwise an oscillation between different images could never be observed.

Apparently Irigaray's concern is to trace the roots of patriarchal
thought ever deeper, even into language as such. But this claim implies false conclusions, as Irigaray does not distinguish sufficiently
between content (e.g., Freud's theories on female sexuality) and formal apparatus. She assumes that the contents—the patriarchal conceptions—are already outlined in the logic of science or of language
itself. For example, when Freud speaks of woman only *per negationem* in comparison to man, the objection is, however, justified
that binary thinking is not appropriate where an adequate theory of
sexuality is sought. This objection does not imply, however, that

dichotomy must be rejected as a logical form. (When dealing with binary oppositions, I explained why it is erroneous to assume such an implication.) Further, the fact that a neurotic fixation on erections can be observed in psychological contexts does not justify the rejection of any kind of measurement. The core problem with the methods of quantification in the humanities does not lie in the fact that these methods originate from a phallocentric thrust, but that they do not offer the means to understand contexts of human action and aesthetic experience.

While Irigaray searches for the roots of masculine hegemony at the level of what she calls Logos, the problem of patriarchy is not closely addressed where it actually arises. What need to be scrutinized, instead of the opaque concept of Logos, are the power discrepancies between the sexes that still shape our everyday lives in many ways. Shifting the question from the sociopolitical level to the level of Logos also works against the aim of overcoming gender asymmetries that Irigaray has in mind. Given her broad critique, there is only one available strategy: to associate women with the counterconcept, that is, the irrational. As the passages quoted at the beginning indicate, Irigaray consistently went this route. However, to choose this option means to subscribe to the traditional image of the feminine developed under patriarchal conditions. This critique is not unchallenged. Scholars following Irigaray's ideas counter this critique—frequently raised—by pointing to the difference between the symbolic feminine and real women.[79] This argument fails to acknowledge, however, that Irigaray stresses the irrational with the explicit intention of overcoming the alienation of female sexuality—and with it the entire self-understanding of real women. Irigaray certainly deviates from the common cliché in that she reevaluates irrationality, but what does this achieve? Irrationality is both a theoretical and a practical dead end. When dealing with the androcentric underdetermination of the feminine, such as found in Freud, a critique can only be made plausible, even among women, when expressed in argumentative language.[80] Where the sphere of praxis is concerned, the power

discrepancies between the sexes, and men's power to define associated with it, cannot be overcome through an insistence on ambiguity.
Women must have access, in terms of equal participation, to public
discourse—including the academic world—and to the decisionmaking processes that concern the community. A concept of autonomy is
necessary for a theoretical account of such involvement. This means
nothing less, however, than that issues which were addressed in the
history of modern philosophy with the concept of practical reason
need to be reconsidered. Do they contain elements that allow for a
redefinition or transformation that renders them instrumental to current feminist theory? I shall return to this question shortly.

Irigaray engages in a legitimate cause as she joins those who draw
attention to the limitations of scientific rationality in the face of a culture that grants it priority. In this context, it also appears legitimate
to vote for ambiguity and ambivalence. Issues of this kind could be
discussed, for instance, in a theory of art. But the difficulties addressed previously result when ambiguity retains connotations of
femininity.

Is the subject shaped by instrumental reason?

A further variation of the feminist critique of reason focuses on the
sphere of praxis. It is directed against the attempt to justify actions
through universal principles and, at the same time, against philosophical concepts of practical reason that analyze the procedure of deciding which normative principles can be universalized.

One author who voices this kind of critique with special emphasis
is Judith Butler. For her, universalist approaches in moral philosophy
are not of immediate interest; only in the course of unfolding her
main concern does she turn to this kind of theory. Butler rejects any
form of fixation of feminine identity. Whenever the woman is attributed a definite identity—regardless of how that identity is defined—
this means, as she argues, a normative fixation that excludes other

possibilities. Butler diagnoses a suppression of heterogeneity here, noting that this problem always arises when feminist politics claims a we.[81] She therefore advocates a different approach: "On the contrary, if feminism presupposes that 'women' designates an undesignatable field of differences, one that cannot be totaled or summarized by a descriptive identity category, then the very term becomes a site of permanent openness and resignifiability." As Butler explains, this means to release the term *woman* into a "future of multiple significations, to emancipate it from the maternal or racialist ontologies to which it has been restricted, and to give it play as a site where unanticipated meanings might come to bear."[82] It probably needs no further explanation that Butler's antiessentialist motive is legitimate.[83] But it remains to be asked how she takes up this motive in her philosophical reflections. In this regard, a number of difficulties emerge.

For Butler, to fixate feminine identity means to orient women toward the traditional model of the subject. In this context, she draws on the concept of the subject as discussed in contemporary deconstructive discourse, where the term *subject* refers to an identity, the constitution of which requires the abjecting of whatever is interpreted as the other. Clearly "a process of subjection is presupposed in the subjectivating process."[84] In reference to Irigaray, Butler states that this subject is "always already masculine" and explains, "Psychoanalytically, that version of the subject is constituted through a kind of disavowal or through the primary repression of its dependency on the maternal."[85] From this perspective, "the instrumental military subject"[86] becomes a paradigm of subject *toto genere*.

Butler also discusses universalist conceptions of morality, arguing that the strategy of abjecting the other can also be found here. She is convinced that the masculine instrumental subject is identical with the philosophical concept of practical reason as it was developed by transcendental philosophy, and she directs this critique against transcendental pragmatics and discourse ethics. Butler believes that any form of universalist moral theory comes down, in the end, to cultural imperialism: "How is it that we might ground a theory of politics in a speech situation or subject position which is 'universal,' when the very category of the universal has only begun to be exposed for its own highly ethnocentric biases?"[87] She goes on to explain that "to assume from the start a procedural or substantive notion of the universal is of necessity to impose a culturally hegemonic notion on the social field. To herald that notion then as the philosophical instrument that will negotiate between conflicts of power is precisely to safeguard and reproduce a position of hegemonic power by installing it in the metapolitical site of ultimate normativity."[88]

Careful reading reveals that Butler, unreflectedly, intermingles two different issues. On the one hand, she has in mind a phenomenon that we often encounter in the past as well as the present and does indeed call for criticism. She refers to the kind of process whereby a particular group of people takes the values that are accepted as binding in its own culture, pronounces them universally valid, and practices coercive measures against all who are committed to different sets of values. On the other hand, Butler contends that a philosophy which maintains a universalist conception of morality provides the theoretical backing for this mode of coercion. She does not, however, seek to justify her understanding with reference to specific texts from the Kantian tradition of moral philosophy. Thus Butler fails to take into account that the claim made by these positions lies in quite the opposite direction.

There is not, as Butler put it, "*a* procedural or substantive notion of the universal,"[89] but two incompatible conceptions of universality. The procedural concept does not amount to a dogmatization of specific values. On the contrary, its character is strictly formal. The main point is that only norms which everyone—all those affected by a particular action—can consent to in an unconstrained discourse can claim validity. Butler suspects that a recourse to a position "that places itself beyond the play of power, and which seeks to establish the metapolitical basis for a negotiation of power relations, is perhaps the most insidious ruse of power. That this position beyond power lays claim to its legitimacy through recourse to a prior and implicitly universal agreement does not in any way circumvent the charge, for what rationalist project will designate in advance what counts as agreement? What form of insidious cultural imperialism here legislates itself under the sign of the universal?"[90] Butler fails to acknowledge, however, that the consensus framed by discourse theory is not supposed to be justified from an external perspective; whether or not a consensus has been achieved is also something everyone who is involved must agree on. Butler disregards this central point of discourse ethics since she does not go into the difference between formal and substantive universalism. Instead of discussing that difference, she shares the "affect against the universal," diagnosed and systematically questioned by Axel Honneth as a characteristic of poststructuralist thought.[91] What Butler does not take into account is that transcendental pragmatics and discourse ethics themselves lead into a critique of ethnocentrism and (not just cultural) imperialism. The assessment that a universalist understanding of morality results in oppressive actions against particular human beings proves therefore to be erroneous. Equally untenable is the suspicion that this philosophical tradition is based on the perspective of the man who is abjecting the woman.

An attentive reading also reveals that the context in which Butler voices her rejection of the universalist tradition is a theory that rests on ideas just like those formulated in this tradition of moral philosophy. This contradiction is not obvious only because she does not reflect the premises of her argumentative thrust. Since Butler opposes the instrumental subject, the thought on which this critique is based, although not made explicit, must run as follows: "No woman may be used as a mere instrument for the purposes of masculine self-realization, since all individuals must be recognized as persons and must also be respected in their differentness." Without the background of this kind of norm, Butler's critique cannot be understood. This norm corresponds precisely to what Kant regards as the one formal law of practical reason, which he elaborates in his conception of the categorical imperative. A correspondence of this kind is not limited to

Butler. Feminist criticism generally cannot be articulated without appealing to normative foundations that are binding for everybody.

A similar problem arises when Butler formulates her political concern. She demands "a social theory committed to democratic contestation within a postcolonial horizon."[92] She conceives of that contestation as follows: "Inasmuch as poststructuralism offers a mode of critique that effects this contestation of the foundationalist move, it can be used as a part of such a radical agenda."[93] However, there is a tension between these two statements. By calling the kind of radical program she has in mind "democratic," Butler is formulating a normative foundation, which has a formal-universalist character. Ideally, in a democracy, all citizens have the right to participate on equal terms in the processes of deliberation and decisionmaking concerning the laws passed in their state. This idea implies that nobody may be excluded from the processes of decisionmaking for belonging to a certain race, class, ethnic, or religious group or because of his or her sex. The contradiction found here is this: While rejecting all attempts to ground political action on basic universal norms, Butler, in pleading for democracy, appeals to just this kind of norm herself.

It is important to see Butler's anti-imperialist and antimasculinist impulse in light of her primary concern—to reject any binary conception of gender identity and create an alternative vision of a free play of differences. Even this ideal, though, is conceivable only on the basis of a formal concept of equality. The free play Butler imagines, in which "unanticipated meanings might come to bear," will be free only if everyone can participate on equal terms. Butler indirectly appeals to a norm by demanding that everybody must be granted the same room for pursuing their self-chosen paths to happiness. As is well-known, this norm was one core element in the philosophy of law of the Enlightenment. Thus Butler, albeit inexplicitly, adopts a concept from the context of a theory of practical reason. (Incidentally, the tension between explicit critique and implicit assumption of normative foundations is not unique to Butler; it characterizes the writings of a number of authors commonly classified as postmodern thinkers.[94] One frequently encounters a disregard for the fact that the call for plurality and for the acknowledgment of differences is based on a universalist conception of justice.)

Detached emotions

An in-depth study of considerations typical of the feminist critique of reason reveals a number of plausible arguments, as well as a tendency toward overdrawn objections. Therefore it is necessary to reformulate the critique in a way that avoids this tendency. In order to develop a more precise form of analysis, it seems appropriate to return to the original bone of contention. As indicated at the beginning of this chapter, the fact that the concept of reason commonly has masculine connotations calls for a feminist critique. With regard to the roots of this gendered use of the term, research in the history of philosophy can make a substantial contribution. In the first half of the eighteenth century reflections on the differences between the sexes became a common part of the philosophy of law and political theory. While the philosophy of Descartes had initiated egalitarian conceptions, the idea was (re)introduced that each sex has—and is obliged to cultivate—specific types of character, oriented toward complementing each other.[95] In connection with the division of labor between the sexes that emerged in the course of industrialization, each sex has been expected to develop a specific style. As men were allocated to the public sphere, it has been seen as their ability and also their task to cultivate the use of reason in the realms of theoretical knowledge as well as politics, economy, and law. Women, by contrast, have been denied such competencies. In correspondence with their allocation to the domestic sphere, they have been expected to represent a counterpart to man's capacity for reason.

A sentimental design of femininity characterized the bourgeois conception of social order. One telling example is the ideal image we find in Rousseau's *Emile:*

"I would prefer a simple and roughly educated girl a hundred times over a blue stocking and aesthete who installs a literary court and make[s] herself the president. An aesthete is a scourge for her husband, her children, her friends, her servants, for the entire world. From the height of her genius she despises all her feminine duties and only thinks of becoming a man of the kind of Mademoiselle l'Enclos. Outside she always appears ridiculous and is rightfully criticized since criticism cannot stay away as soon as you desert your status and adopt a new one for which one is not made . . . even if she would indeed have talents she would devaluate them by her arrogance. Her dignity consists in remaining unknown; her fame is the respect of her spouse; her pleasures consist in the happiness of her family . . . If there were only reasonable men, every educated girl would remain spinsters their entire lives."[96]

Another example is Kant's presumption that women are incapable of letting their actions be guided by the moral law, in other words, by practical reason: "I hardly believe that the fair sex is capable of principles . . . One should not demand sacrifices and generous self-restraint. A man must never tell his wife if he risks a part of his fortune on behalf of a friend."[97] Besides this, Kant makes pejorative remarks on intellectual women that closely resemble those of Rousseau.[98]

This kind of masculinization of reason constitutes the actual scandal for the feminist critique of reason—especially since these clichéd ways of thinking and gendered norms are still prevalent today.[99] In order to focus on this core problem, feminist critique must proceed in a manner that differs from the approaches discussed above. As already pointed out in this chapter, the actual target of the critique is not the faculty of reason (in both its theoretical and practical use) per se; rather, it is the view that this faculty is part of the masculine character. This specification of the feminist concern also allows for a more refined critique of the classics. For instance, neither Rousseau nor Kant assumes that women lack the capacity for reason.[100] Rather, given women's social position, cultivating these abilities would be unseemly.[101]

What the modern classics, in their reflections on reason and gender, ultimately have in mind is not different faculties but different styles of behavior in men and women. This way of viewing the topic—as a question of gendered style of behavior—has prevailed up to the present (although it is expressed in an altered form today, since the concept of seemliness has become obsolete). Consequently the feminist critique of reason has to develop an additional mode of proceeding. Consider how reason and masculinity are correlated in ordinary language. We encounter ambivalence here. Reason, when assigned to men, does not always refer to the faculty of judgment in the realms of theory and praxis; rather, it often designates a specific way of conduct. We are dealing with two different forms of correlation between reason and masculinity. Characteristically, each form operates with a specific opposition. In the first case, reason or rationality is contrasted with a lack of that faculty; in the second case emotion is the opposite. The latter concept corresponds with the well-known model of masculinity characterized by toughness and distance toward others. This model is part of the common idea of a gendered division of labor, according to which women are expected to cultivate emotional faculties, particularly empathy and care for others. For the feminist critique of reason it is important to deal specifically with each of the two modes of correlating reason and masculinity. A different thrust of the critique is required in each case. On the one hand, we need to reject ways of thinking that exclude women from rational discourses in science, politics, law, and so on; on the other hand, the problem lies in the construction of an identity that emphasizes strategic rationality at the cost of the cultivation of emotions. Addressing the second problem, the feminist critique points out that enforced toughness creates the behavioral basis of patriarchal domination. Where the term *reason* is used to characterize the detached behavior commonly attributed to men, the semantic content undergoes a significant change. The realm of reason is limited to instrumental rationality—a rational calculation of one's own advantage and a calculating treatment of others. The cultural background for this limitation is illuminated in a number of studies that place strategic masculine behavior in a theory of modernity. Some feminist scholars, for instance, turned to analyses of the modern world by Weber, Horkheimer, and Adorno—in particular to investigations of the oppressive character of instrumental rationality—searching for the concepts of patriarchal dominance that these authors provide.[102]

The separation of reason and emotion was already viewed as a problem by authors who maintained the polarized character of the sexes. They tried to solve this difficulty with their conception of marriage, holding that husband and wife together should form one whole person. However, in the face of the problems discussed here, the only viable option seems to be to not to start with any division of human competencies—not to conceive of men and women merely as halved persons in the first place. The concept calling for gender-specific characters is *toto genere* outdated. A plausible alternative to that concept lies in the idea that men and women should have equal opportunities to individually unfold their emotional capacity as well as their ability to reason (which in this case is no longer restricted to instrumental rationality).[103]

Unfortunately, many studies voicing a critique of reason from a feminist perspective do not address this point with sufficient clarity. The fact that there are good reasons for criticizing the style of behavior that (at least in Western culture) has been regarded as masculine is often taken as implying that the philosophical discourse on the concept of reason has become obsolete. But this is too hasty a conclusion. The philosophical debate on reason is not focused on an attitude aiming at detachment and strategic action, but on our capability for judgment in theoretical as well as practical matters. Moreover, it is part of such a philosophical inquiry to lay the theoretical foundations for a critique of dominant behavior. As I pointed out in the course of reading Butler, to criticize a certain mode of behavior for its instrumentalizing character requires, as a precondition, an appeal to principles of justice and equal treatment—principles that have been specified in the philosophical debate on practical reason.

Hence the conceptual pair reason/emotion must be approached differently, depending on whether it is used in a study of behavior or in a philosophical inquiry on the foundations of human knowledge and action. Although it is appropriate to question a psychological image of personality built on the severance of emotions, a philosophical debate is not *eo ipso* dubious if it differentiates between reason and sense perception or between duty and inclination. Although it may be necessary to question such philosophical distinctions, what is relevant is the proficiency of these distinctions in elaborating epistemological issues and problems of moral philosophy, not their pertinence to traditionally masculine character traits.[104] (That a de-differentiation at this point leads to difficulties has also become clear in the field of feminist ethics. The debate on the work of Carol Gilligan—and other authors defending a specifically feminine morality—has shown the following: Although it is essential to reevaluate women's achievements in the curative realm—which is associated with the feminine in the cliché of a gendered division of labor—it is equally important to acknowledge the intrinsic character of philosophical issues. Take, for example, philosophers engaged in a controversy over the question whether, in order to establish an appropriate concept of morality, priority goes to an orientation toward universal principles or an orientation toward moral sentiment. Those philosophers will not find it any easier to settle their dispute if they are confronted with the demand to respect the equal rights of men and women—although this demand, taken by itself, is perfectly legitimate.)[105]

Similar questions arise where feminist critics contend that the concept of reason belongs to a theory that ultimately understands humans as disembodied. In this kind of critique, different intentions seem to be intertwined. On the one hand, the question is raised: Which self-understanding underlies our everyday behavior? Should it turn out that the way we see ourselves is marked by an oblivion of the body, critique is indeed called for. A concept of the human being that emphasizes our rational abilities and ignores existential conditions such as birth, gender, illness, and death is marked by reductionism and leads to the problems just exposed with regard to a severance of emotions. However, where epistemological issues are concerned, this kind of critique does not apply. In the epistemological context it may well become necessary to differentiate between our perspective as first person—from which we experience that we are able to judge in theoretical and practical matters—and bodily processes that can be observed in human beings as they perform cognitive acts. To argue that, in the course of this differentiation, the use of the term *reason* again reveals a repression of corporality would erect a taboo on philosophical analysis.[106]

Let us return to the reason/emotion dyad. If we take into account that different issues can be addressed with the help of this dyad, we realize that the feminist critique of the traditional masculine ideal of behavior should lead to other conclusions than those often reached. Instead of assuming that through this critique the concept of reason as such has been unmasked as masculine, the task should be to bring back into view the entire range of philosophical issues that have been discussed under the heading reason. For instance, in the face of the current understanding of the term in the sense of rationality, it is important to reconstruct the considerations that have led modern philosophers to distinguish between reason and rationality, and also between theoretical reason and practical reason. However, as I advocate such a rereading, my interest does not lie in any kind of return. In the face of reductionist approaches, my point is to take up the debate on a level of greater sophistication. Thus I am not proposing that any traditional conception of reason be simply appropriated. On the contrary, a feminist perspective implies the task of unveiling and repudiating the still common, often tacit transition from an elaboration of the general concept of reason to a theory of masculine character traits. The central point of the feminist critique of reason lies not in the thesis of the irrevocably masculine character of the rational but in overcoming the traditional masculinization of reason.

4

FOR A
NONESSENTIALIST POLITICS

Moral foundations

CHAPTERS 1–3 IN THIS VOLUME can be read as prolegomena for a theory of feminist politics. The ultimate aim of feminist philosophy—whose point of departure is the fact of manifold
discrimination against women—is to provide theoretical foundations
for a feminist politics. This is not to say that feminist philosophy is a
subdiscipline of political philosophy or the theory of law. Rather,
issues from different areas of philosophy need to be addressed, as I
have shown, to spell out the feminist concern as comprehensively as
possible. The term *feminist politics* is used in different ways. Basically
a broad meaning and a narrow meaning can be distinguished. In the
broader sense, the concept refers to the entire realm of praxis; it
covers all feminist-motivated efforts to change given gender
relations, including individual efforts in the education of children
and on the level of personal relations. In its narrow meaning it refers

to coordinated efforts that aim to influence legislation and economic decisions. The reflections in this chapter are relevant to either under-standing of feminist politics. I focus primarily on feminist politics in the narrow sense, investigating which theoretical foundations philos-ophy can provide. These reflections on foundational questions will also support feminist efforts to overcome gender asymmetries in other spheres of life.

Some questions concerning politics in the narrow sense have caused heated debates. First, is there a feminist *we?* Does feminist politics concern all women, particular groups, or individuals in their diversity? Who is entitled (or called on) to speak up for whom? A fur-ther controversy has evolved around the issue of what exactly is the problem that feminist politics has to challenge. Is the actual bone of contention a relation of domination and subordination or is it a lack of recognition of difference? The way this question is decided will in-fluence the choice of strategies and targets. Although these contro-versies tend to encourage mutually exclusive options, closer scrutiny reveals that the problems are complex and require a disentangling of different strands of thought that have been tacitly intermingled.

Why does discrimination against women belong to the terrain of moral philosophy? The claims women articulate in the public forum are often received as the demands of an interest group comparable to unions or lobbies. Understood in this way, feminist politics has to ne-gotiate with its opponents. However, this understanding is too lim-ited. Two distinct perspectives need to be recognized. On the one hand, a politics that seeks to improve the rights of women must ne-gotiate, especially where concrete measures are decided, such as the allocation of government funds to promote the education of women. Nonetheless, feminist concerns as such cannot be the object of a pol-itics oriented toward a conciliation of interests, for two reasons. First, discrimination belongs to the type of problem in which compromises can only be called cynical; second, it presents an injustice that con-cerns everyone, not just those affected. The core problem of discrim-ination does not belong among matters that can be settled by specific legislative measures; in order to locate it properly, we must turn to the moral foundations of law. Contemporary debate on the philosophy of law acknowledges that it is inadmissible to negotiate or vote on whether or not fundamental rights are granted to individuals. The state does not provide this kind of rights; only their concrete implementation requires legislative action.[1] The implications of this for a comprehensive concept of feminist politics have not been fully explored. Any theory seeking to provide an in-depth study of the problem of discrimination has to start with issues of moral philosophy.

Why is it that the central concern of a politics aiming to overcome gender asymmetries can't be the object of compromise? This question can only be answered on the basis of a universalistic conception of morality. I would like to explain this with reference to Kant, along the lines of my previous discussion of this topic.[2] There are two good reasons, I think, for choosing this approach. First, most contemporary universalistic conceptions have appropriated Kant's thinking to such an extent that they have established a "Kantian tradition." Second, authors who believe that a consistent feminist theory requires the rejection of any universalistic conception of morality often refer explicitly to Kant.[3] Bear in mind that discrimination against women on account of their sex presents the genuine target of feminist critique. To illustrate, I use the example of a woman who is equally qualified as her male colleague and achieves the same results but is denied pay equity.

Obviously feminist criticism cannot do without a concept of equality. The asymmetry of payment can be called unjust only on the premise of a demand like this: If women do the same work as men, they should get the same salary. This demand expresses the idea that women and men have to be taken equally seriously in their achievements. In order to justify an idea like this, we need to refer to the principle that every single person must be respected equally—without considering sex, age, ethnic and religious identity, or other particularities. Here we enter the debate on the central elements of a universalistic concept of morality. (The idea of equality is addressed in terms of moral philosophy. This does not mean any prejudgment in regard to specific issues of legal theory discussed today concerning, for instance, equal opportunity or affirmative action. The moral philosophical concept can, however, contribute to the clarification of these issues.) As we address the basic principle of setting aside all specific characteristics by which individuals or groups distinguish themselves, one question immediately arises: What is the characteristic that we all share and allows each individual to claim equal respect? It is the experience that we—from the perspective of the first person—have the freedom to take a position toward given conditions generated by nature and history (discussed in Chapter 1). In the present context, one implication is of particular relevance: If we are impeded without good reason from making a free decision in that sense, we suffer an injury. Our genuine competence is being reduced or we are—in the worst case—robbed of it entirely. Apart from actual pain we may suffer, the core of these forms of being injured is that we are not treated as human beings. Thus, when there is a need to stress (e.g., from a feminist position) that every individual must be respected in the same manner, this demand can only be spelled out as follows: It must be recognized that human beings—women as well as men—have the ability to make decisions and act accordingly, or as Kant puts it, the ability to choose their ends on their own.[4]

Universalistic conceptions of morality are centered around this human competency. According to Kant, the one formal moral law that is the moral yardstick for our actions can be expressed in this manner: Whenever I face a decision, I must examine who will be affected by the action I have in mind, and whether or not those individuals will be respected in the way I intend to treat them, as persons who themselves have the competency to decide and to act. The formulation of the categorical imperative that is most relevant here is: "So act that you use humanity, whether in your own person or in the person of any other, always at the same time as an end, never merely as a means."[5] According to Kant, two different implications need to be distinguished: The categorical imperative includes a prohibition as well as an obligation. The first says that human beings are to be treated "never merely as a means," that is, in a way that instrumentalizes them against their will. But the obligation goes further since it is not limited to respecting the prohibition. Our moral duty to take into account that human beings have the capacity to determine their ends by themselves implies, according to Kant, not only that we are not allowed to diminish the freedom of others without good reasons. We are obliged to help others as far as possible (and compatible with the moral imperative) where they are unable to realize their self-chosen ends on their own. In Kant's phrase, "duties of love"[6] can be deduced from the categorical imperative. I highlight these two distinct implications because they are both relevant to feminist theory.

What does the prohibition mean for us? Kant offers a procedure that we can use to determine whether we are about to use others "merely as a means." In regard to every intended action, we must ask whether the persons affected by the action would give their consent—whether the end we seek can also be their end.[7] If we apply this method to our example from the working world, the given injustice can be identified more specifically. It is a double injustice. On the one hand, an asymmetry of payment can be described as an instrumentalization against the will of the persons affected. When women have to work more to obtain the same salary as their male colleagues, then this extra work goes to their employers for free. The problem is therefore that part of the work of women is done without compensation. It can be assumed that no woman would agree to such an arrangement voluntarily—that no woman shares these ends of the employer willingly. But often women have no choice but to agree to work under such conditions. At this point, the critical potential of Kant's approach becomes obvious: Kant equips us with a means to demonstrate the coercive character of such a work "contract."

The second injustice that can be made visible in this manner is discrimination against women on account of their sex. The problem described above would exist if even one person felt forced into an unjust employment contract through the exploitation of difficult circumstances. An additional dimension arises if this person is paid less because she is a woman. From the perspective of moral philosophy this must be opposed since the woman in question is not taken seriously as an independent person: Her salary classification is not determined by her individual qualifications and achievements but by her sex. Clearly the woman in this case is not treated as a person who has the capacity to choose her ends on her own but as part of a biologically defined group. (The objections formulated above with regard to any assumption of a natural order of the sexes prove relevant in this context.) The full extent of the problem becomes visible if one questions—in accordance with Kant—who is affected by each action. If only one woman received less pay on account of her sex, all women would be affected. The reason that is given for unequal treatment suggests the validity of a thesis that may be spelled out like this: To belong to the female sex means to be able to produce only inferior job performances. Such a thesis implies an instruction to instrumentalize all women against their will—in the way just explained on the foundation of the categorical imperative. This point raises a significant lack of consciousness among many women. They can look back on a respectable career and declare they experienced no discrimination in their lives. This is hardly comprehensible considering the many ways the term *woman* is still associated with inferiority. Think of all the jokes about "lady drivers." They too confront us with the problem just explained: A male driver who violates traffic laws is blamed individually. The term *idiot* or other pejorative expressions indicate that he is taken seriously as an independent person; if the same violation is committed by a woman, however, then the entire female sex is held responsible.

Even this trivial example makes it clear that the concept of person belongs to the inalienable foundations of feminist political theory. This is important to state, not least because of the pathos of antihumanism expressed by some authors.[8] They need to be asked how else they can justify their feminist intentions. More generally, how can we demonstrate that discrimination against women—or against other

people—does in fact exist? If it is inadmissible to use respect or disrespect for a person as an analytical category, how will the claimed
injury be recognized? And why should discrimination be fought at
all, if not because of the demand that women must be respected in
their self-determination in the same way as men?[9] The reluctance
common today to adopt the concept of person may be due to a misunderstanding. Often this term is taken to imply a common identity
for all human beings. This view suggests to many the threat of a
leveling of individual differences. To the contrary, the thesis that all
individuals must be treated as persons (i.e., the thesis defended above
with reference to Kant) does not presuppose a shared essence but
only the shared capability to choose their ends for themselves. The
suspicion of essentialism therefore proves unjustified. The concepts
of the person and the individual do not stand in opposition to each
other but in close relation. Anyone who voices the demand to protect and support the peculiarity of all individuals should ask where
this peculiarity comes from. Our individual course through life is
formed to a great extent by our decisions (as outlined in Chapter 1).
Therefore the ways in which we differ from one another result from
the fact that individuals are persons. Only because we can act are we
able to develop an unmistakable identity. It is necessary, particularly
from a feminist perspective, to uncover the problems that result from
assigning a common identity to people who are viewed in that way.
Yet where such a critique is justified, and where individual differences
need to be emphasized, the point is precisely that each individual
must be respected as a person.[10]

   With the help of Kant's philosophy we can further specify the relevance of the person concept. When the categorical imperative is
applied to the phenomenon of discrimination, a moral problem can
be detected. It has two aspects, which makes us aware of a double
duty. First, everybody has to examine to what extent they are themselves involved in the disregard and oppression of women. (Not just
men have to ask themselves this question.) This duty clearly results
from the prohibition against instrumentalizing others against their

will. There is one implication that should not go unnoticed: A moral duty arises also for those who are affected by discrimination, namely, the duty to resist. With this, we have reached the point where the idea of law originates from morality. The argumentation here rests on a thought that is implied in the categorical imperative as quoted above but often escapes notice: The obligation to respect human beings as an end concerns not only the way I act in regard to others but also the way I act in regard to myself. As Kant explains, the categorical imperative can be read like this: "Do not make yourself a mere means for others but be at the same time an end for them."[11] Therefore every individual has the duty of asserting his or her own worth as a human being in relation to others.[12] In this manner the moral imperative implies that I have the right to resist others when they limit my self-determination without good reason.

This right (unlike my right to vote, for example) has not been provided to me by the state; I have already always had it through the fact that I am a human being (i.e., that I have the competency for self-determination). Kant uses in this sense the term *natural right,* which he opposes to *civil right*.[13] According to this, because of my peculiar human nature, I have the right to demand from others that they respect me. Here we face the moral foundation of law; in Kant's formulation, rights can be seen "as the (moral) capacities for putting others under obligation."[14] But how can I oblige others? Moral education and consciousness-raising are important, but experience teaches us not to expect that all people will always act in accordance with the moral law. We need an additional dimension of obligation so that our prospect of being respected as human beings is increased. It is precisely this need that the civil law seeks to meet (viewed exclusively from the perspective of theoretical foundation). Thus we have a moral claim to create legal structures in the sense of positive law. This does not mean that every concrete act of legislation does justice to the outlined moral claim. Rather, for all single states it is true that their legislation is historically situated (i.e., that the given social asymmetries often leave their imprints). Therefore we need to distinguish between the historically contingent codes on the one hand, and the morally based idea of justice on the other. The latter is of crucial importance as an instrument of criticism: Only by appealing to this idea can we criticize the existing laws for reproducing social privileges.

From this thought results the core concern of the philosophy of law: to unfold the idea of justice. One aim of these theoretical efforts is to provide the means for making visible—and overcoming—structures of discrimination that have not been constrained or have even been strengthened by existing laws. With this intention the topic of equality moves into the foreground. How do we have to conceive the state so that it provides the legal preconditions for all individuals to be respected in the same manner as human beings? In an attempt to solve this problem, contract theories have been developed in the philosophy of the Enlightenment. The contemporary philosophy of law still foregrounds this approach, although it has required extensive modifications. How the conception of the contract must be evaluated from a feminist perspective will be discussed later. At this point, it should be obvious why this excursus on the relation of morality and law was important. From what was presented here in general, the argument can be derived that it is morally imperative to object to discrimination against women on account of their sex. The implications of this moral obligation include the need to develop a legal theory focusing on justice between the sexes and to call for corresponding changes in state legislation and international law.

The feminist *we*

Moral philosophy contributes to clarifying the question addressed at the beginning of this chapter: Does feminist politics concern all women, particular groups, or individuals in their diversity? Now we can see that these options do not exclude each other. On the one hand, discrimination against women on account of their sex concerns all women, even if in the concrete case only individual women are affected. This has to be explained more precisely. The thesis that all women are affected is not to be confused with the perpetrator/ victim schema that was characteristic of early criticism of patriarchy and proved to be an oversimplified grid of categories. In many cases, discrimination cannot be put down to single protagonists; it does not always result from explicit misogynist opinions or deliberate acts of discrimination. Common language patterns and traditional customs—cultural practices in Foucault's sense—are also among its sources, often in a way that is not immediately recognizable. (Consider the latent condescension in the kiss on the hand, a form of greeting for women still practiced in some conservative circles.) Here we encounter the danger of another oversimplification: to operate with the plain opposition of men versus women does not allow an adequate description of the problem of discrimination. Insofar as traditional cultural practices are supported by both sexes, women too are involved in creating the conditions for discrimination against women. This observation does not contradict the thesis that all women are affected by discrimination against women on account of their sex.

It is rather misleading to use the term *discrimination* in the singular, since there are various, overlapping forms of discrimination. From an international perspective, a majority of women are discriminated against not only on account of their sex but also class, race, ethnicity, religious belief, age, and so on. Numerous studies have explained how women are often located at the intersection of several disadvantaged groups.[15] These studies document the continuous learning process that took place in feminist theory as well as politics. In the first phase—focusing on the critique of patriarchy—it was important to make the problem of sex discrimination visible; during the 1980s an increasing number of women argued that the categories used in the beginning of feminist criticism did not do justice to their specific situation. Thus awareness was enhanced with regard to the situatedness of feminist theory. Because intellectual discourse has predominately been maintained by a small segment of society, feminist analyses first focused on the situation of the bourgeois middle class. They failed to pay due attention to the mechanisms of exclusion characteristic for their society that affected people with lower income and people of color—meaning double discrimination for many women. A feminist theory that does not reflect the complex constellations of oppression may even be a kind of accomplice.[16] I have already noted that women, in the context of everyday life, participate in discrimination against women, and feminist scholars are not immune to this danger either.

Some may view this complexity as a reason to question the relevance of a universalistic conception of morality. If the competency to decide and act that we all share is chosen as the point of departure for feminist theory, does this not imply the demand that specific situations must be ignored? This question is based on a misunderstanding. Two lines of argument, both inalienable, need to be distinguished. First, all specific group memberships must be ignored in order to explain that—and why—everybody must be treated with the same respect. Second, it has to be examined what it means to pay this respect. Taking someone seriously means looking at this individual's situation as closely as possible. Thus if we criticize feminist studies that are blind in regard to the specific situation of certain groups of women, we orient ourselves, at least implicitly, toward the basic moral demand that everybody must be equally respected. As we reflect the preconditions for going into the differences between groups as well as individuals, we face the issues elaborated in the universalistic conceptions of morality.

The need to distinguish different forms of discrimination exists not only with respect to the diversity of disadvantaged groups but also in structural regard. The term *discrimination* in colloquial usage covers different mechanisms of oppression. Obviously concrete programs of emancipatory politics can only be successful if the mechanisms at work in a specific situation are identified. Therefore, as Iris Young has stressed, it is not enough to establish the fact that particular groups are disadvantaged; we have to take into account that members of different groups are often affected by the same kind of disadvantaging while the individual members of one particular group are at the same time subjected to different mechanisms. Young differentiates "five faces of oppression": exploitation, marginalization, powerlessness, cultural imperialism, and violence.[17] This typology helps clarify which group of persons (e.g., those suffering from Eurocentrism or racism) is affected by which mechanisms. In regard to women, Young explains how they suffer from all named forms of oppression.[18] This is not the place to discuss the suggested typology in detail; I just wish to point out that such a structural investigation, too, is founded on the basic moral demand (as explained above). Young analyzes specific suffering with the aim of promoting changes that are tailored specifically to provide each individual with equal and just conditions.

To reflect on the connection between concrete problem analyses and a universalistic conception of morality is the way additional approaches to feminist criticism are opened up. Research by Onora O'Neill offers a good example. She has demonstrated that the categorical imperative allows us to reveal a dimension of oppression that is often ignored. O'Neill investigates what it means to examine, in Kant's sense, whether or not the people affected by my action could give their consent to my ends. She first emphasizes that the term *consent* implies voluntariness; only where the possibility of *not* consenting is given can we say that someone does consent to a certain way of proceeding. On the basis of this clarification, O'Neill turns to life situations that typically confront women today. Picking examples from sexual relations as well as the workplace, she reveals characteristic misconceptions. Common social arrangements are often received as if the women involved voluntarily gave in to conditions that imply disrespect for them. But if one asks what options are available, then it can be seen that women often have no other choice. Thus what first seemed to be based on free will proves to be a matter of forced instrumentalization.[19]

To stress the main point once more: Morality, as defined in a universalistic approach, is not only compatible with attending to a specific situation, but it cannot otherwise be translated into action. At this point it is important to take into account that Kant shows two different implications of the categorical imperative. Each provides a framework for spelling out feminist concerns in detail. While the aspect of prohibition demands an exploration of the manifold ways in which women are instrumentalized against their will, the obligation—as specified in Kant's concept of the duties of love—implies that we have to ask which kinds of support women need in order to be able to choose their own path and pursue it. From the second perspective, the categorical imperative leads us to examine how women's freedom of decision is reduced by popular prejudices. Parents still tend to enable the best possible education for their sons rather than their daughters; certain professions are still called women's work, while others are seen as men's domain; many women, unlike men, still feel forced to choose between profession and family; women are still underrepresented in top political positions and decisionmaking bodies; and so on. A closer look at asymmetries like these reveals the need for a whole bundle of measures. While it is necessary to raise consciousness and suggest changes in the education of children in order to combat prejudice, it is also imperative to explore what can be achieved by means of legislation. The obstinate perpetuation of the described limitations on women can also be observed in countries in which women are long since de jure equal to men. This indicates that the instrument of formal equal rights alone does not suffice. In view of this problem, well-known demands for legal measures providing specific support to women have been voiced. Note that I am talking about the implications of the moral law. Programs under debate today in the areas of social laws or welfare state conceptions prove—with regard to their general direction of argumentation—justifiable on the basis of the duties explained in universalistic moral philosophy. The same applies to quota systems in areas that have remained male domains, despite the long-standing formal equality of women.[20] (Quotas may not be advisable in every case. My point is directed toward the common objection that quota systems are incompatible with a moral claim. Once the moral basis has been established, the question needs to be shifted to pragmatic calculation, and here it may well turn out that other measures are more effective.)

The task of feminist philosophy—to confront all the single sections of the discipline with the fact of gender hierarchies—also applies to ethics. The reflections just unfolded shed doubts on a widely accepted understanding of a feminist approach to moral philosophy. The concept of feminist ethics is often defined in a way that equates this project with the studies initiated by Carol Gilligan on a theory of feminine morality.[21] This equation has to be analyzed in several aspects. Concepts of an ethics of care have their roots in thoroughly legitimate motives. We certainly need to criticize that in the history of moral theory the paradigm of moral behavior was frequently explained with the virtues traditionally assigned to men, and it is just as necessary to claim recognition for the performances of women in the realm of caring. But neither of these two motives forces us to oppose two moralities. Where this is attempted, as in Gilligan's distinction between a feminine care perspective and a masculine justice perspective, this results in grave problems. As a closer look reveals, the assumption of two moralities that are equally valid contravenes the concept of morality in its entirety.[22]

We also encounter problems of the kind already explained in regard to concepts of feminine writing and feminine epistemology. Yet the most poignant conflict comes into sight when we consider that assuming a moral division of labor between the sexes corresponds with traditional gender relations. Then it turns out that the concepts advocating a feminine morality clearly stand in opposition to the feminist project. In view of these difficulties, I am suggesting another definition. The term *feminist ethics* should be used, in my opinion, as an umbrella term that has the general aim of confronting moral philosophy with the fact of gender hierarchies. From this general direction a number of specific tasks arise, including the project of confronting masculine bias in the history of moral philosophy or studying the moral experiences of women and examining whether they give cause for changes in the core concepts of moral philosophy.[23] But primarily it has to be brought into focus that discrimination against women on account of their sex is incompatible with any moral claim.[24]

This definition of the term feminist ethics contradicts in certain regards the considerations that characterize an ethics of difference.[25] Yet there is also a shared motive. It is mandatory to strive for a new ethics, aiming at an improved form of relations between the sexes shaped by mutual respect—in a new "choreography" of genders, as Derrida has expressed it.[26] But the plausibility of this project is lost if it is explicated in the following way: "The two sexes must respect each other because they each can contribute a different moral competence."[27] In this case the familiar problems arise again. In contrast, a feminist ethics in the sense proposed here does not see the new choreography in the form of an opposition of two sex rows—as in dances like the polonaise that do not accidentally belong to the courtly tradition.[28] The point is that every person—regardless of sex—has the same right to be respected independently of whether or not the individuals share certain virtues and interests. Susan Wolf argues similarly when discussing a completely different theoretical field of contemporary philosophy. Charles Taylor's conception of a politics of recognition gives her reason to insist on the claim of every single woman to be recognized because of herself. As Wolf explains, discrimination against women is different from discrimination against ethnic, national, or religious minorities and therefore cannot be overcome with the same means. In a certain way the situation of women is opposite to that of minorities: For women, discrimination cannot be eliminated with ensuring group status since it would lead to a "distorting type of recognition." This distortion, Wolf says, is done to women by not acknowledging them as "individuals with their own mind, own interest, own gifts."[29]

But let us return to the issue of the feminist "we." It should be clear why the different views addressed above—which seem at first incompatible—can be valid at the same time. Context is crucial. If we ask who is affected by discrimination against women on account of their sex, all women have to be included. If, on the other hand, concrete measures are demanded, they can be developed only by considering the specific situation of particular women and the mechanisms effective in each case of oppression. In this case, the *we* of those affected will include only small groups. Solidarity, however, should not be forgotten in this context. It is one of the strengths of political movements that individuals and groups in their specific suffering find support from others. Therefore the *we* that carries concrete demands can include a significant number of people who are not directly affected. If a problem arises here, it is the danger of paternalism. Even the best intentions of solidarity become counterproductive if there is no readiness to learn how the women who receive this support experience and interpret their situation themselves. This was plain to see after 1989. While well-meaning feminist speakers from Western countries traveled to the former socialist states in Eastern Europe and delivered their talks with missionary enthusiasm, many of the women in the audience found the critical categories offered unsuitable for an analysis of their history and situation.[30] Experiences like these show that advocates need to cultivate sensitivity to differences.

Yet there is also the danger that a *we* is defined in an unnecessarily narrow way that causes a division among those who are discriminated against in one and the same manner. This danger usually arises in the context of an understandable motivation. For example, let us consider the history of particular groups facing discrimination on account of a certain feature, for instance, because they are nonwhite, nonheterosexual, or women. Often a specific pattern is apparent in the history of such groups. As the affected individuals begin to understand that they share their painful experience with others and communicate those shared experiences, it becomes evident that many have internalized the disdain shown for them. It is therefore vital to look for ways out of this self-contempt. In the course of this process, it seems obvious to choose the incriminating feature as a point of departure, awarding a new meaning to it. In this manner, subcultures begin to grow that offer self-confidence vis-à-vis the hegemonic culture. Characteristic for this development are slogans like "black is beautiful," as well as specific lifestyles such as the ones that emerged in the gay and lesbian subculture in U.S. urban centers.

These motives are certainly comprehensible. That they may, nevertheless, have problematic consequences has been shown, for instance, by Anthony Appiah.[31] As he explains, the price for belonging to such an alternative culture lies in the renunciation of part of one's self-determination. Individuals can only become insiders if they agree to organize their lives around the incriminating feature. The danger here is that a well-known problem repeats itself in reverse: The individuals see themselves confronted once again with certain expectations regarding their behavior. Therefore Appiah raises the question of whether one tyranny is not merely replaced by another.

Discussions of the feminist *we* must also address essentialism. Although this term is sometimes employed as a sweeping objection against all forms of saying *we,* it also has a legitimate use. Theories assuming a shared identity—whether attributed to all women or all feminists—must be rejected. This insight is long-standing[32] but needs constant updating. Today it must be applied, for instance, to attempts undertaken in the context of the multiculturalism debate to understand the aims of the women's movement analogously to those of oppressed ethnic or religious minorities. (The problem arising here has been discussed already with regard to Charles Taylor's work.) As has been pointed out several times, the paradigm of identity politics[33] is ultimately incompatible with feminist concerns. But the critique of essentialism is overdrawn when it insinuates that every feminist *we* is based on the assumption of a shared identity.[34] (Similarly exaggerated is the demand to dismiss the term *woman* since it evokes the idea of a shared female nature. Victoria Baker states rightfully, referring to the logic of definitions: "Simply by defining 'woman,' we do not thereby commit ourselves to the existence of formal or timeless characteristics of 'woman's nature.' . . . We will not be obliged to assume that the designation serves as a means to support an attribution of identity, of essence or of universality.")[35] The interpretation that I am suggesting focuses exclusively on a shared concern: The feminist *we* (whether formulated in regard to all women or particular groups) signals agreement only on a commitment against oppression. I do not intend to deny that people can only say *we* if they can establish some common ground. But what is common in this case is not a shared "nature" but a shared problem— the fact of being discriminated against on account of belonging to the female sex. This shared problem is nothing inherent in women, as their essence, but it has been externally imposed on them and is therefore intended to be overcome.[36] In short, the sweeping essentialism objections lack accuracy; they fail to notice that it makes a big difference whether the demands articulated on behalf of a *we* are directed toward the preservation of shared characteristics or toward the protection of the right and the chances of every single woman to determine her way of life for herself—and to reject gender roles in which ideas of an essential femininity manifest themselves.

To prevent misunderstandings, I emphasize that the idea of self-determination employed here does not imply an individualist utopia. Again we have to differentiate. First, while it is true that women share the fate of being discriminated against, the experiences of being treated with a lack of respect are made by each individual herself. It is a specific woman who is not considered for a job although she is better qualified than her male coapplicants; it is a specific woman who is sexually harassed; and so on. Even if such experiences are shared, it is not the group as such that suffers; rather, an oppressed group shares injuries that are part of individual biographies. This has consequences for feminist politics. Although it is indispensable to unite in speaking up and acting in public in accordance with the just explained meaning of the feminist *we,* the target must lie in creating such conditions that no woman has to suffer from discrimination on account of her sex. Second, to liberate individual women from structures in which they experience oppression does not mean to strive for their social isolation. On the contrary, this kind of liberation allows new patterns of social life to emerge. If, for instance, the individual sees herself no longer forced into traditional family structures, then she is free to explore other forms of relationships. From this perspective Marilyn Friedman has explained the relevance of friendships: As self-chosen relationships they offer the possibility of distancing oneself from the traditional family model without being isolated.[37]

If the task is to protect the individual from oppression, this does not imply a predecision in regard to concrete legal measures; on this theoretical level it remains open whether and when specific regulations in support of women should be introduced. Generally, in regard to this question two points have to be considered. First, if individuals who have been affected by one and the same problem stand up against it jointly, this does not mean *eo ipso* that specific rights are claimed for this group. Second, if in a certain situation we weigh whether the instrument of group rights promises success from a feminist perspective, then our focus can only lie in whether this instrument can be more effective in sparing women the experience of discrimination than are all other means. We need to separate the aims of feminist politics, on the one hand, and the issue of which legal measures are best suited to achieve them, on the other.

The topic of the feminist *we* has yet another dimension. Looking at discrimination, as suggested here, from the perspective of moral philosophy leads to a change of emphasis: The problem no longer concerns primarily the affected. Of course, it is important that these persons articulate their suffering; but a moral interpretation of discrimination directs us to look at the causes. Not to raise this issue would result in a perspective that in analogy would correspond with the thesis that racist patterns of behavior are only a topic for those affected by them. Discrimination against women on account of their sex is a problem that concerns not only the affected but all who try to orient their way of acting along moral principles. Consequently feminist aims are not only women's business. In view of this, it is necessary to understand the feminist *we* in a comprehensive manner that goes beyond women in general. This insight has existed partially for years, if not in this wording. Historically, processes in which parliamentary bodies consisting exclusively of male delegates decided in favor of women's right to vote, women's equal access to state-funded institutions of education, and so on, are a case in point. Therefore it is hard to understand why many men today reject the term *feminism*. Considering that the principle of the same respect for all individuals is the foundation of the concept of modern democracy, opponents of feminism should be asked, How can you be a democrat without being committed to feminism?

Women as citizens; or, Why the social contract theory should be reformulated

If the demand for just gender relations is well founded, then the question arises how this demand should be translated into action. This issue too calls for a critical analysis. We need to ask why the civil codes we typically find in Western democracies do not prevent the injustices many women have to suffer. Only if we examine this issue with great care will we be in a position to search for well-targeted means to overcome the existing asymmetries. Clearly it is not a case of a single cause at work. Choosing a course of analysis that leads, so to speak, from the periphery to the center, I address first a type of problem generated by the application of laws, not by the laws themselves. For example, in court trials, women's testimony often is not taken as seriously as that of men. In the case of sexual crimes, for instance, male judges may believe the word of the accused man over that of the accusing woman.[38] In regard to such injustices, instruments need to be developed that secure an application of the law in accordance with the principles of fairness and political correctness. However, not all forms of discrimination against women that occur in the framework of the law can be reduced to a problem of application. This has to be stressed especially in regard to those people who reject the entire project of feminist legal theory with the argument that gender asymmetries generated in the legal context are attributable exclusively to problems of application. (When I used the term *periphery* for the issue of application, my intention was to indicate that the genuine and most challenging questions of legal theory are not yet visible on this level. For those affected, this kind of gender asymmetry is no marginal matter.)

Turning to the laws themselves, we can again detect different causes for gender discrimination. Negative effects for women result from both the specific formulations of laws and the basic theoretical conceptions of the state. Discrimination effects have been generated from both laws that are intended to be gender neutral and differential laws designed to support women. First we encounter the familiar problem of androcentrism. As has been well documented, laws that are supposedly gender neutral are often formulated with masculine views in mind. Where laws refer to paradigmatic life circumstances, the model, considered valid in general, is de facto characteristic for men but not for women. For instance, male career patterns are inappropriately generalized. As I have done before,[39] I would like to give an example from the academic realm. If fellowships for habilitations[40] are exclusively awarded to people younger than forty, then applicants who are mothers have lower chances. The reason for this is not so much the limited time devoted to pregnancy, birth, and breast-feeding, but rather the traditional division of labor that makes the mother responsible for the care of the children over a period of time that goes far beyond the initial phase. Therefore the age limit—allegedly gender neutral—implies an indirect exclusionary mechanism. Since for applications of this kind the lists of publications, conference papers, and so on, are crucial, only women who do not have children will be able to compete with their male fellow applicants. The result is, as Catharine MacKinnon pointedly remarks, the paradox that women must appropriate male life patterns to claim equal treatment.[41] The age clause for fellowships reinforces the common cliché according to which family and profession are alternatives for women but not for men.

What triggers such obstacles must be understood if they are to be eliminated. The problem is not the idea of neutral formulations as such but the subversion of the claimed neutrality. A counterstrategy needs to be developed. First, every law that claims neutrality has to be examined *in concreto* for gender blindness. The task is to check whether the regulation in question (in the face of the different situatedness of men and women) leads or could lead to discrimination against women. If so, the next step is to ask which kind of measure is best suited to prevent such consequences. Should a truly neutral formulation be sought, or are regulations needed that provide for a differential treatment of men and women? This question cannot be decided in general but only in reference to the concrete case.

There is nothing absurd about searching for truly neutral formulations. I emphasize this because some people argue that gender-neutral formulations necessarily lead to women being measured against a scale meant for men. Feminist criticism proves this notion false. Whenever we criticize discrimination against women, we assume that a comparison on the basis of neutral criteria is possible. For example, we can only complain about unjust salaries if we evaluate the achievements of men and women on an outside scale and judge them to be equal. Of course, a further differentiation has to be made here. When I say that existing laws have to be examined *in concreto* for possible gender blindness, I do not have a simple test in mind. If the task were only to make women as a gender visible, then this could prove to be counterproductive. Usually it is women in specific situations who face discrimination (e.g., those who have children compared with those who do not). Therefore it is necessary to find out precisely which conditions of life, abilities, needs, and so on are relevant for the law in question. Such detailed analyses are also a prerequisite if a legal text that has turned out to be androcentric is to be replaced by a truly (and not only allegedly) neutral formulation. For example, feminist analysis has resulted in the demand that the regulations for the awarding of habilitation fellowships must be reformulated to provide a higher age limit for persons who have raised children or an age limit that is graded according to the number of children. But the fact that such neutral formulations are indeed possible does not say anything about when this approach should *de facto* be chosen. Feminist politicians have in a number of cases decided that regulations providing for a differential treatment of women are the more promising way.

Laws that explicitly refer to women may also have (and indeed have had) discriminatory consequences. This can be observed especially where legislation takes the traditional situatedness of women in the family into account. If, for instance, women who have given birth are assigned a maternity leave of a year or more (a time span that goes beyond the usual period of breast-feeding), then this is based on the idea that the care of children is primarily the task of the mother, not the father. From a feminist perspective it therefore needs to be pointed out that such legal measures reflect traditional gender roles and consequently fortify the common asymmetries between the sexes. On the basis of this objection, efforts are currently under way in a number of countries to promote, through appropriate changes in the law, a more balanced distribution of the work of child-rearing.

Labor law issues show that there is not one single form of feminist politics. Rather, one and the same basic claim—the fight against discrimination—can be translated into contrary strategies according to each concrete situation. For example, labor unions first considered it mandatory to call for a legislation that takes the double burden of women at work and at home into account, whereas today legislation is used as an instrument to overcome traditional gender roles. Significantly, the legislation on night work initiated by the women's movement has undergone a radical shift. Prohibitions against women working at night, which women in labor unions originally fought for, have been removed in many countries or are currently under revision due to objections voiced by today's feminist theorists and politicians.[42] Similar changes have taken place in regard to women in the military. Clearly the concept of gender-neutral laws is of great importance. Legislation that seeks to challenge the traditional order of the sexes needs to establish truly inclusive regulations. For this reason, in several countries jobs must be offered without gender specifications, and decisions must be made only on the basis of the relevant qualifications.

This does not imply, however, that legal measures providing specific support to women necessarily lead to a stabilization of traditional gender roles. Rather, the instrument of specific regulation can also be used for overcoming discrimination. Here the issue of social rights needs to be addressed. It has repeatedly proved to be true—for other underprivileged groups as well as women—that, for a limited span of time, affirmative action is necessary so that the rights granted *formaliter* also can be taken de facto. Considerations in the contemporary philosophy of law focusing on the concept of substantial equality of opportunity can in this respect be appropriated for the feminist project.[43] But social rights are not the only means for the specific promotion of women. It also needs to be discussed to what extent quotas can help achieve the overall goal. (Presenting this as a pragmatic issue follows my earlier point that moral philosophy has no compelling objection against quotas.)[44]

Let us move from the level of concrete legal regulations to that of foundational questions of legal theory. In countries that are constitutionally based on the concept of modern democracy, concrete legislation has often led to injustices for women. Therefore it seems appropriate to ask whether the various effects of discrimination— even if they can be referred to individual legal texts—have a common origin. Does the modern state have a masculine design? This question calls for an investigation of the social contract, beginning with the classic variations of this concept. If we take the contract theories developed by authors such as Hobbes, Locke, Rousseau, and Kant, then this question can quickly be answered yes. All the different approaches converge on the following point: The partners in the social contract are exclusively thought of as men.[45] (A further aspect of exclusion is that citizenship is also withheld from men who are wage workers.) What is the significance of this diagnosis in regard to the theoretical foundations of democratic states? Contemporary feminist scholars hold diverging opinions on this question. Some argue as follows: First, the originally exclusive definition of citizenship is to be seen as historically contingent. Second, the history of the Western states since the French Revolution can be characterized by a process of increasing inclusion; the men of the Fourth Estate and then women fought for and achieved formal equality.[46] Third, the concept of the social contract has gone through decisive modifications, so that the basic thought of liberty and equality for all individuals is now more consistently formulated. Fourth, a redefinition of citizenship is needed, given that an understanding of the term still exists that does not include women in the same way as men. However, many feminist authors see in such a line of argumentation a grave misunderstanding. The way in which contract theory portrays the single contract partner, they object, draws its central definitions from modernity's characteristic image of the man. Because the exclusion of women is implied in the definition, the concept of the contract partner cannot be extended to include women without risking inconsistency. Carole Pateman therefore stresses the "incongruous character of an alliance between feminism and contract."[47] From this perspective, special attention needs to be paid to studies seeking to demonstrate that the problem has not been completely overcome, even in the most advanced contemporary theories of justice, such as that of Rawls.[48]

This contradictory evaluation of contract theory has led to a multifaceted debate that cannot be reported here in detail.[49] I will limit my remarks to its central themes, with two aims in mind. While analyzing the specific objections raised against the social contract, I will show that feminist legal theory is well advised if it does not reject the social contract approach *in toto* but reformulates it from the viewpoint of justice between the sexes.

The objection has repeatedly been raised that contract partners are thought of as isolated individuals. "The assumption in this case is that human individuals are ontologically prior to society."[50] A number of authors assume that the conception of the contract is based on a social atomism[51] which neglects the circumstance that people always need to be raised in a human community before they can step out as individuals. They believe that a theory which ignores the relational background of individuality relies on an androcentric perspective. The experiences of women, to whom Western culture traditionally assigns the care of children, remain unconsidered.[52] For some critics the problem of an atomistic social ontology continues within contemporary conceptions of justice, including the work of Rawls, Nozick, and Dworkin.[53] It is undoubtedly legitimate to reject a concept of individuality which neglects the fact that the individual is always tied into various community contexts. But it must be asked whether all the authors defending the idea of the social contract indeed operate with such a concept. Suggestions for alternative readings argue that contract theory does not claim to develop a comprehensive concept of individuality in the first place. Rather, the single person is only taken into account insofar as it is necessary for a theory of the state. Authors such as Charles Taylor[54] and Will Kymlicka[55] warn in this sense of an ontological misunderstanding that is bound to miss the actual point: taking a stand for the rights of each individual.

The philosophy of the Enlightenment offers a much richer understanding of individuality than its critics commonly acknowledge. This fact is revealed as soon as one takes into account not only the theories of the state but also reflections from other fields such as philosophical anthropology, philosophy of history, ethics, and aesthetics that have been elaborated by thinkers of the Enlightenment. Contrary to an atomistic understanding, we have to ask, If the central aim of feminist theory and practice is overcoming the multiple forms of discrimination against women, is this not also about taking a stand for the rights of all individual women? (As explained above, discrimination, even if it affects an entire group of people, still is experienced, or rather suffered, by the affected individual.) The fact that contract theory's point of departure is the single person—the contract partner—does not warrant the thesis according to which the feminist project must completely dismiss the contractarian approach.[56] It seems more appropriate to elaborate a revised definition of citizenship that takes the rights of women into account in the same manner as the rights of men.

An important piece of evidence for the masculine character of the liberal tradition is frequently seen in the value attached to the concept of autonomy. This way of arguing is usually based on an interpretation of autonomy in the tradition of object-relations theory, especially the research of Chodorow (introduced in Chapter 3). Here autonomy refers to the tendency of male children to excessively detach themselves from the mother.[57] But is it legitimate to assume this psychological meaning wherever the term *autonomy* is encountered in a philosophical context? A more thorough examination reveals that it is also used in a number of ways that do not correspond with the psychological paradigm. Enlightenment philosophy includes the following terminology: When a rigid isolation is addressed, the expression used is *autarchy,* not *autonomy*.[58] Used in a political context, *autonomy* does indeed imply a rejection, but one that is primarily directed against a hierarchical structure, not people. The actual point of *autonomy* lies in being the opposite of *heteronomy*. Therefore this concept presents an instrument for the criticism of paternalism and oppression.

Where this understanding is employed to articulate political demands, it allows for a twofold thrust. The call for autonomy, on the one hand, intends self-legislation in the sense of the equal participation of all individuals in the decisionmaking processes concerning the community. On the other hand, it demands the chance for self-determination to be provided through protecting individuals and groups from encroachments—by other people or institutions of the state. In view of this usage, the thesis that the concept of autonomy must be rejected *toto genere* as masculine does not seem plausible. It rather must be asked: Can a feminist criticism of the different forms of gender hierarchy be formulated at all if it is not demanded at the same time that women should be empowered for autonomy in this dual sense? Have not present feminist endeavors with their various accents appropriated both intentions? Iris Young, for instance, has both intentions in mind when she votes for active participation of all citizens (in a critical discussion of the passive aspect of the distributive paradigm) as well as recognition of group differences.[59] Feminists have also appropriated the thought that free space for self-determination has to be demanded not only for groups but also for the individual, for instance, in the current discussion of the concept of privacy. One core issue in this debate is the fact that women living in the traditionally shaped domestic sphere are too little protected from assaults, such as (sexual) violence.[60] If it is imperative to strive for a "new definition of the private,"[61] this means that women demand autonomy in the form of self-determination (also over their own bodies).[62]

The diverse aspects mentioned so far still create an incomplete picture because they confine themselves to autonomy as discussed in political theory. In Kant the term *autonomy* primarily refers to his concept of morality, not issues of the philosophy of law. For Kant, the core of this term lies in moral autonomy, as explained in his theory of the moral law. If we take into account here that the categorical imperative also includes the obligation to care for others, we can see clearly that the philosophical concept of autonomy cannot be identified with the kind of detachment that object-relations theory observes in boys.[63]

Good reasons for a feminist critique arise from the definition of contract partners in classical texts. The problem is not limited to the exclusion of women. To achieve the status of full citizenship, a person must belong to the male sex, meet certain economic requirements, and found a family. Therefore we have to examine which legal design the family gets in this context. In connection with the assignment of the woman to the domestic sphere, a hierarchical conception of marriage and family is developed. As we can see in Rousseau, Kant, or Fichte, the woman is put under the authority of the husband, who is assigned the position of head of the family, as well as the corresponding authority of decision.[64] That this conception is problematic from a feminist perspective is obvious. The principle of self-determination, which forms a central element in the contract conception, is not applied to women. A whole bundle of problems results from this—four of which are mentioned in the following discussion. The most obvious point is probably that women, because of their sex, are refused participation in public decisionmaking processes that affect their conditions of life. In the ever popular thesis that politics is men's business, this line of thought from classical liberalist legal theory continues to be effective. An analogous problem is created by the way the woman is positioned in the family. As Heidemarie Bennent states in regard to Rousseau, the claim to replace the old contract of rule by a new contract, free of subordination, does not extend to the realm of marriage and family.[65] This problem has an effect today, not only in the widespread master of the house cliché but also in advanced contemporary legal theories that contain traces of the hierarchical family conception. As Susan Moller Okin has shown,[66] this is even true for Rawls's reformulation of contract theory insofar as the contract partners are thought of as heads of households.[67] Although this expression is gender neutral, it may easily be interpreted in the sense of the traditional family structures. A further problem of classic contract theory results from the conception of the domestic sphere as a private space and therefore largely beyond the reach of the state's influence. Thus the life of women is located in a space predominantly unregulated by law. Under these conditions, women hardly have legal means at their disposal to defend themselves against disregard and abuse. One indication for the lack of legal protection is the continuing debate over rape within marriage in many countries. (Women's vulnerability in the domestic sphere was a central point of criticism at the beginning of the women's movement. The well-known slogan "the personal is political" referred precisely to this problem.)[68]

We need to analyze how the relation of public and private sphere has been conceived. The tasks typically assigned to women all refer to

performances in the service of the public sphere. Sons are educated
to carry out their occupations in politics and economy; women have
the duty to compensate emotionally for the psychic pressure that
men experience in the competition characteristic of bourgeois society.[69] Rousseau demands, accordingly, "The whole education of
women ought to relate to men, to be useful to them, to make herself
loved and honored by them, to educate them in their youth and care
for them when grown, to counsel them, to console them, to make
their lives agreeable and sweet—these are the duties of women at all
times."[70] In regard to such ideas, it would be wrong for feminist criticism to limit itself to targeting the asymmetry of the outlined relation between the sexes. This becomes particularly clear as one
examines the impact these ideas had on later theories.[71] For instance,
grave consequences have resulted from the fact that the term *work*
has also been defined with reference to the characteristic constellation of public and private sphere. Marx and Engels, despite their
trenchant rejection of liberalism, in this point retained the bourgeois
conception. This continuity has in the meantime been examined by a
number of authors whose results I can only briefly summarize here.
First we have to realize that the term *production* is ambivalent, referring on the one hand to all activities "that are necessary for the continuation of the human species, including breastfeeding and the
raising of children as well as the production of food" and, on the
other hand, only to activities that serve the production of commodi-
ties.[72] Critics believe the source for this ambiguity to be the fact that
Marx and Engels tend to associate household work with the biology
of women. One case in point is "German Ideology," where a "natural" division of labor between the sexes is explicitly assumed. This
presents a glaring inconsistency. The basic concept of historical materialism is not applied to the living conditions of women. In this sense
Alison Jaggar states, "No Marxist theory provides a satisfactory historical account of the sexual division of labor."[73] The problem is exac-
erbated in that the term *production* is usually defined in
gender-neutral language. In this manner a double marginalization of

women is covered up. It is concealed that Marxist theory does not devote thorough examination to labors that are carried out in the domestic sphere, and it is also concealed that it indirectly affirms the popular practice by which women who work outside the home are often assigned work comparable with domestic labor—a practice that usually entails a disadvantage in salary. This deficit in economic analysis was so consequential that up to the Frankfurt School gender was not seen as an independent principle of social order from which a specific kind of dominance emerges.[74] (The gender blindness of the common definition of the term *work* can also be found outside the Marxist tradition, up to contemporary economic theory.)[75]

It is self-evident that these feminist objections against the modern state result in the demand for a reconceptualization. Answering this demand means focusing on not only the problems themselves but also their manifold interactions.[76] A number of studies have discussed the measures necessary to ensure women their full rights, including civil, political, and social rights.[77] One essential aim of these considerations on the citizenship of women is a redimensioning of the domestic sphere. It has been demanded, for instance, that caring for children must be understood as socially necessary work and evaluated accordingly.[78] Informed by this debate, feminist politicians have developed suggestions for labor law measures that do not handicap but support the sharing of domestic work among men and women.[79] What are the theoretical prerequisites for such demands? To what extent is a withdrawal from the original conception of the modern state required to make the intended reconceptualization possible?

Here we need to address the question of how the patriarchal features of classic contract theory are to be interpreted. Is it possible to eliminate them, or do they amount to unavoidable implications of contract theory? As already noted, a number of authors believe that they originate in the concept of the contract itself. Since the most distinct presentation of this thesis is found in Carole Pateman, I will briefly summarize and discuss her critique. Pateman's central point is that there is not just one contract; a closer look discovers two different forms of contract. As they enter the social contract, the equal and free male citizens agree simultaneously on a sexual contract. This double contract guarantees their dominance over women in a dual way. It ensures, on the one hand, "men's political rights over women" and guarantees, on the other, "orderly access by men to women's bodies."[80] For Pateman, the gender hierarchy already laid out in the original pact is the reason for the contradictions that appear wherever contracts are signed by women. In an analysis of Kant's reflections on the marriage contract, Pateman explains this problem in greater detail. She emphasizes that Kant denies women the maturity that is decisive for men to be full citizens and to sign contracts, while he nonetheless assigns them the ability to enter the marriage contract. Pateman locates a further contradiction in pointing out that Kant, while characterizing the marriage contract by the principle of mutuality (since he speaks of a "mutual use of the sexual characteristics"), assumes at the same time that the woman consents to her subordination to her husband through signing the marriage contract.[81] For Pateman, these examples show that ensuring patriarchal dominance has been so important to the contract theoreticians that they have accepted even obvious inconsistencies. Therefore she sees only one viable option: From a feminist perspective, the concept of the contract has to be dismissed *toto genere*.[82] But this conclusion is not compelling, as I will now show.

Different lines of thought are intertwined here. Let us first reconsider the core of the contract conception, as explained in connection with the concepts of person and autonomy. Recall that the principle of self-legislation can be defined consistently without implying the subordination of any person or group. If, for instance, Rousseau emphasizes that the social contract is about the "obedience to the law which one has been given by oneself,"[83] it is not comprehensible why it should be impossible to include all individuals, regardless of their sex or their class, ethnicity, religion, and so on, in this self-government. (What I said above in my response to Judith Butler's criticism of the instrumental subject is of relevance in this context.) In short, there is no reason not to take the universalistic claim of the contract theory seriously.

At the same time, we need to notice that in contemporary political theory there is the danger of confusing two issues. Self-determination is sometimes understood in the sense of developing a special identity. In this context, it is often pointed out (with reference to de Saussure and Derrida) that the determining of a specification cannot be thought—or performed—without the exclusion of other options or the abjection of the other. This observation might not be easily dismissed; however, it does not provide a justification for the thesis that the political concept of self-determination inevitably implies a hierarchy between insiders and outsiders. Such a thesis confuses two different levels. It leaves unconsidered that the development of a special identity always presupposes—in spite of all differences—the shared competence to choose one's ends, and that the contractualist defense of the rights of the individual refers to autonomy only in this formal sense. It is one of the core concerns of contract theory that all individuals must have the same possibilities to choose their ends and to connect to groups of their choice. Thus it would be a serious misunderstanding to interpret the autonomy/heteronomy dyad as introduced in Kant's moral philosophy in such a manner that the self-determination of people necessarily has as a precondition that others are being determined (i.e., coerced) by the self.[84] In light of the quest for the most consistent feminist theory, it seems almost disastrous that confusion on this point has become so widespread in postmodern approaches to political theory.[85]

The universalistic character of the contract conception is only one of the elements that have to be discussed here. Let us now turn to the fact that the classical theories of the social contract are shaped patriarchally. For an in-depth examination of this fact, it is crucial to first address the ambivalence that usually marks the use of the term *citizen*—an ambivalence that can be demonstrated with the help of the French terms *bourgeois* and *citoyen*. Obviously those theorems of the classics, which deny women the right to self-determination to a great degree, correspond with the normative ideas of the bourgeoisie of the eighteenth century and also with the economic realities of bourgeois society. (The latter aspect was illustrated above with Rousseau's reflections on the pressure of competition and domestic emotional compensation.) Therefore it is correct to assume that Enlightenment authors tended to use the term *citizen* in a way that uncritically blends the concepts of citoyen and bourgeois. In this manner, the ideas of the bourgeoisie have influenced contract theory. But the implications of this form of blending should not be overestimated. As just explained, the central concern of contract theory is to advocate a universalistic approach, not to defend bourgeois hierarchies. That we are indeed confronted with an oscillation between the concepts of citoyen and bourgeois is illustrated by the internal contradictions in classical texts that Pateman has pointed out. I believe, however, that these inconsistencies require an interpretation that differs from the one suggested by Pateman. They do not warrant the thesis that contract and gender hierarchy are indissolubly linked. On the contrary, the fact that tension exists between two concepts that were tacitly intermingled indicates that patriarchal ideas contradict the core of contractualist thinking. Consequently it is imperative to separate contract theory and the bourgeois order of the sexes in a consequent manner. This will clear the way for an examination of the relevance of contract theory for a feminist conception of citizenship. In this context, the question arises, Does Pateman, albeit unadmittedly, presuppose central elements of contractualist thinking? Is it not obvious that any critique of concrete injustices—such as the subordination and sexual exploitation of women in wedlock—can be made plausible only by an appeal to the principle that all individuals have the right to self-determination?[86]

My call for a consequent uncoupling of the two concepts is not limited to the classics but also refers to the fact that patriarchal structures of thinking are still found in contemporary formulations of the contract conception. In this regard, too, it is not a sufficient reason for a complete distancing from this approach to the philosophy of law. If, for instance, Rawls's "A Theory of Justice" has been rightfully criticized for not paying enough attention to asymmetries in the family, this objection reveals a limited inconsistency but not an unavoidable weakness of his whole project. Rawls himself could appropriate this criticism and explain in a later study that the principles of justice he developed need to be applied to institutions whose inner structure is determined by the traditional order of the sexes.[87]

The feminist objections to Rawls are not limited to the existing traces of a patriarchal idea of family but often address the central claim of his theory. Feminist authors, like scholars focusing on other groups facing discrimination, frequently criticize the conception of the original position. According to them, Rawls's argument that the contract partners have to deliberate under a "veil of ignorance" when making decisions on fundamental principles of justice leads inevitably to the well-known problem of gender blindness.[88] In regard to the ubiquitous phenomenon of androcentrism,[89] this objection seemed plausible to many. But on closer inspection this supposed plausibility disappears. Let us assume the veil of ignorance was perforated in such a manner that the individuals in the hypothetical original state would know about their sex. Could this provide a solid basis for the normative claim to justice between the sexes? Dealing with this question, we first need to acknowledge that there is no good reason why the veil of ignorance should be permeable only for this piece of information. Why should the individuals know about their sex but not about their sexual orientation, social standing, ethnic and religious membership, and so on? If the veil is damaged at one point, it cannot be kept from tearing completely. With the additional information, the decisive point of Rawls's conception would in the end get lost. The single individuals or groups would confront each other with their special interests and negotiate compromises but not general principles of justice. "Translated into . . . practical politics, this would mean that there would be only persons pleading for special interests . . . only lobbyists but no legislators, only prosecutors and defense attorneys but no judges," states Ruth Anna Putnam.[90] To formulate this problem with regard to the general line of argument that I am suggesting here: A theory of justice that starts with particular interests loses the insight of moral philosophy that discrimination is a problem which concerns not only those affected but everybody.

How is it that criticism articulated in the interest of groups facing discrimination repeatedly risks such a loss? As indicated, the reason lies in a rash identification of the veil of ignorance with gender blindness. In order to expose the misconception contained in this view, I first need to note that, according to Rawls, the contract partners are barred only from taking a look at how *they themselves* will be positioned in the community whose normative regulation is under debate. The veil of ignorance metaphor refers exclusively to this lack of information. Apart from not knowing their own position, the individuals are well aware of the problems that typically arise when people live together, and also of possible social asymmetries. This is the very point of the entire construction of the hypothetical contract.

According to this basic idea, each individual must deal with the following question: Assume I am in the most underprivileged position. Which principles would appear to me in this condition appropriate as a foundation for an order of the community? If we consider this, it immediately becomes evident how the problem of hierarchical gender relations can be introduced into this conceptual frame. At the point where the contract partners are informed about possible social asymmetries, they also need to be confronted with the fact that gender is traditionally a category of social order through which women experience manifold discrimination. Accordingly, everybody deliberating in the original position must tackle the question that starts as follows: Assume I am an individual belonging to the female sex. Which principles would appear to me in this condition appropriate as a foundation for an order of the community? With this in mind, the problem of gender blindness can be addressed more precisely. An objection of that kind is called for where a contractualist conception does not acknowledge gender discrimination and therefore does not include this specific question—yet it is called for *only* where this is the case. This means that such an objection to Rawls's theory is justified only insofar as his elaborations of the contract conception in their early stage lacked an explicit engagement with gender asymmetries. It would be counterproductive as well as erroneous to raise the reproach of gender blindness in regard to the veil of ignorance, since it is through this part of Rawls's conception that all single contract partners can take discrimination seriously as a problem of justice.

This discussion of the objections to contract theory characteristic of feminist discourse has already revealed, in an indirect manner, the potential of this theory to provide the foundations for a politics aiming at justice between the sexes. Additionally, one specific aspect needs to be highlighted. Contemporary variations of the contract conception are not limited to explaining the justification of the claim for formal legal equality of all individuals, regardless of their specific group membership. Of course, it is one of their major achievements to provide this justification, and we have to consider that the claim for equal rights for women (e.g., with regard to active and passive suffrage, state-funded education, or freedom of speech and assembly) has always been based on contractualist considerations, even if this has remained unreflected or has been rejected explicitly. More recent legal theoretical debate has shown that the principle of equality, central to contract theory, also implies that underprivileged individuals and groups have to be promoted specifically to ensure substantial as well as formal equality of opportunity.[91] I am emphasizing this aspect of contract theory because it provides a sound way of reasoning for feminist politics. If we recall how plans for a specific promotion of women's interests are sometimes articulated, then deficits of argumentation become obvious that invite the criticism of all those who oppose these plans anyway. For instance, the term *reverse discrimination* has suggested to many critics that the targeted asymmetry between the sexes is to be continued in reverse. Another notorious example is that some special legal measures for women are presented under the heading "recognition of difference," suggesting the thesis of an alterity of women—the problematic of which has been pointed out already.[92] On the basis of contract theory, however, a different path of argumentation opens up. Now it can be shown that such plans do not diverge from the principle of equal treatment (e.g., by calling for new privileges) but are a consistent application of the principle of equality. Evidence for this can be found in the issues that lead to calls for specific support, since they center around questions such as, What has to happen so that job and family are compatible for women in the same manner they are for men? The importance of appealing to the principle of equality to legitimate measures that specifically address one group in the community can be seen where legal regulations in regard to persons of gay or lesbian orientation are discussed. Let us take as an example the current debate in many countries on the inclusion of gay and lesbian partnerships into the laws regulating marriage. In public opinion, this topic is often understood as if it were about special treatment by which the otherness of the persons in question is acknowledged. The problem with this view is that, as the focus is on difference, it maintains the very perspective that has supported discrimination on account of sexual orientation. This dangerous congruence can be avoided if contract theory is adopted as an argumentative basis.[93] In this case, the individual under the veil of ignorance, who is informed about possible social asymmetries, is also confronted with the problem of discrimination on account of sexual orientation. Therefore it must deal with the following question: Why should I—in the case that I find myself as an individual of homosexual orientation—not have the same opportunity as everybody else to live with my chosen partner in a legally protected form, including the laws regulating matters of health and pension as well as inheritance?[94]

A politics that aims at overcoming discrimination is well advised to use the tool of contractualism. But contract theory can only provide the necessary foundations if the asymmetries defined by gender or sexual orientation are included in the reflections of the individual who is deliberating in the original position. Therefore, from a feminist perspective, we must strive for a reformulation of contract theory—with equal emphasis on the contract and its rereading.

NOTES

Introduction:
Feminist Philosophy under Post-feminist Conditions

1. The grammatical form should not be misinterpreted. The singular -"feminist philosophy"- does not imply that there is only one theory (that would require to be tested for internal coherence); rather it is to be read as a general notion.

2. See for example: *Hypatia. A Journal of Feminist Philosophy* (Bloomington, IN, since 1983); *Die Philosophin* (The Woman Philosopher) (Tübingen, since 1990); the book series documenting the conferences of the International Association of Women Philosophers (founded in Würzburg in 1974). The most recent volume of this series is Birgit Christensen et al., eds., *Knowledge/Power/Gender. Philosophy and the Future of the 'condition féminine'* (Zurich 2002).

3. See for instance: Marion Heinz/Sabine Doyé (eds.), *Feministische Philosophie. Bibliographie 1970–1995* (Feminist Philosophy. Bibliography 1970–1995) (Bielefeld 1996); Marion Heinz/Meike Nordmeyer (eds.), *Feministische Philosophie. Bibliographie 1996–97* (Feminist Philosophy. Bibliography 1996–97) (Bielefeld 1999); Marion Heinz/Meike Nordmeyer (eds.), *Feministische Philosophie. Bibliographie 1998–99* (Feminist Philosophy. Bibliography 1998) (Frankfurt am Main 2003); Alison M.Jaggar / Iris Marion Young (eds.), *A Companion to Feminist Philosophy* (Oxford, UK, 1998); Judith Evans, *Feminist Theory Today. An Introduction to Second-Wave Feminism* (London 1995); Andrea Nye, *Philosophy and Feminism at the Border* (New York 1995); Heftschwerpunkt Feministische Theorie—Zwischenbilanzen (Special Issue "Feminist Theory—Interim Balances), in: *Deutsche Zeitschrift für Philosophie* (German Journal of Philosophy) 46 (1998), pp.780–848.

4. It is true not only with regard to philosophy that feminist research still faces marginalization. As Ute Gerhard points out, "the social critique voiced by the new feminism (. . .) has until now had no systematic impact on contemporary sociological theory." Ute Gerhard, "'Illegitime Töchter'. Das komplizierte Verhältnis zwischen Feminismus und Soziologie ('Illegitimate Doughters'. The Complex Relationship Between Feminism and Sociology)" in: Jürgen Friedrichs/M.Rainer Lepsius/Karl Ulrich Mayer (eds.), *Die Diagnosefähigkeit der Soziologie* (Sociology's Diagnostic Competence) (Opladen 1998), p.345. As Gerhard explains, this deficit presents a step backwards, since sociological "classics" such as Tönnies, Durkheim and Simmel have attributed central significance to issues of gender and the women's movement of their time (ibid. pp. 346–365).

5. See Margaret Maruani, "Die gewöhnliche Diskriminierung auf dem Arbeitsmarkt (The Common Discrimination on the Labor Market)," in: Irene Dölling/ Beate Krais (eds.), *Ein alltägliches Spiel. Geschlechterkonstruktionen in der sozialen Praxis* (An Everyday Game. Gender Constructions in Social Praxis) (Frankfurt am Main 1997), pp.48–74.

6. In the world's poorest countries the sustained gender asymmetry entails a drastically reduced life expectancy for women, compared to the men in these regions. This fact is analysed in: Amartya Sen, "More than 100 Million Women are Missing," in: *The New York Review of Books*, 37, 20, 1990, pp.61–66. See also: Amartya Sen, "Inequality Reexamined" (Cambridge, MA, 1995), pp.122–125. With regard to the gender aspect of neo-liberal globalisation see: Eva Kreisky/ Birgit Sauer, "Geschlechterverhältnisse im Kontext politischer Transformation (Gender Relations in the Context of Political Transformation)," in: *Politische Vierteljahresschrift. Sonderheft 28* (Political Quarterly. Special Issue 28), 38,1997, pp. 29–32.

7. For an overview see "part 6. Rezeption und Kritik philosophischer Theorien der Gegenwart (Reception and Critique of Contemporary Philosophical Theories)" in: Heinz/Nordmeyer (eds.), *Feministische Philosophie. Bibliographie 1996–97* (Feminist Philosophy. Bibliography 1996–97), pp. 142–164.

8. For an analysis of the relations between post-modern theories and the notion "post-feminist" see: Patricia Mann, *Micropolitics. Agency in a Postfeminist Era* (Minneapolis 1994).

9. See Susan Falludi, *Backlash. The Undeclared War Against American Women* (New York 1991).

10. Nancy Fraser, "The Uses and Abuses of French Discourse Theories for Feminist Politics," in Nancy Fraser and Sandra Lee Bartky (eds.), *Revaluing French Feminism. Critical Essays on Difference, Agency and Culture* (Bloomington 1992), p. 191.—Many authors point at a close relation between theoretical and socio-political developments. They suggest to correlate the "post-feminist" turn of thought to those changes in the women's movement that are commonly seen as either a crisis or the beginning of a new wave. See Ute Gerhard, "Frauenbewegung in der Flaute? (Is the Women's Movement Currently in a Lull?)" in: *Transit*, 10,1995, pp.117–135; Imelda Whelan, *Modern Feminist Thought. From the Second Wave to 'Post-Feminism'* (New York 1995); Special Issue "Third Wave Feminisms," *Hypatia* 12,3,1997. These sociological and political theoretical issues cannot be discussed here in detail.

11. See for instance Iris Marion Young, "Fünf Formen der Unterdrückung," in: Herta Nagl-Docekal/ Herlinde Pauer-Studer (eds.), *Politische Theorie. Differenz und Lebensqualität* (Political Theory. Difference and the Quality of Life) (Frankfurt am Main 1996), pp.99–139. Engl: "Five Faces of Oppression," in: Iris M.Young, *Justice and the Politics of Difference* (Princeton, N.J., 1990), pp.39–65.

12. See chapter 2, "Feminist Philosophy in New Directions," in: Eve Browning Cole, *Philosophy and Feminist Criticism. An Introduction* (New York 1993), pp.24–50. One danger needs to be heeded here. Where complex social relations are discussed, attention tends to shift in such a manner that the specific problems of sex discrimination move out of focus. Cornelia Klinger explains this danger with regard to Foucault's concept of power. See: "Periphere Kooptierung. Neue Formen der Ausgrenzung feministischer Kritik—Ein Gespräch mit Cornelia Klinger (Peripheral Cooptation. New Patterns of the Marginalisation of Feminist Critique—A Conversation with Cornelia Klinger)," in: *Die Philosophin* (The Woman Philosopher) 9,18,1998, p.99. Klinger also diagnoses a similarly problematic shift where current studies on lesbian and gay identity are connected with the claim that feminist research has become obsolete. As Klinger stresses, "the axis masculinity/femininity is not identical with the axis heterosexuality/ homosexuality." Ibid., pp. 486–508.

13. With regard to the specific field of philosophy of science this kind of reservation is voiced in: Jack Nelson and Lynn Hankinson Nelson, "No Rush to Judgment," in: *The Monist*, 77,4,1994,pp.486–508.

14. I have discussed this type of objection more comprehensively in: Herta Nagl-Docekal, "Was ist feministische Philosophie? (What is Feminist Philosophy?)," in: Herta Nagl-Docekal (ed.), *Feministische Philosophie* (Feminist Philosophy), second ed.(Wien 1994), pp.7–38.

15. See the definition provided by Alison M.Jaggar and Iris M.Young: "Introduction," in: Alison M.Jaggar and Iris M.Young (eds.), *A Companion to Feminist Philosophy*, pp.1–6.

16. See for instance: Harriet Baber, "The Market for Feminist Philosophy," in: *The Monist*, 77,4,1994, p.188. Similarly Helen Longino notes "(We) can reach the idea of feminist science through that of doing science as a feminist." Helen Longino, *Science as Historical Knowledge. Values and Objectivity in Scientific Inquiry* (Princeton1990), p.188.

17. Harriet Baber rightly argues that this point of view promotes the development of "pink-collar ghettos." Harriet Baber, "The Market for Feminist Philosophy," p.419.

18. Apart from the bibliographies quoted above, an overview is provided by: Cornelia Klinger, "Das Bild der Frau in der patriarchalen Philosophiegeschichte. Eine Auswahlbibliographie (The Image of the Woman in the Patriarchal History of Philosophy. A Selected Bibliography), in: Herta Nagl-Docekal (ed.), *Feministische Philosophie* (Feminist Philosophy), 244–275.

19. A number of publications aim to eliminate this information deficit. See for instance: Mary Ellen Whaithe (ed.), *A History of Women Philosophers*, vol. I-IV (Dordrecht 1989ff.); Elisabeth Gössmann (Hg.), *Archiv für philosophie- und theologiegeschichtliche Frauenforschung* (Archive for Women's Studies in the His-

tory of Philosophy and Theology) (München 1984 ff.); Marit Rullmann et al. (eds.), *Philosophinnen* (Women Philosophers), Bd.1: Von der Antike bis zur Aufklärung (vol 1: Fom Antiquity to Enlightenment), Bd.2: Von der Romantik bis zur Moderne (vol. 2: From the Romantic Era to Modernity), second ed., (Zürich 1994); Ursula I. Meyer and Heidemarie Bennent-Vahle (eds.), *Philosophinnen Lexikon* (Encyclopedia of Women Philosophers), second edition (Aachen 1996).

20. It is important to note that the analysis of the "Canon" from a feminist point of view is no longer guided exclusively by the aim to uncover patriarchal patterns of thinking. One focus of recent studies in the history of philosophy is the search for theoretical concepts that allow to be reformulated and utilized for feminist theory. The fruitfulness of this double perspective is evident in the book series: Nancy Tuana (ed.), *Re-Reading the Canon*, University Park, PA; see for instance the volumes on Plato (1994), Kant (1997), Hegel (1996), Foucault (1996) and Derrida (1997).

21. Herta Nagl-Docekal, "What is Feminist Philosophy?," p.11. In the context of this definition I explore the manifold specific issues of research implied in this general concept of feminist philosophy; therefore there is no need to discuss this variety of tasks here. See also Herta Nagl-Docekal "Von der feministischen Transformation der Philosophie (On the Feminist Transformation of Philosophy)," in: *Ethik und Sozialwissenschaften* (Ethics and Social Sciences), 2(1992), 4, pp.523–531, and Herta Nagl-Docekal "Anknüfungen und Einsprüche. Ein Versuch, auf sehr unterschiedliche Kommentare zur feministischen Philosophie einzugehen (Picking Up and Objecting. An Attempt to Respond to Some Very Different Comments on Feminist Philosophy)," ibid., pp.577–592.

22. Some people contend that feminist thinking must cultivate a style of its own that is not characterized by the idea of reasoned argumentation and the need to formulate objections. This opinion is, however, incompatible with the claim to do science. Philosophical research, too, cannot dispense with the pondering of arguments. Thus the demands for an alternative style support—albeit unintentionally—the view of those who have argued all along that feminism and philosophy form irreconcilable opposites. A different—and legitimate—matter is the call for fairness that demands to distinguish between the refutation of an argument and a contemptuous treatment of the person who formulated it.

23. A differentiating mode of discussing philosophical issues is often answered with a sweeping dismissal that is positively qualified with the expression "radical." Yet this term is misleading: In order to get to the "root" (Latin "radix") of a given problem, sweeping judgments are hardly helpful. Rather, what is required is an in-depth study of the issues in question. Taken in this sense, the feminist approach suggested in this book does indeed claim to be radical.

Chapter 1

1. See Claudia Honegger, *Die Ordnung der Geschlechter: Die Wissenschaften vom Menschen und das Weib* (Frankfurt/Main, 1991).

2. An overview of the egalitarian thinking characteristic for the period from the middle of the seventeenth to the middle of the eighteenth century is offered by

Hannelore Schröder, "Olympe de Gouges' 'Erklärung der Rechte der Frau und Bürgerin' (1791): Ein Paradigma feministisch-politischer Philosophie," in Herta Nagl-Docekal, ed., *Feministische Philosophie*, 2nd ed. (Vienna, 1994), pp. 202–228.

3. The structure of this disadvantaging will be more closely investigated in Chapter 4 of this book.

4. To avoid choosing only single studies from the large number published, I would like to refer to a more comprehensive compilation: Cornelia Klinger, "Das Bild der Frau in der patriarchalen Philosophiegeschichte: Eine Auswahlbibliographie," in Nagl-Docekal, *Feministische Philosophie*, pp. 244–276.

5. See Michael Mitterauer, "Diktat der Hormone? Zu den Bedingungen geschlechtstypischen Verhaltens aus historischer Sicht," in Hubert Ch. Ehalt, ed., *Zwischen Natur und Kultur: Zur Kritik biologistischer Ansätze* (Wien, 1985), pp. 63–92.

6. A clear demarcation of both terms is necessary if the philosophical distinction is to be further detailed. But for the sake of readability in the following I will use the term *behavior*—when no ambiguity results from it—in its everyday meaning referring to deliberate decisions.

7. This list is formulated—in reference to Konrad Lorenz—by Bernd Lötsch and Peter Weish in their accompanying text to the documentary film *Fressen und gefressen werden* (Wien, 1982), p. 37.

8. Lötsch and Weish, *Fressen und gefressen werden*, p. 37.

9. Konrad Lorenz, *Das sogenannte Böse: Zur Naturgeschichte der Aggression* (Wien, 1963), chap. 7: "Der Moral analoge Verhaltensweisen."

10. In the section "Rationality and gender blindness in the sciences" in Chapter 3 of this book, I argue that the traditional criteria of scientific objectivity must be subjected to feminist criticism. Here I emphasize only that the problems to be discussed in this regard will not question this objection against the arbitrary selection and anthropomorphizing depiction of animal behavior.

11. In the context of analytical philosophy it has also been demonstrated as impossible "to search in nature for a foundation of the rationality of virtous behaviour." See, for instance, John McDowell, "Zwei Arten von Naturalismus," in *Deutsche Zeitschrift für Philosophie* 45, 5 (1997): 687–710. McDowell emphasizes, "Rationality opens the possibility for the deliberating subject to distance himself from *all* rationales for his supposed requirements (p. 692)."

12. The manifold attempts at naturalizing the existing hierarchy of the sexes are documented in Elvira Scheich, ed., *Vermittelte Weiblichkeit: Feministische Wissenschafts- und Gesellschaftstheorie* (Hamburg, 1966).

13. This matter will be discussed in Chapter 4 of this book.

14. See B. Rensch, "Geschlechtlichkeit," *Historisches Wörterbuch der Philosophie* (Darmstadt, 1974), 3:443.

15. As Hilge Landweer has made clear, it must be stated at the same time that these decisions always have the idea of the bodily differences of the sexes as their point of reference as a prerequisite. "Especially if one intends to dissolve the normative connection of sexuality and reproduction," she writes, "one has to distinguish between the sexes. Otherwise one has to reckon with the passing or accidental emergence of individuals." She also emphasizes in regard to the issue of an adequate

definition of *gender* that the "relevance of generativity" cannot be circumvented. Hilge Landweer, "Generativität und Geschlecht: Ein blinder Fleck in der sex/gender-Debatte," in Theresa Wobbe and Gesa Lindemann, eds., *Denkachsen: Zur theoretischen und institutionellen Rede vom Geschlecht* (Frankfurt/Main, 1994), p. 153. See Wobbe and Lindemann, "Geschlechterklassifikation and historische Deutung," in Klaus E. Müller and Jörn Rüsen, eds., *Historische Sinnbildung* (Reinbek bei Hamburg, 1997), pp. 142–164.

16. As Hilge Landweer has noted, "mortality, birth and therefore generativity are specific challenges for every culture, which are responded to with appropriate distinctions and practices with principally infinitely variable contents." Hilge Landweer, "Kritik und Verteidigung der Kategorie Geschlecht: Wahrnehmungs und symboltheoretische Überlegungen zur sex/gender-Unterscheidung," *Feministische Studien*, November 1993, p. 36.

17. See Andrea Maihofer, "Die Historizität des Geschlechtskörpers," in *Geschlecht als Existenzweise*, pp. 21–39.

18. With the help of a number of informative examples of the development of feminine characteristics, this is shown by, among others, Frigga Haug, *Sexualisierung der Körper*, 2nd ed. (Hamburg, 1988).

19. Edith Stein, *Zum Problem der Einfühlung* (Halle, 1917), p. 45.

20. Stein, *Zum Problem der Einfühlung*, p. 45. See the entire section "Die Gegebenheit des Leibes," pp. 44–53. See also Edmund Husserl, *Gesammelte Werke (Husserliana)* (The Hague, 1950–), 4:159. Gesa Lindemann uses the differentiations suggested by Plessner and Schmitz to "demarcate the body that we are in its specific spatiality from the body that we have." Gesa Lindemann, "Zeichentheoretische Überlegungen zum Verhältnis von Körper und Leib," in Annette Barkhaus et al., eds., *Identität, Leiblichkeit, Normativität: Neue Horizonte anthropologischen Denkens* (Frankfurt/Main, 1996), p. 152. See Helmuth Plessner, *Die Stufen des Organischen und der Mensch* (Berlin, 1975); and Hermann Schmitz, *System der Philosophie*, vol. 11/1 (Bonn, 1965).

21. *Leibwahrgenommener Leib* in the German original (Trans.), *Zum Problem der Einfühlung*, Stein, p. 47.

22. *Körper* and *Leib* both translate as *body* in English. In this and other philosophical texts, *Körper* means the body as perceived from the outside, while *Leib* means the body as perceived and experienced from the inside. The difference is often rendered in English this way: *Körper* = physical body, *Leib* = lived body (Trans.).

23. In the following I will not always adhere strictly to this linguistic differentiation, although it is objectively correct. For the sake of readability I will often simply use the term *body* and hope that the meaning is clear from the context.

24. Barbara Duden, *Geschichte unter der Haut* (Stuttgart, 1991). See also "Zur Exegese vergangener Körpererlebnisse: Ein Gespräch mit Barbara Duden," *Die Philosophin* 7 (1993): 63–68. Duden criticizes the effect that with the rejection of the experience of corporality in favor of outer perception, women were in a certain way expropriated of their bodies. See Barbara Duden, *Der Frauenleib als öffentlicher Ort* (Hamburg, 1991). For a critical position toward this point of view, see Regula Giuliani, "Körpergeschichten zwischen Modellbildung und haptischer Hexis—Thomas Laqueur and Barbara Duden," in Silvia Stoller and Helmuth Vetter, eds., *Phänomenologie und Geschlechterdifferenz* (Wien, 1997),

pp. 148–165. On the perception of the female body in medieval times, see Linda Lomperis and Sarah Stanbury, eds., *Feminist Approaches to the Body in Medieval Literature* (University Park, 1993).

25. Husserl, *Gesammelte Werke*, 4:212, 215, 240. See also Felix Hammer, *Leib und Geschlecht: Philosophische Perspektiven von Nietzsche bis Merleau-Ponty und Phänomenologischer Aufriß* (Bonn, 1974), pp. 104f.

26. Elisabeth List formulates the problem thus: "Pain is located in the body; nonetheless, to speak of physical pain is misleading. Pain is always perceived pain and therefore a subjective phenomenon." Elisabeth List, "Schmerz: Der somatische Signifikant im Sprechen des Körpers," in Jörg Huber and Alois Martin Müller, eds., *Die Wiederkehr des Anderen* (Basel, 1996), p. 232.

27. In his discussion on our creative competence in this regard, Edmund Husserl differentiates two kinds of sensuality, namely, the "ur-sensibility, which does not contain any traces of reason, and the secondary sensibility, which has emerged from the production of reason" (Husserl, *Gesammelte Werke*, 4:334f.). But it remains to be investigated to what extent this distinction is valid today. The phenomena that Husserl cites, such as sensible emotions and drives, are from the viewpoint of contemporary historical anthropology not at all primary, unaltered experiences (as will be further elaborated for the concept of sexual drive).

28. Hilge Landweer, "Fühlen Männer anders? Überlegungen zur Konstruktion von Geschlecht durch Gefühle," in Stoller and Vetter, *Phänomenologie und Geschlechterdifferenz*, pp. 249–273. As Landweer shows, observable differences between men and women in the emotional realm are not caused by sex difference in the physiological sense, "but by the complex interaction of gender norms and gender-codified rules for the expression of emotions" (p. 271).

29. Maurice Merleau-Ponty, *Phänomenologie der Wahrnehmung* (Berlin, 1966), p. 189.

30. Merleau-Ponty, *Phänomenologie der Wahrnehmung*, p. 189.

31. For an overview of the critiques voiced from a feminist perspective as well as the references to Merleau-Ponty, see Sonia Kruks, "Existentialism and Phenomenology," in Alison M. Jaggar and Iris M. Young, eds., *A Companion to Feminist Philosophy* (Oxford, 1998), pp. 68–70; and Silvia Stoller, "Merleau-Ponty im Kontext der feministischen Theorie," in Regula Giuliani, ed., *Merleau-Ponty und die Humanwissenschaften* (Freiburg, 1999).

32. Judith Butler, *Gender Trouble: Feminism and the Subversion of Identity* (New York, 1990), p. 64.

33. See the entire chapter "Prohibition, Psychoanalysis, and the Production of the Heterosexual Matrix," in Butler, *Gender Trouble*, pp. 35–78.

34. In this context, Alison Assiter suggests a new reading of Plato's Symposium. In her interpretation, it becomes evident that sexual desire cannot easily be ascribed to rational planning in the service of social power claims. "The Platonic reading of sexual desire brings to light some limitations of one type of 'constructivism' about sexuality. Even if sexuality can be willed, sexual desire cannot. Sexual desires cannot be willed or chosen because, by their very nature, they lie partly outside the domain of will and conscious control. . . . Desire can neither be a product of conscious will nor of social and historical forces." Alison Assiter, *Enlightened Women: Modernist Feminism in a Postmodern Age* (London, 1996), pp. 138f.

35. Carol Bigwood suggests that exactly on this point the thought of Merleau-Ponty can be useful for feminist theory. Under the title "Is Any Body Home?" she criticizes Butler's tendency to deny our corporality all autonomous sexual impulses while Merleau-Ponty believes it important to take our body seriously, not only in regard to its cultural significance but also in its own weight. The way in which Bigwood tries from there to think together the natural and the cultural body leaves open many questions, however. Carol Bigwood, "Renaturalizing the Body (with a Little Help from Merleau-Ponty)," *Hypatia*, Special Issue, Feminism and the Body, Fall 1991, pp. 54–73.

36. Jean Grimshaw states, too, that this is a contradiction. To assume, she explains, that there is something like perverted behavior, one must have already dismissed the idea that nature would be "something which dictates or determines everything that humans do." Jean Grimshaw, *Feminist Philosophers: Women's Perspectives on Philosophical Traditions* (Brighton, 1986), p. 105.

37. See Andrea Maihofer, *Geschlecht als Existenzweise* (Frankfurt/Main, 1995), esp. pt. 1, pp. 19–108.

38. Luce Irigaray has drawn attention to this procedure with special emphasis. See Luce Irigaray, "This Sex Which Is Not One," in Elaine Marks and Isabelle de Courtivron, eds., *New French Feminisms: An Anthology* (New York, 1981), pp. 99–106. (A more detailed analysis can be found in Chapter 3 of this book.)

39. As will be explained in Chapter 4 of this book in greater detail, it is not enough for an extensive definition to see an immoral treatment of people only in the violation of integrity; rather, the refusal of possible help and support also presents a moral problem.

40. Catharine A. MacKinnon, "Geschlechtergleichheit: Über Differenz und Herrschaft," in Herta Nagl-Docekal and Herlinde Pauer-Studer, eds., *Politische Theorie: Differenz und Lebensqualität* (Frankfurt/Main, 1996), pp. 140–173.

41. See Catharine A. MacKinnon, *Only Words* (Cambridge, Mass., 1993).

42. Andrea Maihofer seems to go even further with this connection when she suggests that the logical structure of the complete disjunction itself should be understood as historically contingent, and should be referred to as the "hegemonic" attitude of "modern Western thought." See Maihofer, *Geschlecht als Existenzweise*, p. 74.

43. As will be shown at the end of the chapter, this disjunction has not become obsolete because there have been or are very different theories on the moment of death. Martha Nussbaum has explained that we cannot do without binary oppositions in certain contexts: "I believe that death in the most binary of all thinkable ways is opposite to life as well as freedom to slavery, hunger to appropriate nutrition and ignorance to knowledge." Martha Nussbaum, "Menschliches Tun und soziale Gerechtigkeit: Zur Verteidigung des Aristotelischen Essentialismus," in Micha Brumlik and Hauke Brunkhorst, eds., *Gemeinschaft und Gerechtigkeit* (Frankfurt/Main, 1993), p. 326.

44. Starting from this thematic core, Alison M. Jaggar and Susan R. Bordo explain six points in which the basic traits of Cartesianism are seen in current criticism. They further make it clear that in the English-speaking world this criticism is acquiring explosive force with regard to the analytical mainstream. Not only feminist-motivated objections but also those of Richard Rorty are oriented toward a

thesis according to which "Catesianism . . . reached its culmination in the positivism and neo-positivism of Anglo-American analytic philosophy." Alison M. Jaggar and Susan Bordo, introduction to *Gender/Body/Knowledge: Feminist Reconstructions of Being and Knowing* (New Brunswick, N.J., 1989), p. 3.

45. See the explanations on both variants of "constitution theory," pp. 27–39.

46. For a lucid and understandable description of this point, see Manfred Frank, "Über Subjektivität: Rede an die Gebildeten unter ihren Reduktionisten," in Jörg Huber and Alois Martin Müller, eds., *Die Wiederkehr des Anderen* (Basel, 1996), pp. 83–102.

47. Moira Gatens discusses this problem in regard to historical materialism. Further investigation would be required to determine whether her outline of an ethological monism drawing on a Deleuzian reading of Spinoza offers a plausible alternative. Moira Gatens, "Ethologische Körper: Geschlecht als Macht und Affekt," in Marie-Luise Angerer, ed., *The Body of Gender: Körper, Geschlecht, Identitäten* (Wien, 1995).

48. Eve Browning Cole, *Philosophy and Feminist Criticism: An Introduction* (New York, 1992), pp. 68f. If in the last phrase of the quoted passage Browning Cole also sees the moral basis for living together anchored in the body, she comes close to attempts that try to derive morality "phylogenetically." The problems arising from this have already been shown.

49. This has already been demonstrated by Descartes's critics. See, for instance, Gottfried Wilhelm Leibniz, *Monadologie* (Jena, 1720); Immanuel Kant, *Kritik der Urteilskraft* (Berlin, 1790).

50. Moira Gatens explains when and in what theoretical context the terms "sex" and "gender" actually became a point of discussion within feminist research. First she tries to locate who originally developed the terminology. Her inquiries led to the conclusion that feminist authors obtained the terms from a psychoanalytical study: Robert J. Stoller, *Sex and Gender* (London, 1968). Cf. Moira Gatens, *Imaginary Bodies: Ethics, Power, and Corporality* (London, 1996), pp. 3ff. For early evidence of the feminist reception of this dyad, see Ann Oakley, *Sex, Gender, and Society* (London, 1992).

51. The term *gender* in English originally referred only to grammatical gender. In German translations, however, the equivalent term *genus* did not gain acceptance. Instead complementary adjectives were favored, of which none has found unreserved recognition. *Sex,* for example, is often translated with *biological gender,* whereas *gender* turns into terms like *social gender, symbolic gender,* or *gender identity,* the use of which always depends on the corresponding focus.

52. Among those who favor the argument that on close examination the differentiation of *sex* and *gender* only represents a "transferred biologism" are Regine Gildemeister and Angelika Wetterer, "Wie Geschlechter gemacht werden," in Gudrun-Axeli Knapp and Angelika Wetterer, eds., *Traditionen: Brueche* (Freiburg, 1992), p. 206.

53. In this sense Joan Wallach Scott wrote: "In its most recent usage, 'gender' seems to have first appeared among American feminists who wanted to insist on the fundamental social quality of distinctions based on sex. The word denoted a rejection of the biological determinism implicit in the usage of such terms as 'sex' or 'sexual difference.'" See Scott, *Gender and the Politics of History* (New York, 1988).

54. A notable background for the outline of the program came from Marxist theory of science, for which *class* represents a central concept in research. In dependence on this model (but also as a response to the reproach that from the perspective of class differences other conflict constellations are reduced to a minor role), *gender* and later *race* were given priority as categories of analysis. See Scott, *Gender and the Politics of History*, pp. 28–52, "Gender: A Useful Category of Historical Analysis." The phrase *category of analysis* is meant to indicate a certain kind of questioning: All academic disciplines should be challenged with the question of to what degree *gender* (explicit or implicit) is relevant to their research.

55. That the term *gender* today is employed in two ways, as critical device and normative restriction, can also be found in Linda Nicholson, "Was heißt 'gender'?" in Institut für Sozialforschung, ed., *Geschlechterverhaeltnisse und Politik* (Frankfurt/Main, 1994), pp. 188f.

56. At this point Nicholson's ideas lose their critical sharpness. According to Nicholson, historical and cultural diversity could only become consistently valid if at the same time the perspective of a "historically less variable body compared to the majority of other personality and behavior features" (p. 202) is abandoned. This argumentation presumes that the assumption of consistent biological conditions necessarily entails a naturalistic idea of gender. But this means that Nicholson now employs precisely the logic of a biological foundation of norms, which she actually rejects. The recurring feminist variation of the naturalistic fallacy poses a problem to which I will return later on.

57. Significant for this change of language is the founding of the magazine *Genders* in 1988.

58. During a seminar discussion, Derrida explained that abandoning binary ideas of "sexual opposition" smooths the way for "a very different sexuality, a multiple one. At that point there would be no more sexes . . . there would be one sex for each time. . . . We are in the order of the incalculable, of undecidability. . . . This is sexual difference. It is absolutely heterogeneous." See the documentary report "Women in the Beehive: A Seminar with Jacques Derrida," in Alice Jardine and Paul Smith, eds., *Men in Feminism* (New York, 1987), p. 199.

59. "Women in the Beehive," p. 198.

60. Sally Haslauger puts it this way: "(many) feminists aim for a day when no one will fall within the category of women." Haslauger, "On Being Objective and Being Objectified," in Louise M. Antony and Charlotte Witt, eds., *A Mind of One's Own: Feminist Essays on Reason and Objectivity* (Boulder, 1993), p. 101. A comment on this thought can be found in Steven Burns, "Reason and Objectification," *Ethik und Sozialwissenschaften* 3, no. 4 (1992): 542–544. For a critical view, see Herta Nagl-Docekal, "Anknuepfungen und Einsprueche: Ein Versuch, auf sehr unterschiedliche Kommentare zur Feministischen Philosophie zu antworten," *Ethik und Sozialwissenschaften* 3, no. 4 (1992): 590f.

61. Thomas Laqueur, *Making Sex: Body and Gender from the Greeks to Freud* (Cambridge, Mass., 1990).

62. Laqueur, *Making Sex,* p. 18.

63. For a great deal of evidence concerning the scientific revolution in views of sexual difference from the history of science since 1750, see also Londa Schiebinger, *The Mind Has No Sex? Women in the Origin of Modern Science*

(Cambridge, Mass., 1989), esp. chap. 7, "More Than Skin Deep: The Scientific Search for Sexual Difference," pp. 189–213.

64. Schiebinger, *Mind Has No Sex?* p. 173. The effect this correlation had on scientific research will be discussed more deeply in Chapter 3 of this book.

65. In this sense Andrea Maihofer, for example, emphasizes, "The different body parts are not at all ahistorically the same with only historically different meanings." *Geschlecht als Existenzweise*, p. 72.

66. For a lucid summation of Foucault's elaborations on this matter as well as their influence on the feminist debate, see Lois McNay, "The Foucauldian Body and the Exclusion of Experience," *Hypatia: A Journal of Feminist Philosophy*, Special Issue, Feminism and the Body, Fall 1991, pp. 125–139.

67. Maihofer, *Geschlecht als Existenzweise*, p. 73.

68. Sometimes the term *effect* in Butler is used in the sense of *fictional* or *imaginary*. This is true especially for her book *Gender Trouble*. On closer examination, however, it resembles the same idea. *Effects* should be thought of as they are produced in the theater, where, for example, the impression of water is created on stage by means of ingenious lighting. Applied to *sex*, this means again that corporality is not given but discursively created.

69. Judith Butler, *Bodies That Matter* (New York, 1993), p. 9.

70. Butler refers especially to Michel Foucault, "Nietzsche, die Genealogie, die Historie," in Foucault, *Von der Subversion des Wissens* (Frankfurt/Main, 1987), pp. 69–90; as well as Foucault, *Sexualität und Wahrheit*, 3 vols. (Frankfurt/Main, 1983–1986).

71. Butler, *Bodies That Matter*, p. 251.

72. Butler, *Bodies That Matter*, p. 10.

73. As Reinhard Kleinknecht—in a more general analysis and without special reference to gender theory—has shown, it is characteristic for the contemporary debate "that in dealing with the problem of perception quite often the epistemological and ontological aspects get confused." "Der Schleier der Maja: Die Wahrnehmungswelt als Erscheinung der objektiven Welt," in Winfried Loeffler and Edmund Runggaldier, eds., *Vielfalt und Konvergenz der Philosophie: Vortraege des V. Kongresses der Oesterreichischen Gesellschaft für Philosophie* (Wien, 1999), pp. 133–139.

74. That Butler makes the epistemological insight of the insuperability of language "ontologically absolute" is also pointed out by Andrea Maihofer: "The semiological perspective turns into a semiological idealism. Or, in analogy to the history of philosophy, Kant's transcendental idealism turns into Fichte's ontological one." *Geschlecht als Existenzweise*, p. 48.

75. Maihofer, *Geschlecht als Existenzweise*, p. 32.

76. Donna Haraway, *Simians, Cyborgs, and Women: The Reinvention of Nature* (London, 1991), p. 208. De Beauvoir did not intend to doubt the existence of sex, as I will show later on.

77. Michelle Renée Matisons elaborates that Haraway does not offer any answers to questions like these but rather escapes into neologisms. Terms like *cyborg* or *natural social* only pretend to offer a solution, while omitting a discussion of the problem based on reasoned argument. "The New Feminist Philosophy of the Body: Haraway, Butler, and Brennan," *European Journal of Women's Studies*

5, no. 1 (1998): 16. Matisons illustrates this deficit in special reference to Donna Haraway, *Modest Witness at Second Millennium: FemaleMan Meets Onco-Mouse* (New York, 1997).

78. Meanwhile it has been emphasized a number of times that Foucault could be interpreted quite differently. The presented constructivist interpretation does not consider that Foucault did not aim at reducing the body to discursive formations, but to place the body in its corporality within the field of view of the criticism of power. See Alison Assiter, *Enlightened Women: Modernist Feminism in a Postmodern Age* (London, 1996), esp. chap. 8, "A Critique of Constructivist Accounts of Sexuality," pp. 129–141.

79. This objection is raised by (among others) Alison Assiter: "Human bodies, for some, are in danger of slipping altogether out of the picture . . . sexuality becomes a matter of free will, of free choice . . . there are only free floating wills, taking on sexual identities and sexual desires as they wish" (p. 135). Assiter especially refers to Sheila Jeffreys, *Anticlimax* (London, 1989). Susan Wendell also argues against the suggestions of Haraway and Butler of a discursively available corporality. By referring to our suffering of pain, she not only objects theoretically to this idea but exposes it also as an expression of callousness. Wendell, *The Rejected Body: Feminist Philosophical Reflections on Disability* (New York, 1996), p. 169. Further differentiation in this direction can be found in Elisabeth List, "Schmerz—Selbsterfahrung und Grenzerfahrung," in Maria Wolf et al., eds., *Körper/Schmerz: Intertheoretische Zugänge* (Innsbruck, 1998), pp. 143–160.

80. Especially revealing are passages in which Butler refers to Simone de Beauvoir. In this context sexuality becomes merely a style of corporeal performance, "a way of wearing one's flesh as a cultural sign." Judith Butler, "Gendering the Body: Beauvoir's Philosophical Contribution," in Ann Garry and Marilyn Pearsall, eds., *Women, Knowledge, and Reality: Explorations in Feminist Theory* (Boston, 1989), p. 256. In some places Butler even presupposes physiological differences. "Surely differences do exist which are binary, material and distinct, and we are not in the grip of political ideology when we assent to this fact." See Butler, "Variations on Sex and Gender: Beauvoir, Wittig, and Foucault," in Seyla Benhabib and Drucilla Cornell, eds., *Feminism as Critique: Essays on the Politics of Gender in Late Capitalist Societies* (Cambridge, Mass., 1987), p. 135.

81. As Isabell Lorey demonstrated, the problem also becomes apparent in Butler's ambiguous use of *sex*. "'Sex' on the one hand always already signifies the socially situated body"; on the other, "however, it signifies the sexually differentiated anatomy." In the latter case, "the 'binary' anatomical marks . . . are a fact." Isabell Lorey, "Der Körper als Text und das aktuelle Selbst: Butler und Foucault," *Feministische Studien* 2 (1993): 12, "Kritik der Kategorie Geschlecht." Lorey refers especially to Butler, "Variations on Sex and Gender," pp. 128–142.

82. Some interpreters believe that the different views Butler presents cannot be regarded simply as inconsistencies. Rather, they articulate a process of learning, particularly since Butler in *Bodies That Matter* also considered criticism of her earlier work. I do not elaborate on this thesis since I am primarily interested in examining certain types of arguments, not in judging the whole oeuvre of individual authors.

83. Elizabeth Grosz, "Nietzsche and the Stomach for Knowledge," in Paul Patton, ed., *Nietzsche, Feminism, and Political Theory* (London, 1993), p. 50.
84. See the quotation in note 80 from Butler, "Gendering the Body," p. 256.
85. Enlightening in regard to the whole debate is Donn Welton, ed., *Body and Flesh: A Philosophical Reader* (Malden, Mass., 1998).
86. A similar opinion is held by Andrea Maihofer (among others): "The single body parts are not at all ahistorically the same only with historically different meaning." Significantly, Maihofer is pleading subsequently to "understand the body with its sex characteristics *itself* as socially constructed or produced" (*Geschlecht als Existenzweise*, p. 729).
87. See Jutta Weber, "Sprechen wovon sich nicht sprechen lässt? Zum Naturbegriff in der aktuellen feministischen Debatte," *Feministische Studien* 2 (1997): 109–120.
88. Andrea Maihofer, for example, supports the thesis that the "assumption of an ahistorical, naturally sexed body" inevitably leads to gender classification "based upon it" (*Geschlecht als Existenzweise*, p. 22). To operate with the "sex/gender"-dyad necessarily means, according to Maihofer, that "the sexual biology and morphology is seen as *cause* for particular forms of consciousness, social roles, identities, and conditions" (p. 69; italics added). To clarify again the problem that I perceive here: such an inevitability was and still is assumed within patriarchal thinking. Feminist theory can only consistently maintain its point if it does not adopt the naturalistic fallacy but questions it instead. Natural facts (not only our sexed bodies but also the geological and climatic conditions of our environment, etc.) are—like our historical precondition—*subject* to our actions. Without such subjects, actions are not possible at all; that does not mean, however, that these are their *cause*—any more than marble is the cause of a sculpture. Therefore I do not perceive the differentiation of *nature/culture*, as Maihofer does, as "a constitutive moment of a ruling patriarchal gender discourse" (p. 90) but as the indispensable starting point for an argumentative rejection of the latter.
89. Donna Haraway evidently is also led by the logic of the naturalistic fallacy, as she supposes that social norms, which oblige women to be sexually passive, can only be defeated on the basis of a new term for *sex*. Such an alternative term, she imagines, could remove by definition the biological sex of woman. "Claims of biological determinism can never be the same again," she writes, "when female 'sex' has been so thoroughly re-theorized and revisualized that it emerges as practically indistinguishable from 'mind.'" *Simians, Cyborgs, and Women*, p. 199.
90. See C. G. Hempel, "Wissenschaftliche und historische Erklärungen," in Hans Albert, ed., *Theorie und Realität*, 2nd updated ed. (Tübingen, 1972), pp. 237–262.
91. See Karl Otto Apel, "Szientistik, Hermeneutik, Ideologiekritik," in *Wiener Jahrbuch für Philosophie* 1 (1968): 15–45.
92. The following remark by Linda Nicholson seems significant in this respect: "To the cultural context of research belongs a culturally defined knowledge of the meaning of the body and its relation to culture" ("Was heißt 'gender'?" p. 210). As is obvious here, one may speak of historical or cultural variability only

if at the same time the body as the subject of divergent interpretations is already presupposed.

93. Georg Wilhelm Friedrich Hegel, *Enzyklopaedie der philosophischen Wissenschaften*, §410, in *Works*, 10:236. Hegel mentions that the subject of *Verleiblichung* leads to a number of complex questions, which makes the development of a specific discipline—a psychological physiology—desirable (§401).

94. See Ch. Grawe, "Kultur, Kulturphilosophie," in *Historisches Wörterbuch der Philosophie*, vol. 4 (Darmstadt, 1976), col. 1309.

95. Helmuth Plessner, "Lachen und Weinen," in *Gesammelte Schriften,* vol 7, *Ausdruck und menschliche Natur* (Frankfurt/Main, 1982), pp. 234f.

96. Merleau-Ponty, *Phänomenologie der Wahrnehmung*, p. 196.

97. Also illuminating in this regard are Plessner's observations about how we experience an outburst of corporeal spontaneity while laughing or crying in the context of a particular situation. Cf. Helmuth Plessner, *Philosophische Anthropologie: Lachen und Weinen. Das Lächeln* (Frankfurt/Main, 1970).

98. Cf. Carol Hagemann-White, "Wir werden nicht zweigeschlechtlich geboren," in Carol Hagemann-White and Maria S. Rerrich, eds., *Frauen-Männer-Bilder* (Berlin, 1988), pp. 224–235. In this context Hagemann-White refers to Uli Wellner, "Zur Biologie der Geschlechterdifferenzierung," in Heide Kellner, ed., *Geschlechtsunterschiede* (Weinheim, 1979), pp. 93–126.

99. Carol Hagemann-White had this problem in mind when she wrote: "Two sexes are above all a social reality" ("Wir werden nicht zweigeschlechtlich geboren," p. 229). But as far as she pleads for giving up the idea of natural sex differences and instead using a "zero-hypothesis" (p. 230), she gets caught in the very problems exemplified above in regard to the second variation of the constitution thesis.

100. The problem of gender attribution is examined by Stefan Hirschauer, *Die soziale Konstruktion der Transsexualität* (Frankfurt/Main, 1993). Cf. Marjorie Garber, *Verhüllte Interessen: Transvestitismus und kulturelle Angst* (Frankfurt/Main, 1993).

101. Iris Marion Young shows that girls in Western culture are taught from the very beginning to match the image of the passive, secluded, and weak woman in "Throwing Like a Girl: A Phenomenology of Body Comportment," in *Throwing Like a Girl and Other Essays in Feminist Philosophy and Social Theory* (Bloomington, 1990), pp. 141–159. Similarly, one should also consider the immense anguish male children suffer when they do not equal the image of the strong man.

102. The subject of incorporated images of femininity is taken up in the already quoted studies by Frigga Haug and Iris Marion Young. In regard to incorporated ideal images of masculinity, see Sabina Braendli, "'Die unbeschreibliche Beherrschung und Ruhe in Haltung und Geberden'. Koerperbilder des buergerlichen Mannes im 19. Jahrhundert," *Oesterreichische Zeitschrift für Geschichtswissenschaften* 8, no. 2 (1997): 274–281.

103. Hubert Ch. Ehalt, "Über den Wandel des Termins der Geschlechtsreife in Europa und dessen Ursachen," in *Zwischen Natur und Kultur: Zur Kritik biologistischer Ansaetze* (Wien, 1985), pp. 93–168.

104. My intention agrees in large part with that of Barbara Holland-Cunz, who favors "recommencing the categories 'sex/gender'" on the grounds that "the

logic of material corporality" precedes all constructions. *Soziales Subjekt Natur: Natur- und Geschlechterverhaeltnis in emazipatorischen politischen Theorien* (Frankfurt/Main, 1994), p. 206.

105. Alison M. Jaggar, for example, writes: "Where human nature is concerned, there is no line between nature and culture" (*Feminist Politics and Human Nature* [Totowa, N.J., 1983], p. 111). It is certainly true that our social life influences our biological constitution, this "complex interplay" (p. 110) can only be addressed on the basis of a precise differentiation.

106. Elizabeth Grosz supports the thesis of a conversion of nature into culture and vice versa, referring to the model by Moebius: "The Moebius strip has the advantage of showing the inflection of mind into body and of body into mind, the ways in which, through a kind of twisting or inversion, one side becomes another" (*Volatile Bodies*, p. xii; cf. p. 210). How this inversion should be imagined she does not explain. The image of the loop does not suffice for the reason that philosophical problems cannot simply be answered by metaphors.

107. Simone de Beauvoir, *The Second Sex*, trans. E. M. Parshley (New York, 1973), p. 301.

Chapter 2

1. See Christina von Braun, *Nichtich: Logik, Lüge, Libido*, 3rd ed. (Frankfurt/Main, 1990), p. 181.

2. See especially Sigmund Freud, *New Introductory Lectures on Psychoanalysis*, trans. James Strachey (New York, 1965), "Lecture XXX. Femininity."

3. Some examples can be found in von Braun, *Nichtich*, pp. 177–181.

4. See Linda Nochlin, "Why Have There Been No Great Women Artists?" in Thomas B. Hess and Elizabeth C. Baker, eds., *Art and Sexual Politics* (New York, 1973), pp. 1–39.

5. An overview of these developments can be found in Linda Krumholz and Estella Lauter, "Annotated Bibliography on Feminist Aesthetics in the Visual Arts," *Hypatia* 5, no. 2 (1990): 158–172.

6. See Cornelia Klinger, "Von der Kritik an der 'ästhetischen Ideologie' über 'cunt art' und 'écriture féminine' zum Diskussionsstand einer feministischen Ästhetik heute," *Deutsche Zeitschrift für Philosophie* 46, no. 5 (1998): 809.

7. See Estella Lauter, "Re-enfranchising Art: Feminist Interventions in the Theory of Art," *Hypatia* 5, no. 2 (1990): 22f.

8. Inadequate encouragement given to the talents of girls or women is the central topic of a lecture that Simone de Beauvoir delivered in 1966 in Japan: "La femme et la création," in C. Francis and F. Gonhier, eds., *Les Ecrits de Simone de Beauvoir: La Vie—L'Ecriture* (Paris, 1979): 458ff.; English: "Women and Creativity," in Toril Moi, ed., *French Feminist Thought: A Reader* (Oxford, 1987), pp. 17–32. Simone de Beauvoir refers here to a mental experiment proposed by Virginia Woolf: If instead of William Shakespeare a girl had been born into the same family and with the same talent, she would not have produced artistic achievements because cooking and sewing would have been taught to her and she would have been married off early. See Virginia Woolf, *A Room of One's Own* (London, 1929).

9. For example, Heidemarie Seblatnig, *Einfach den Gefahren ins Auge sehen: Künstlerinnen im Gespräch* (Wien, 1988).

10. A more detailed presentation of this case can be found in Elsa Honig Fine, *Women and Art* (Montclair, N.J., 1978); Griselda Pollock, "Women, Art, and Ideology: Questions for Art Historians," *Women's Studies Quarterly* 15, no. 1–2 (1987): 2–9.

11. On the undervaluation of the quilt by U.S. art criticism, see Patricia Mainardi, "Quilts: The Great American Art," in Norma Broude and Mary D. Garrard, eds., *Feminism and Art History: Questioning the Litany* (New York, 1982), pp. 331–346.

12. Alessandra Comini shows this problem through the examples of Käthe Kollwitz, Paula Modersohn-Becker, and Gabriele Münter: "Gender or Genius? The Woman Artists of German Expressionism," in Broude and Garrard, *Feminism and Art History*, pp. 271–292.

13. Estella Lauter, "Re-enfranchising Art," p. 23.

14. Estella Lauter, "Re-enfranchising Art," p. 23.

15. This broad conceptual determination seems to guide the collecting activity for the chapter "Kunst-, Literatur- und Sprachtheorie," in Marion Heinz and Sabine Doyé, eds., *Feministische Philosophie: Bibliographie, 1970–1995* (Bielefeld, 1996), pp. 351–384. I refer to the extensive information supplied in this context.

16. See Herta Nagl-Docekal, "Für eine geschlechtergeschichtliche Perspektivierung der Historiographiegeschichte," in Wolfgang Küttler, Jörn Rüsen, and Ernst Schulin, eds., *Geschichtsdikurs*, vol. 1, *Grundlagen und Methoden der Historiographiegeschichte* (Frankfurt/Main, 1993), pp. 233–256.

17. Walter Benjamin, "Über den Begriff der Geschichte," in *Illuminationen: Ausgewählte Schriften* (Frankfurt/Main, 1977), p. 253.

18. See Ines Lindner et al., eds., *Blick-Wechsel: Konstruktionen von Männlichkeit und Weiblichkeit in Kunst und Kunstgeschichte* (Berlin, 1989); Elisabeth Bronfen, *Nur über ihre Leiche: Tod, Weiblichkeit und Ästhetik* (Munich, 1992); Irene Nierhaus, *ARCH 6: Raum, Geschlecht, Architektur* (Sonderzahl, 1999); Ursula Simek, "'Es ist die schönste Familie, die man denken kann': Die Familie als musikalische Akademie," in Hana Havelková, ed., *Gibt es ein mitteleuropäisches Ehe- und Familienmodell?* (Prague, 1995), pp. 87–96.

19. It is also necessary to think about how traditional forms of masculinity are expressed in art. Ilsebill Barta notes, "A critical and not affirmative or identificatory confrontation with the image of men in art and with the self-presentation of men in art has only been enabled by feminist scholarship." Foreword to *Frauen, Bilder, Männer, Mythen: Kunsthistorische Beiträge* (Berlin, 1987), p. 9.

20. For the political aspect of all cultural production, see Joan Wallach Scott, *Gender and the Politics of History* (New York, 1988); especially the introduction, pp. 1–11.

21. See Silvia Bovenschen, *Die imaginierte Weiblichkeit: Exemplarische Untersuchungen zu kulturgeschichtlichen und literarischen Präsentationsformen des Weiblichen* (Frankfurt/Main, 1979).

22. This conception corresponds with the effort to destroy the "woman myth." Angelika Maiworm, *Räume, Zeiten, viele Namen: Ästhetik als Kritik der Weiblichkeit* (Weingarten, 1984).

23. Peter Gorsen explains "aesthetical androgynism," referring to Meret Oppenheim, in G. Nabakowski, H. Sander, and P. Gorsen, eds., *Frauen in der Kunst* (Frankfurt/Main, 1980), 2:156f.
24. See the interviews with Viennese women artists in Seblatnig, *Einfach den Gefahren ins Auge sehen.*
25. For an informative overview of the feminist debate over psychoanalysis—including the developments after Freud—see Teresa Brennan, "Psychoanalytic Feminism," in Alison M. Jaggar and Iris Young, eds., *A Companion to Feminist Philosophy* (Oxford, 1998), pp. 27–279.
26. Juliett Mitchell, *Psychoanalysis and Feminism: Freud, Reich, Laing, and Women* (New York, 1975), p. 301. The quoted formulation can be found in the context of a critical discussion of Simone de Beauvoir's objections to Freud.
27. Sigmund Freud, "First Lecture: Introduction," in *A General Introduction to Psycho-Analysis* (New York, 1935), pp. 17–24.
28. Freud, "First Lecture," p. 46.
29. Freud, "First Lecture," p. 47.
30. Freud, "First Lecture," p. 48.
31. Freud, "First Lecture," p. 48.
32. Freud, *New Introductory Lectures on Psychoanalysis*, p. 134 (to quote only one passage).
33. Freud, *New Introductory Lectures on Psychoanalysis*, p. 134.
34. Freud, *New Introductory Lectures on Psychoanalysis*, p. 132.
35. Freud, *New Introductory Lectures on Psychoanalysis*, p. 132.
36. Freud, *New Introductory Lectures on Psychoanalysis*, p. 132. Freud here insinuates that his imagined audience will refuse its consent, so that he can proceed: "If you reject this idea as fantastic and regard my belief in the influence of lack of a penis on the configuration of femininity as an *idée fixe*, I am of course defenceless." (Defenselessness is rather true for the audience, since the anticipated objection has not moved Freud to cut this passage from his manuscript.)
37. Freud, *New Introductory Lectures on Psychoanalysis*, p. 133.
38. Freud, *New Introductory Lectures on Psychoanalysis*, p. 117.
39. Freud, *New Introductory Lectures on Psychoanalysis*, p. 118.
40. Freud, *New Introductory Lectures on Psychoanalysis*, p. 113.
41. Freud, *New Introductory Lectures on Psychoanalysis*, p. 118.
42. Freud, *New Introductory Lectures on Psychoanalysis*, p. 118. Luce Irigaray explains that this thesis lays the foundations for the entire problem of Freud's views on women in *The Speculum of the Other Woman* (Ithaca, 1985).
43. Freud, *New Introductory Lectures on Psychoanalysis*, p. 118.
44. Freud, *New Introductory Lectures on Psychoanalysis*, p. 126.
45. Freud, *New Introductory Lectures on Psychoanalysis*, p. 126.
46. Freud, *New Introductory Lectures on Psychoanalysis*, p. 131.
47. Freud, *New Introductory Lectures on Psychoanalysis*, p. 130.
48. Freud, *New Introductory Lectures on Psychoanalysis*, p. 129.
49. Freud, *New Introductory Lectures on Psychoanalysis*, p. 129.
50. Freud, *New Introductory Lectures on Psychoanalysis*, p. 126.
51. Freud, *New Introductory Lectures on Psychoanalysis*, pp. 559f.
52. Freud, *New Introductory Lectures on Psychoanalysis*, p. 125.

53. Freud, *New Introductory Lectures on Psychoanalysis*, p. 125.

54. Freud, *New Introductory Lectures on Psychoanalysis*, p. 126.

55. Freud, *New Introductory Lectures on Psychoanalysis*, p. 127.

56. Freud notes "that girls hold their mothers responsible for their lack of a penis and do not forgive her for their being thus put at a disadvantage" (*New Introductory Lectures on Psychoanalysis*, p. 124).

57. When castration is not, as in mother and daughter, depicted as already fulfilled, but as with the boy is a threatened punishment, the threat comes from the father. See *New Introductory Lectures on Psychoanalysis*, p. 129.

58. *New Introductory Lectures on Psychoanalysis*, p. 124. Freud, despite his different theoretical claim, in the end finds the biological difference decisive for the sexual identity of men and women. Thus at the beginning of the new women's movement he stood at the center of the critical debate with psychoanalysis. See Germaine Greer, *The Female Eunuch* (London, 1970); Shulamith Firestone, *The Dialectic of Sex* (New York, 1970); Kate Millet, *Sexual Politics* (New York, 1970). Juliet Mitchell tries to relativize this objection in the context of a reading of Freud inspired by Lacan. But she, too, cannot avoid diagnosing at least residues of a biologistic thinking in Freud. See Mitchell, *Psychoanalysis and Feminism*.

59. See Sigmund Freud, *New Introductory Lectures on Psychoanalysis*, p. 129 or pp. 116f. Juliet Mitchell remarks: "Freud was inclined to make quips against feminism. One suspects that the intention was to make the militant women feel that they were vainly, and somewhat madly, tilting at windmills" (*Psychoanalysis and Feminism*, p. 303).

60. Within this theoretical frame the term of the marriage contract—which the woman signs—leads to an aporia, which is discussed in Chapter 4 of this book.

61. See Freud, *New Introductory Lectures on Psychoanalysis*, p. 54.

62. An analogous situation can be found in Freud's cultural theoretical considerations. As Ingvild Birkhan has shown, in "Totem and Taboo," the beginnings of religion, ethics, society, and art are shaped by the reprojection of the dominant position of the father. See "Fin-de-siècle Vienna: A Movement for or Against Womanhood? Some Thoughts on Weininger and Freud," in Herta Nagl-Docekal and Cornelia Klinger, eds., *Continental Philosophy in Feminist Perspective: Re-Reading the Canon in German* (University Park, Pa., 2000), pp. 255–280. See Sigmund Freud, "Totem and Tabu," in *Standard Edition of the Complete Psychological Works of Sigmund Freud*, ed. and trans. J. Strachey (New York, 1955), 13:ix–99. See also Renate Schlesier, *Mythos und Weiblichkeit bei Sigmund Freud* (Frankfurt/Main, 1990).

63. Freud, *New Introductory Lectures on Psychoanalysis*, p. 117.

64. Freud, *New Introductory Lectures on Psychoanalysis*, p. 118.

65. See Freud, *New Introductory Lectures on Psychoanalysis*, p. 130. Freud is not the first to use this comparison. As Astrid Deuber-Mankowski shows, it can be found in Baudelaire's elaborations on the female author. See Astrid Deuber-Mankowski, "Woman: The Most Precious Loot in the 'Triumph of Allegory': Gender Relations in Walter Benjamin's Passagenwerk," in Nagl-Docekal and Klinger, *Continental Philosophy in Feminist Perspective*, pp. 281–302.

66. Freud himself belonged to a history of reception, for instance, of the mockery by Nietzsche or long before him by Kant or Rousseau on the masculinization of intellectual women.
67. Freud, *New Introductory Lectures on Psychoanalysis,* p. 135.
68. Similar to the distinction suggested by Carol Gilligan (*In a Different Voice: Psychological Theory and Women's Development* [Cambridge, Mass., 1988]) of a masculine "justice perspective" and a feminine "care perspective," Freud, too, makes a differentiation in this regard. While he assumes that the woman has "little sense of justice" compared to the man, he assigns to her a specific competency, apparently only little developed in men: He speaks of the "invaluable social achievements" that the woman furnishes in the family on the basis of motherly ties (*New Introductory Lectures on Psychoanalysis,* p. 134).
69. Freud, *New Introductory Lectures on Psychoanalysis,* p. 116.
70. The way in which Freud proceeds in the quoted passage on the contrary supports the objection: "We, on the other hand, standing on the ground of bisexuality, had no difficulty in avoiding impoliteness. We had only to say: 'This doesn't apply to *you.* You're the exception; on this point you're more masculine than feminine" (*New Introductory Lectures on Psychoanalysis,* pp. 116–117).
71. See Elaine Marks and Isabelle de Courtivron, eds., *New French Feminisms: An Anthology* (New York, 1981); Toril Moi, ed., *French Feminist Thought: A Reader* (Oxford, 1988; for an explanation of terms, see esp. pp. 4–7); Nancy Fraser and Sandra Lee Bartky, eds., *Revaluing French Feminism: Critical Essays on Difference, Agency, and Culture* (Bloomington, 1992).
72. Some readers might raise the question whether the term *French feminism* is appropriate, since most authors subsumed under this term have distanced themselves from feminism. I believe that this only appears to be a contradiction since the term *feminism* has different meanings. As I discuss later, the rejection formulated by authors such as Cixous or Kristeva refers to a certain form of argumentation in the women's liberation movement—the egalitarian conceptions—but not to the entire spectrum of approaches that this concept (at least in the anglophone as well the German-speaking sphere) contains today. From the perspective of this broad meaning, which comprises all efforts to challenge the subordination of women, the term *French feminism* seems justified. (See also the explanation of the term in the introduction to this book.)
73. Next to the theories of Lacan and Derrida, Kojèves and Hippolyte's interpretations of Hegel, Lévi-Strauss's reading of Saussure, and Althusser's discussion of Marx belong to the intellectual background of these feminist theories. See Elaine Marks and Isabelle de Courtivron, "Why This Book?" in *New French Feminisms,* p. xii.
74. See Hélène Cixous, "The Laugh of the Medusa," in Marks and de Courtivron, *New French Feminisms,* p. 252. See also the editors' introduction, "Why This Book?" p. xii.
75. Toril Moi formulates this assessment in her book *Sexual/Textual Politics: Feminist Literary Theory* (London, 1985), p. 121.
76. Moi, *Sexual/Textual Politics,* pp. 118f.
77. Moi, *Sexual/Textual Politics,* p. 119.

78. See also Rosi Braidotti, *Patterns of Dissonance: A Study of Women in Contemporary Philosophy* (Cambridge, U.K., 1991), esp. chap. 5, "The Becoming-Woman of Philosophy, 1. Derrida," pp. 98–107.

79. Cixous, "Laugh of the Medusa," p. 255.

80. Cixous, "Laugh of the Medusa," p. 246.

81. Cixous, "Laugh of the Medusa," p. 246.

82. Cixous, "Laugh of the Medusa," p. 257.

83. Cixous, "Laugh of the Medusa," p. 263.

84. Cixous, "Laugh of the Medusa," p. 245.

85. Cixous, "Laugh of the Medusa," p. 249.

86. Cixous, "Laugh of the Medusa," pp. 247, 255.

87. Cixous, "Laugh of the Medusa," p. 251.

88. Cixous, "Laugh of the Medusa," pp. 263f.

89. The tendency toward such a conception of the mother–child dyad, based on so many exclusions, is quite common. It can also be seen in Donald Winnicot and other representatives of object-relation theory. See Axel Honneth, *Kampf um Anerkennung: Zur moralischen Grammatik sozialer Konflikte* (Frankfurt/Main, 1992), pp. 154–172.

90. If, as Honneth (*Kampf um Anerkennung*, p. 158) states, Winnicot points out how much the child "in the first months of his life . . . depends for the practical extension of its behavior upon the care of the *mother*," then the suspicion of biologism cannot be rejected. Since care for a baby is not restricted to breast-feeding but includes various tasks that are not tied to the abilities of the female body, it is a sign of bias if a theory does not make room, for instance, for a father who changes diapers at night and then hums his child back to sleep. See Donald W. Winnicott, "Die Theorie von der Beziehung zwischen Mutter und Kind," in *Reifungsprozesse und fördernde Umwelt* (Frankfurt/Main, 1984).

91. In this sense Charles Taylor notes: "The very form of a work of art shows its character as *addressed*." Taylor, "The Politics of Recognition," in Amy Gutmann, ed., *Multiculturalism and the "Politics of Recognition"* (Princeton, 1994), p. 34. Taylor refers here to Michail M. Bachtin, "The Problem of the Text in Linguistics, Philosophy, and the Human Sciences," in *Speech Genres and Other Late Essays*, ed. Caryl Emerson and Michael Holquist (Austin, 1986), p. 126.

92. Even if one considers the situation of the traditional nuclear family, it is not understandable why the beginning of language acquisition is thought to come from the direction of the father. As Bettina Schmitz contends, the breaking up of the original identification with the mother that happens in the mirror stage is once again mediated by the mother: "Another person, who holds the child, must through his or her supporting presence ensure that the unity of 'je' and 'moi' becomes imaginable. Lilli Gast points out that a weakness of Lacan's approach consists in his tendency to overlook this precondition. . . . The mirror stage can be introduced only through the interaction with another person, especially with the mother and her body." "Heimatlosigkeit oder symbolische Kastration? Subjektivität, Sprachgenese und Sozialität bei Julia Kristeva und Jacques Lacan," in Jan Beaufort and Peter Prechtl, eds., *Rationalität und Prärationalität* (Würzburg, 1998), p. 343.

93. This problem was pointed out, among others, by Kelly Oliver who—with a critical reference to Judith Butler—stressed that "women cannot merely jump outside of the symbolic." "Julia Kristeva's Feminist Revolutions," *Hypatia*, Summer 1993, p. 101.

94. As Braidotti shows, Cixous in this point precisely follows Derrida's evaluation, according to which feminism must be qualified as phallic and therefore rejected as an erroneous approach. See Braidotti, *Patterns of Dissonance*, p. 243.

95. Braidotti comments: "What has Cixous done except confirm the centuries-old association of the female with pathos and the male with logos, of women with literature and men with philosophy? And what would be so new and symbolically subversive about it?" Braidotti, *Patterns of Dissonance*, p. 242.

96. This problem is also taken up by Rita Felski: "By claiming that women's writing must be radically other than anything which has gone before, feminism sets itself the hopeless task of generating a new aesthetic by means of a negation of the entirety of existing cultural and literary traditions. As a result, an accusation often leveled at women's writing by feminist critics is that it is not different enough, that it fails to excise all traces of male influence from its language, structures or themes." *Beyond Feminist Aesthetics: Feminist Literature and Social Change* (Cambridge, 1989), p. 43.

97. Barbara Sichtermann, *Wer ist wie? Über den Unterschied der Geschlechter* (Berlin, 1987), p. 68.

98. For a thoroughly formulated objection to conceptions of feminine art, see Felski, *Beyond Feminist Aesthetics*. But the title could lead to misunderstandings; Felski does not use the term "feminist" in the broad sense common today, but defines it as follows: "By 'feminist aesthetics' I mean . . . any theoretical position which argues a necessary or privileged relationship between feminine gender and a particular kind of literary structure, style or form" (p. 19).

99. Eva Waniek, too, criticizes Cixous's reference in the end to a "binarily schematized basis" by which "an implicit mutually exclusive definition for feminine/against masculine is pregiven." *Hélène Cixous: Entlang einer Theorie der Schrift* (Vienna, 1993), p. 49.

100. Freud, *New Introductory Lectures on Psychoanalysis*, p. 134.

101. A similar critique is raised by Eva Waniek in her discussion of Cixous: "It seems appropriate to distance oneself from the conception of 'feminine writing,' since linguistic and narrative patterns here are interpreted only as the expression and result of a libido through which they are bound to the real sex and therefore biologistically reasoned in the end." "(K)ein weibliches Schreiben," *Die Philosophin* 5 (1992): 56f.

102. Sigrid Weigel notes an even greater threat: In her discussion of the term "feminine" in Walter Benjamin's depiction of artistic production, she reaches the conclusion that the idea according to which "the genius incorporates the feminine" is finally accompanied by the destruction of the feminine. Into the artistic creation thus understood "'the feminine' enters as substance; but it is exhausted, it 'dies' in it." "Die Verdoppelung des männlichen Blicks und der Ausschluß von Frauen aus der Literaturwissenschaft," in Karin Hausen and Helga Nowotny, eds., *Wie männlich ist die Wissenschaft?* (Frankfurt/Main,

1998), pp. 43–61. See Walter Benjamin, "Denkbilder," in *Werkausgabe* (Frankfurt/Main, 1980), 4:438.

103. See Hayden White, *Metahistory: The Historical Imagination in Nineteenth-Century Europe* (Baltimore, 1973), p. 34.

104. As Gertrude Postl explains, Kristeva's differentiation can be characterized as "a projection of the functions of primary and secondary processes as Freud developed them onto language." *Weibliches Sprechen: Feministische Entwürfe zu Sprache und Geschlecht* (Vienna, 1991), p. 154. See also Kristeva, *Revolution in Poetic Language*.

105. In psychoanalytical terminology she expresses it thus: "Matricide is essential, the condition sine qua non of our individuation." Julia Kristeva, *Soleil noir: Dépression et mélancolie* (Paris, 1987), p. 38.

106. More accurately, Kristeva believes that the symbolic order as Freud and Lacan describe it is characteristic for the Mosaic-monotheistic culture. See Dorothy Leland, "Lacanian Psychoanalysis and French Feminism: Toward an Adequate Political Psychology," in Fraser and Bartky, *Revaluing French Feminism*, p. 128.

107. Bettina Schmitz rightfully emphasizes that a critical discussion of Kristeva which does not acknowledge the degree to which her entire theory formation rests on language-theoretical conceptions would be shortsighted. *Arbeit an den Grenzen der Sprache: Julia Kristeva* (Königstein, 1998).

108. Allison Weir states, "Kristeva wants to argue that the symbolic order is not absolutely identical with the father's law." "Identification with the Divided Mother: Kristeva's Ambivalence," in Oliver Kelly, ed., *Ethics, Politics and Difference in Julia Kristeva's Writing* (New York, 1993), p. 89.

109. Allison Weir explains this aspect of Kristeva's thinking as follows: "The internalization of linguistic and social systems does not necessarily lock the subject into a conformity or identity with a phallogocentric regime; rather, internalization is a prerequisite for full participation as an individuated self in the social world . . . (Kristeva) argues that this internalization can facilitate rather than repress change, for it can foster the expression rather than only the repression of the 'nonidentity,' the heterogeneity, of subjects." *Sacrificial Logics: Feminist Theory and the Critique of Identity* (New York, 1996), p. 12. See also the chapter "Toward a Theory of Self and Social Identity: Julia Kristeva," pp. 145–183.

110. Inge Suchsland, *Julia Kristeva* (Frankfurt/Main, 1992), p. 106.

111. In accordance with this, Bettina Schmitz notes that "the idea that the symbolic, the instance of the symbolic, could be suspended, is repeatedly criticized by Kristeva" (*Arbeit an den Grenzen der Sprache*, p. 208).

112. Inge Suchsland therefore states a relation between Kristeva's understanding of poetic language, on the one hand, and the conception of ideology criticism in Benjamin and Adorno, on the other (Suchsland, *Kristeva*, pp. 105f.). Other authors criticize that Kristeva's considerations are hardly compatible with a theory of feminist-motivated social change. For example, Toril Moi states it is not "clear *why* it is so important to show that certain literary practices break up the structures of language when they seem to break up little else" (*Sexual/Textual Politics*, p. 171). This question cannot be pursued in detail in this chapter devoted to aesthetics.

113. Kristeva, *Revolution in Poetic Language*.

114. This term can be translated as *closed space* or *womb*.
115. See the section entitled "The paradox: Mother or primary narcissism," Julia Kristeva, "Stabat Mater," in Toril Moi, ed., *The Kristeva Reader* (New York, 1986), pp. 161–163. Kristeva explains the extent to which the "mother" is connected to infantile experience: "If . . . one looks at it more closely, this motherhood is the fantasy that is nurtured by the adult, man or woman, of a lost territory; what is more, it involves less an idealized archaic mother than the idealization of the relationship that binds us to her, one that cannot be localized—an idealization of primary narcissism" (p. 161).
116. "She raises doubts about the inherent masculinity of symbolic language," notes Diana T. Meyers, among others. Through this Kristeva opens up the possibility of imagining a completely different order: "There could be nonphallic power manifest in nonphallic symbolic language." Meyers, "The Subversion of Women's Agency in Psychoanalytic Feminism: Chodorow, Flax, Kristeva," in Fraser and Bartky, *Revaluing French Feminism*, pp. 145f. Meyers refers here especially to Julia Kristeva, *About Chinese Women* (London, 1977).
117. The concept of the semiotic refers therefore to nonspeech, which communicates that "which linguistic communication does not account for" (Kristeva, "Stabat Mater," p. 174). It points at the same time at "the weakness of language" (p. 175).
118. In this sense Bettina Schmitz notes: "The semiotic and the symbolic are the two modes of the language process." "Heimatlosigkeit oder symbolische Kastration? Subjektivität, Sprachgenese und Sozialität bei Julia Kristeva und Jacques Lacan," in Jan Beaufort and Alfred Schöpf, eds., *Rationalität und Prärationalität* (Würzburg, 1998), p. 337.
119. Painting, as well as poetry, fulfills this function according to Kristeva. See Julia Kristeva, "Maternité selon Giovanni Bellini," in *Polylogue* (Paris, 1977), pp. 173–224.
120. Schmitz, *Arbeit an den Grenzen der Sprache*, p. 193.
121. See the section "Wie weiblich ist das Semiotische?" in Postl, *Weibliches Sprechen*, pp. 163–177.
122. As she emphasizes, Christianity has identified men with motherhood from the beginning; for instance, "the most intense revelation of God, which occurs in mysticism, is given only to a person who assumes himself as 'motherly.'" Kristeva refers here to Augustinus, Bernhard of Clairvaux, and Meister Eckhart. Kristeva, "Stabat Mater," p. 162.
123. In this sense Diana T. Meyers observes in Kristeva a "resuscitation of the cultural stereotype of women as self-sacrificial mothers" ("Subversion of Women's Agency in Psychoanalytic Feminism," p. 149).
124. This is, as I believe, the core statement of the entire text "Stabat Mater."
125. "La femme, ce n'est jamais ça," Julia Kristeva, interview by Jacqueline Rose, in Kristeva, *Polylogue*, pp. 517–524.
126. "Kein weibliches Schreiben? Fragen an Julia Kristeva" [interview by R. Rossum-Guyon], *Freibeuter* 2 (1979): 79–84.
127. "It seems to me," she notes, "that nothing, neither in the earlier nor in the contemporary publications of women, allows one to state that a specific feminine writing exists" ("Kein weibliches Schreiben," p. 79).

128. In this sense Schmitz emphasizes that Kristeva calls "for the possibility for women to reach the symbolic as women." See Schmitz, *Arbeit an den Grenzen der Sprache*, p. 192.
129. As Domna C. Stanton explains, this problem can be encountered equally in Kristeva, Cixous, and Irigaray: "They reproduce the dichotomy between male rationality and feminine materiality, corporality and sexuality. . . . Ultimately, the maternal-feminine is the mysterious black continent, which Freud . . . debased as la contrée du con." "Difference on Trial: A Critique of the Maternal Metaphor in Cixous, Irigaray, and Kristeva," in Jeffner Allen and Iris Marion Young, eds., *The Thinking Muse: Feminism and Modern French Philosophy* (Bloomington, 1989), p. 167.
130. In a similarly focused critique, Nancy Fraser formulates the objection that Kristeva does not reject clearly intolerable positions, but rather proceeds "additively: She alternates essentialist gynocentric moments with anti-essentialist nominalist moments." Introduction to Nancy Fraser and Sandra Lee Bartky, eds., *Revaluing French Feminism* (Bloomington, 1992), p. 16.
131. Kristeva, "Stabat Mater," p. 184.
132. In the context of her religious-historical considerations, Kristeva relates the genesis of feminism to the fact that Protestantism does not embrace the veneration of the Virgin Mary as it developed in Catholicism and the churches of the East. "The blossoming of feminism in Protestant countries is due, among other things, to the greater initiative allowed women on the social and ritual plane. One might wonder, if, in addition, such a flowering is not the result of a lack in the Protestant religious structure with respect to the Maternal, which, on the contrary, was elaborated within Catholicism with a refinement to which the Jesuits gave the final touch" ("Stabat Mater," pp. 168–169).
133. Norma Broude and Mary D. Garrard, introduction to *The Power of Feminist Art: The American Movement of the 1970s—History and Impact* (New York, 1994), p. 28.
134. Klinger, "Von der Kritik an der 'ästhetischen Ideologie' über 'cunt art' und 'écriture féminine,'" 816.
135. For a detailed overview of the development and different elements of this criticism, see Klinger, "Von der Kritik der 'Ästhetischen Ideologie' über 'cunt art' und 'écriture féminine.'" See also Cornelia Klinger, "Aesthetics," in Jaggar and Young, *Companion to Feminist Philosophy*, pp. 353–360.
136. Klinger, "Von der Kritik der 'Ästhetischen Ideologie' über 'cunt art' und 'écriture féminine,'" p. 801.
137. This program of a feminist hermeneutics is outlined by Seyla Benhabib in "The Debate over Women and Moral Theory Revisited," in Herta Nagl-Docekal, ed., *Feministische Philosophie* (Vienna, 1994), p. 199.
138. See Immanuel Kant, *Observations on the Feeling of the Beautiful and Sublime*, trans. John T. Goldthwait (Berkeley, 1965).
139. Kant, *Observations on the Feeling of the Beautiful and Sublime*, p. 81. The term *noble* refers in this context to one of three subcategories of the sublime, since Kant distinguishes among the terrifying sublime, the noble, and the splendid (p. 48). Beyond this, to what extent is Kant's contrast of "beautiful virtue" and "noble virtue" congruent with Gilligan's differentiation of a feminine "care per-

spective" and a masculine "justice perspective"? But this question cannot be further discussed here.

140. Kant, *Observations on the Feeling of the Beautiful and Sublime*, pp. 76–77.

141. With great thoroughness Ursula Pia Jauch documents that Kant, besides the bourgeois conception of the relation of the sexes, also presents contrasting egalitarian conceptions. *Immanuel Kant zur Geschlechterdifferenz: Aufklärerische Vorurteilskritik und bürgerliche Geschlechtsvormunschaft* (Vienna, 1988).

142. Kant, *Observations on the Feeling of the Beautiful and Sublime*, p. 45.

143. Kant, *Observations on the Feeling of the Beautiful and Sublime*, p. 46.

144. Kant, *Observations on the Feeling of the Beautiful and Sublime*, p. 47.

145. Kant, *Observations on the Feeling of the Beautiful and Sublime*, p. 51.

146. Kant, *Observations on the Feeling of the Beautiful and Sublime*, p. 57.

147. Kant, *Observations on the Feeling of the Beautiful and Sublime*, pp. 76–96.

148. Kant, *Observations on the Feeling of the Beautiful and Sublime*, p. 58.

149. Kant, *Observations on the Feeling of the Beautiful and Sublime*, p. 57.

150. Kant, *Observations on the Feeling of the Beautiful and Sublime*, p. 61.

151. Kant, *Observations on the Feeling of the Beautiful and Sublime*, p. 81.

152. Ursula Pia Jauch in her interpretation of Kant's *Observations* reaches the conclusion that it was an unambiguous priority: "The limits of the sexes become the matrix of orientation for the differentiation of the sublime and the beautiful" (*Immanuel Kant zur Geschlechterdifferenz*, p. 64).

153. According to the biographer Arsenij Gulyga, Kant first read *Emile* at the end of the summer 1762. See Arsenij Gulyga, *Immanuel Kant* (Frankfurt/Main 1981), p. 58.

154. Recent theoretical debate has rendered evident that the conceptions of a separation of "context of discovery" and "logic of justification" in their original formulation are not tenable, since they amount to a demand for value-free scholarship, which is neither fulfillable nor desirable. But the only adequate response to this insight is to seek further differentiations, whereas attempts at a complete dismissal of the mentioned differentiation prove just as questionable (as, for instance, has been worked out in the critical debate on Nietzsche and Foucault). In short, it must still be acknowledged that the argumentative claim of a thesis can be refuted only if it is tested in itself, while a mere recourse to the conditions of its genesis—even if the arguments are correct—is not enough. This topic will be discussed more extensively in Chapter 3 of this book dealing with the theory of science.

155. More detailed elaborations on the points mentioned in the following can be found in Klinger, "Von der Kritik an der 'ästhetischen Ideologie' über 'cunt art' und 'écriture féminine,'" pp. 808f.

156. Klinger, "Von der Kritik an der 'ästhetischen Ideologie' über 'cunt art' und 'écriture féminine,'" p. 809.

157. Barnett Newman, "The Sublime Is Now" [1948], in *Selected Writings and Interviews*, ed. John P. O'Neill (New York, 1990), p. 173.

158. Jean-François Lyotard, "Das Erhabene und die Avantgarde," in Jacques LeRider and Gérard Raulet, eds., *Verabschiedung der (Post-) Moderne?* (Tübingen, 1987), pp. 251–274. Lyotard refers explicitly to Newman in this essay.

159. An elaboration of this statement can be found in Paul Mattick Jr., "Beautiful and Sublime: 'Gender Totemism' in the Constitution of Art," in Brand and Korsmeyer, *Feminism and Tradition in Aesthetics*, pp. 27–48.

160. See Seyla Benhabib, *Situating the Self: Gender, Community, and Postmodernism in Contemporary Ethics* (New York, 1992): 213–225. I refer here only to the methodological aspect; on the level of content, Benhabib suggests distinguishing strong or weak interpretations in regard to postmodernism, not aesthetics.

161. Immanuel Kant, *Logik: Ein Handbuch zu Vorlesungen*, §81, in *Werke in sechs Bänden*, 3:563.

162. Joseph Margolis, "Reconciling Analytic and Feminist Philosophy and Aesthetics," in Zeglin und Korsmeyer, *Feminism and Tradition in Aesthetics*, p. 426. Margolis refers to his essay "Reinterpreting Interpretation," in *Journal of Aesthetics and Art Criticism* 47 (1989): 237–251.

163. Margolis, "Reinterpreting Interpretation," 237–251.

164. We often encounter this problem in the criticism of the term *genius,* especially criticism directed against the thesis according to which a central claim of art is the overcoming of nature. As some feminist authors contend, this thesis mediates the concept of a superiority of men over women. (For a detailed description of this argumentation, see Klinger, "Von der Kritik an der 'Ästhetischen Ideologie' über 'cunt art' und 'écriture féminine.'") Obviously this objection is plausible only for those who before have identified *woman* with *nature.* But why should we agree to this? (Such an equation of woman and nature is also performed by Paul Mattick Jr. in his discussion of the concept of the sublime in "Beautiful and Sublime.")

165. Kant's differentiation between "beauty which is merely dependent" and "free beauty" (*pulchritudo adhaerens* and *pulchritudo vaga*) already points in this direction. See Immanuel Kant, *The Critique of Judgment*, trans. James Creed Meredith (Oxford, 1952), p. 72.

166. As an example of the appropriation of the aesthetic conceptions at hand, see Rita Felski's reference to Adorno's "negative aesthetic," to which I refer below.

167. Rita Felski, too, rejects attempts at a dedifferentiation: "Any attempt to assert the necessary identity of political and aesthetic value in the context of a theory of feminist aesthetics runs into obvious problems" (*Beyond Feminist Aesthetics*, p. 176).

168. Referring to the various attempts to trace cultural productions back solely to historical and social determinants, Janet Wolff speaks of a "genetic fallacy." *Aesthetics and the Sociology of Art* (London, 1983), p. 11.

169. Immanuel Kant, "To Perpetual Peace: A Philosophical Sketch," in *Perpetual Peace and Other Essays*, trans. Ted Humphrey (Indianapolis, 1985), p. 127.

170. Felski, *Beyond Feminist Aesthetics*, p. 31.

171. Theodor W. Adorno, "Reconciliation Under Duress," in Ernst Bloch et al., eds., *Aesthetics and Politics* (London, 1977), p. 160. In this context, the remarks of Birgit Recki on the "double character of art as 'autonomous and fait social'" assumed by Adorno can prove useful. *Aura und Autonomie: Zur Subjektivität der Kunst bei Benjamin und Adorno* (Würzburg, 1988), pp. 92–94.

172. Felski, *Beyond Feminist Aesthetics*, pp. 43f.

Chapter 3

1. Georg Simmel, "Das Relative und das Absolute im Geschlechter-Problem" [1911], in *Schriften zur Philosophie und Soziologie der Geschlechter* (Frankfurt/Main, 1985), p. 200.

2. For an overview of the different topics and positions that have dominated the debate so far, see Genevieve Lloyd, "Rationality," in Alison M. Jaggar and Iris Marion Young, eds., *A Companion to Feminist Philosophy* (Oxford, 1998), pp. 165–173. See also Elizabeth Grosz, "Bodies and Knowledges: Feminism and the Crisis of Reason," in *Space, Time, and Perversion* (New York, 1995), pp. 25–44.

3. Sandra Harding, *The Science Question in Feminism* (Ithaca, 1986), p. 11.

4. See Karin Hausen and Helga Nowotny, eds., *Wie männlich ist die Wissenschaft?* (Frankfurt/Main, 1986); Barbara Schaeffer-Hegel and Barbara Watson-Franke, eds., *Männer-Mythos-Wissenschaft: Grundlagentexte zur feministischen Wissenschaftskritik* (Pfaffenweiler, 1988). For an overview of the feminist critique of the sciences in the Anglo-Saxon realm, see Sue V. Rosser, "Feminist Scholarship in the Sciences: Where Are We Now and When Can We Expect a Theoretical Breakthrough?" in Nancy Tuana, ed., *Feminism and Science* (Bloomington, 1989), pp. 3–16 (this article contains a select bibliography). See also Bonnie B. Spanier, *Im/partial Science: Gender Ideology in Molecular Biology* (Bloomington, 1995).

5. Carol Gilligan, *In a Different Voice: Psychological Theory and Women's Development* (Cambridge, Mass., 1982).

6. For the historical disciplines, Gisela Bock, among others, explains the necessity for such an expansion. See "Der Platz der Frauen in der Geschichte," in Herta Nagl-Docekal and Franz Wimmer, eds., *Neue Ansätze in der Geschichtswissenchaft*, Conceptus Studien 1 (Vienna, 1984), pp. 108–127.

7. Donna Haraway, "In the Beginning Was the Word: The Genesis of Biological Theory," *Signs: Journal of Women in Culture and Society* 6, no. 3: (1981). This distinction is picked up by Sandra Harding in *The Science Question in Feminism*, especially the chapter entitled "'Bad Science' Versus 'Normal Science.'"

8. Annemarie Pieper encountered a number of "telling examples" for gender blindness while studying scientific encyclopedias published in the course of the 18th century: Pieper, *Gibt es eine feministische Ethik?* (Munich, 1998), pp. 14–19.

9. With this general characterization the controversies in the contemporary theory of science on the definition of scientificity will not be subverted. The opinions seem to diverge only when the procedures of reasoning and intersubjective examination have to be defined more closely. To clarify my language use in this chapter, when I speak of *reasoning* and *examination*, I do not mean verification; I accept Karl Popper's thought that we can focus only on falsification.

10. For an overview of the history of this debate from the beginnings to the present, see Lorraine Code, "Epistemology," in Jaggar and Young, *A Companion to Feminist Philosophy*, pp. 173–184; Andrea Nye, *Philosophy and Feminism at the Border* (New York, 1995), esp. pp. 82–115; Alessandra Tanesini, *An Introduction to Feminist Epistemologies* (Oxford, 1999).

11. Lorraine Code, "Is the Sex of the Knower Epistemologically Significant?" *Metaphilosophy* 12 (1981): 267–276; reprinted in *What Can She Know? Feminist Theory and the Construction of Knowledge* (Ithaca, N.Y., 1991), pp. 1–26.

12. "Feminist epistemology should not be taken seriously" is Pinnick's hard judgment. See C. L. Pinnick, "Feminist Epistemology: Implications for Philosophy of Science," *Philosophy of Science* 61 (1994): 646. See also Noretta Koertge, "Feminist Epistemology: Stalking an Un-Dead Horse," in Paul R. Gross et al., eds., *The Flight From Science and Reason*, Annals of the New York Academy of Sciences (New York, 1996), 775: 413–419.

13. See Harding, *Science Question in Feminism*.

14. As Monika Betzler has explained, feminist criticism targets four concepts of objectivity. See "'Objektivität' als epistemische Norm feministischer Erkenntnistheorie," *Deutsche Zeitschrift für Philosophie* 5 (1998): 783–798. Four different meanings of objectivity are also distinguished by Elisabeth A. Lloyd, "Objectivity and the Double Standard for Feminist Epistemologies," *Synthese* 104 (1995): 351–381.

15. See Harding, *Science Question in Feminism*, p. 272.

16. Elisabeth List, "Theorieproduktion und Geschlechterpolitik: Prolegomena zu einer feministischen Theorie der Wissenschaften," in Herta Nagl-Docekal, ed., *Feministische Philosophie*, 2nd ed. (Vienna, 1994), p. 173.

17. See Sandra Harding, *Whose Science? Whose Knowledge? Thinking from Women's Lives* (Ithaca, N.Y., 1991), esp. pp. 191–217. That it is important to work out the parallelity of the mechanisms of "class, gender, and race supremacy" is also emphasized by Donna Haraway, "The Promises of Monsters: A Regenerative Politics for Inappropriate/d Others," in Lawrence Grossberg et al., eds., *Cultural Studies* (New York, 1992), p. 297.

18. A depiction and detailed elaboration of these attempts as well as bibliographical information can be found in Alison M. Jaggar, *Feminist Politics and Human Nature* (Totowa, N.J., 1983), esp. chap. 11: "Feminist Politics and Epistemology: Justifying Feminist Theory," pp. 353–394.

19. See Code, "Is the Sex of the Knower Epistemologically Significant?" p. 182.

20. See Kathleen Lennon and Margaret Whitford, eds., *Knowing the Difference: Feminist Perspectives in Epistemology* (New York, 1994).

21. See, for instance, Lynn Hankinson Nelson, *Who Knows: From Quine to a Feminist Empiricism* (Philadelphia, 1990); and Louise M. Antony, "Quine as Feminist: The Radical Import of Naturalized Epistemology," in Louise M. Antony and Charlotte Witt, eds., *A Mind of One's Own: Feminist Essays on Reason and Objectivity* (Boulder, 1993), pp. 185–226.

22. The expression *situated knowledges* usually refers to the chapter "Situated Knowledges: The Science Question in Feminism and the Privilege of Partial Perspective," in Donna J. Haraway, *Simians, Cyborgs, and Women: The Reinvention of Nature* (London, 1991), pp. 183–202.

23. For a useful Foucault reading, see Wolfgang Detel, *Macht, Moral, Wissen: Foucault und die klassische Antike* (Frankfurt/Main, 1998). Detel comes to the following conclusion: "The regulative power penetrates language and reason, but does not make rationality obsolete. On the contrary, it creates space for rationality and stabilizes our reason" (p. 12).

24. Another example is women in the history of science. See Londa Schiebinger, *The Mind Has No Sex? Women in the Origins of Modern Science* (Cambridge, Mass., 1989).

25. For a more extensive elaboration of this point, see Brenda Almond, "Philosophy and the Cult of Irrationalism," in A. P. Griffiths, ed., *The Impulse to Philosophise* (Cambridge, Mass., 1992), pp. 201–217. Janet Radcliffe Richards warns of a false but common conclusion: No specific methods or knowledges are required to unmask androcentrism in research. She writes, "A feminist awareness that sex-connected anomalies may come up in particular areas, . . . does not constitute expertise in these areas. In fact it is rather the other way round. Until she has enough of a grip on a particular subject, a feminist cannot be adequately aware of the ways in which sex-connected anomalies may lurk within it, or where to look for undiscovered facts that might be of feminist significance." Janet Radcliffe Richards, "Why Feminist Epistemology Isn't," in Gross et al., *Flight from Science and Reason*, 775: 404.

26. Käthe Trettin, "Is a Feminist Critique of Logic Possible?" in Herta Nagl-Docekal and Cornelia Klinger, eds., *Continental Philosophy in Feminist Perspective* (University Park, Pa., 2000), pp. 175–200. Trettin critically discusses Nye's feminist-motivated objections to logic. See Andrea Nye, *Words of Power: A Feminist Reading of the History of Logic* (New York, 1990).

27. Martha Nussbaum, review of Louise M. Antony and Charlotte Witt, eds., *A Mind of One's Own: Feminist Essays on Reason and Objectivity* (Boulder, 1993), *Times Literary Supplement* 41 (1994): 59–63.

28. See Code, "Is the Sex of the Knower Epistemologically Significant?" pp. 175f.

29. The problems shown in the following do not result only when the claimed difference in thinking is immediately assigned to biological difference. They derive also from theories which depict early infantile socialization in a manner suggesting that the two sexes have distinct, specific ways of thinking and feeling. Therefore Harriet Baber directs her criticism at both versions: "The Market for Feminist Epistemology," *Monist* 77, no. 4 (1994): 404. Regrettably, Baber claims that the "deeply entrenched differences in the ways in which men and women see the world" are the main concern of "feminist epistemology" (p. 404). Her criticism loses precision because her claim does not encompass—as she asserts—the entire feminist epistemology (as will be discussed in the following), but only the concepts of gendered forms of knowledge. Even more regrettably, this exaggerated claim is no exception. The term *feminist epistemology* is often reduced and therefore becomes an easy target.

30. Waltraud Ernst, "Von feministischer Wissenschaftskritik zu feministischen Wissenschaftskonstruktionen," *Die Philosophin* 9 (1994): 22.

31. Dorothy Smith, "Women's Perspective as a Radical Critique of Sociology," *Sociological Inquiry* 44 (1974): 7–13.

32. Hilary Rose, "Hand, Brain, and Heart: A Feminist Epistemology for the Natural Sciences," *Signs: Journal of Women in Culture and Society* 9, no. 1 (1983): 73–90.

33. Nancy Hartsock, "The Feminist Standpoint: Developing the Grounds for a Specifically Feminist Historical Materialism," in Sandra Harding and Merrill Hintikka, eds., *Discovering Reality: Feminist Perspectives on Epistemology,*

Methodology, and Philosophy of Science (Dordrecht, 1983), pp. 283–310; *Money, Sex, and Power* (Boston, 1985), esp. chap. 10.

34. Regarding the debate on feminist standpoint epistemologies, see Cornelia Klinger, "Bis hierher und wie weiter? Überlegungen zur feministischen Wissenschafts- und Rationalitätskritik," in Marianne Krüll, ed., *Wege aus der männlichen Wissenschaft: Perspektiven feministischer Erkenntnistheorie* (Pfaffenweiler, 1990), pp. 21–56.

35. Sandra Harding, "Feminism, Science, and the Anti-Enlightenment Critiques," in Linda Nicholson, ed., *Feminism/Postmodernism* (New York, 1990), pp. 94–99.

36. See Betzler, "'Objektivität' als epistemische Norm feministischer Erkenntnistheorie," p. 787; and Code, "Is the Sex of the Knower Epistemologically Significant?" pp. 174, 177.

37. Genevieve Lloyd reaches a similar finding. She, too, states that men and women must be assumed to be differently situated in many regards and therefore develop specific perspectives; she goes on to emphasize that no insuperable boundaries to communication emerge from these differences: "But whatever differences there may be here are in principle accessible to an informed philosophical imagination, regardless of gender." Lloyd, "Rationality," in Jaggar and Young, *Companion to Feminist Philosophy*, p. 172.

38. See also Ernst, "Von feministischer Wissenschaftskritik zu feministischen Wissenschaftskonstruktionen," p. 22.

39. See Alison M. Jaggar, "Feminist Ethics: Projects, Problems, Prospects," in Herta Nagl-Docekal and Herlinde Pauer-Studer, eds., *Denken der Geschlechterdifferenz: Neue Fragen und Perspektiven der Feministischen Philosophie* (Vienna, 1990), p. 162.

40. Referring to different elements of contemporary philosophy, a number of authors discussed in the meantime the dialogic or interactive character of the production of knowledge. See Jane Duran, *Toward a Feminist Epistemology* (Savage, 1991); Lynn Hankinson Nelson, "Epistemological Communities," in Alcoff and Potter, *Feminist Epistemologies*, pp. 121–160; Lorraine Code, "What Is Natural About Epistemology Naturalized?" *American Philosophical Quarterly* 33 (1996): 1–22.

41. Helen Longino explains in this sense her concept of a cognitive democracy: "Scientific knowledge, on this view, is an outcome of the critical dialogue in which individuals and groups holding different points of view engage with each other." Longino, "Subjects, Power, and Knowledge: Description and Prescription in Feminist Philosophy of Science," in Alcoff and Potter, *Feminist Epistemologies*, p. 112.

42. That we can refer only to the best theories so far is also emphasized by Ruth Anna Putnam, "Why Not a Feminist Theory of Justice?" in Martha Nussbaum and Jonathan Glover, eds., *Women, Culture, and Development: A Study of Human Capabilities* (Oxford, 1995), pp. 324–326.

43. That feminist critique of science reaches a false conclusion when it assumes that "the differentiation between the development and the justification of cognition . . . is to be dismissed" is also explained by Elisabeth C. Parzer, "Was kommt nach der modernen Rationalität?" *Die Philosophin* 5, no. 9 (1994): 68.

44. Sandra Harding, "Ist die westliche Wissenschaft eine Ethnowissenschaft?" *Die Philosophin* 5, no. 9 (1994): 27. See Harding, *Is Science Multicultural? Postcolonialisms, Feminisms, and Epistemologies* (Bloomington, Ind., 1998).

45. Putnam, "Why Not a Feminist Theory of Justice?" p. 326.

46. Sandra Harding, "Rethinking Standpoint Epistemology: What Is Strong Objectivity?" in Linda Alcoff and Elizabeth Potter, eds., *Feminist Epistemologies* (New York, 1993), pp. 49–82.

47. Herta Nagl-Docekal, *Die Objektivität der Geschichtswissenschaft* (Vienna, 1992), esp. chap. 4, "Die Objektivität der Historie als Resultat eines mehrdimensionalen Kontrollprozesses," pp. 227–243.

48. Helen Longino argues in this context: Insofar as research starts with problems of orientation, it can be said that our social and cultural values are constitutive for the elaboration of knowledge. Longino, *Science as Social Knowledge: Values and Objectivity in Scientific Inquiry* (Princeton, 1990).

49. On the question of the relation between science and conditions of life, see also Waltraud Ernst, *Diskurspiratinnen: Wie feministische Erkenntnisprozesse die Wirklichkeit verändern* (Vienna, 1999).

50. Putnam, "Why Not a Feminist Theory of Justice?" p. 326.

51. Sandra Harding, "Geschlechtsidentität und Rationalitätskonzeptionen: Eine Problemübersicht," in Elisabeth List and Herlinde Studer, eds., *Denkverhältnisse: Feminismus und Kritik* (Frankfurt/Main, 1989), p. 444.

52. Harding, "Geschlechtsidentität und Rationalitätskonzeptionen," p. 445.

53. Arthur C. Danto, for instance, reaches this conclusion, when he shows that from the perspective of the program of unified science the narrative aspect of the historical discipline cannot come into focus. See Danto, *Analytische Philosophie der Geschichte* (Frankfurt/Main, 1974).

54. See "Is the subject shaped by instrumental reason?" in this chapter.

55. Benjamin Farrington, ed., "*Temporis Partus Masculus:* An Untranslated Writing of Francis Bacon," *Centaurus* 1 (Copenhagen, 1952): 201.

56. Farrington, *Temporis Partus Masculus*, p. 197.

57. Evelyn Fox Keller, *Reflections on Gender and Science* (New Haven, 1985), p. 39.

58. Keller, *Reflections on Gender and Science*, p. 42.

59. Metaphors cannot be equaled with analogies, as has been made clear by Phyllis Rooney. (See Rooney, "Gendered Reason: Sex Metaphor and Conceptions of Reason," *Hypatia* 2, no. 6 [1991]: 77–103.) Yet this insight does not render the question of the genesis of metaphors obsolete. Rooney's argument lacks plausibility where she operates with the term *root metaphor*, referring to linguistic images that have become so self-evident that we no longer understand them as metaphors (p. 87). I believe that the familiarity of an image does not prevent it from being analyzed. Why should we not try to find out how this association emerged? Feminist linguistic criticism can profitably engage in such investigations.

60. Nancy Chodorow, *The Reproduction of Mothering: Psychoanalysis and the Sociology of Gender* (Berkeley, 1978).

61. Chodorow, *Reproduction of Mothering*, p. 88.

62. This term goes back to R. Greenson, "Disidentifying from Mother: Its Special Importance for the Boy," in *Explorations in Psychoanalysis* (New York, 1978).

63. Greenson, "Disidentifying from Mother," p. 122.
64. Greenson, "Disidentifying from Mother," pp. 130f. Susan Bordo formulates a very similar thought. She discusses Descartes's Meditations and reaches the conclusion that the term *knowledge* can be referred to the desire to compensate for the fear of separation. "I will suggest that we understand the 'great Cartesian anxiety,' although manifestly expressed in epistemological terms, as anxiety over separation from the organic female universe of the Middle Ages and the Renaissance. Cartesian objectivism, correspondingly, will be explored as a defensive response to that separation anxiety, an aggressive intellectual 'flight from the feminine.'" See Susan Bordo, "The Cartesian Masculinization of Thought," *Signs: Journal of Women in Culture and Society* 11, no. 3 (1986): 439–456. Because of the similarity of the argumentation the objections against Keller in the following also work for Bordo. For a critical discussion of Bordo, see also Code, *What Can She Know?* pp. 50–54, 134–137.
65. Keller, *Reflections on Gender and Science*, p. 124.
66. Keller, *Reflections on Gender and Science*, p. 132. Keller refers also to June Goodfield, *An Imagined World* (New York, 1981), p. 63.
67. Keller, *Reflections on Gender and Science*, p. 132; see also Goodfield, *Imagined World*, p. 213.
68. An animism is stated in this context also by Val Plumwood, although without the intention to unveil a theoretical dead-end street. See Plumwood, *Feminism and the Mastery of Nature* (London, 1993), p. 136. Briefly, Plumwood's aim is to reject a purely mechanistic concept of nature as reductionist, and this demand is surely justified. But the proposed solutions are not convincing. When Plumwood presents the thesis according to which "mindlike qualities are spread out throughout nature" (p. 134), and when she pleads for assigning to all realms of nature—starting with stones—"intentionality" and "agency" (pp. 134–136), then she falls into the other extreme and dedifferentiates herself.
69. Luce Irigaray, *This Sex Which Is Not One* (Ithaca, N.Y., 1985), p. 23. See also Margaret Whitford, "Luce Irigaray's Critique of Rationality," in Morwenna Griffiths and Margaret Whitford, eds., *Feminist Perspectives in Philosophy* (London, 1988), p. 118.
70. Irigaray, *This Sex Which Is Not One*, p. 22.
71. Irigaray, *This Sex Which Is Not One*, p. 25.
72. Irigaray's reference to Derrida is investigated by Ellen T. Amour, "Question of Proximity: 'Woman's Place' in Derrida and Irigaray," *Hypatia* 12, no. 1 (1997): 63–78.
73. Amour, "Question of Proximity," p. 26.
74. Luce Irigaray, "Is the Subject of Science Sexed?" *Hypatia* 2, no. 3 (1987): 74 (italics added).
75. Irigaray, *This Sex Which Is Not One*, pp. 28f.
76. Irigaray, *This Sex Which Is Not One*, p. 24.
77. Irigaray, *This Sex Which Is Not One*, p. 29.
78. Luce Irigaray, *Speculum: Spiegel des anderen Geschlechts* (Frankfurt/Main, 1980), p. 181.
79. See Whitford, "Luce Irigaray's Critique of Rationality," pp. 119f.

80. Sally Haslanger also formulates this objection (without reference to Irigaray): "Women's insistence on standards of reason should be one way to combat the dogmatism that fuels patriarchy. If we reject the value of rational reflection and reasoned discussion, then what acceptable methods are left to criticize entrenched positions . . . ?" See Sally Haslinger, "On Being Objective and Being Objectified," in Louise M. Antony and Charlotte Witt, eds., *A Mind of One's Own: Feminist Essays on Reason and Objectivity* (Boulder, 1993), p. 86.

81. See Judith Butler, *Gender Trouble: Feminism and the Subversion of Identity* (New York, 1991), p. 142.

82. Judith Butler, "Contingent Foundations," in Seyla Benhabib, Judith Butler, Drucilla Cornell, and Nancy Fraser, *Feminist Contentions: A Philosophical Exchange* (Frankfurt/Main, 1993), p. 50.

83. Butler is not right when she assumes that feminist politics which claims a *we* necessarily is founded on essentialist assumptions. The common ground of women assumed here is that they experience a certain oppression, not that they share certain feminine characteristics. This is further explained in the final chapter of this book. See also Herta Nagl-Docekal, "Rezension zu Judith Butler, Das Unbehagen der Geschlechter," *L'Homme: Zeitschrift für Feministische Geschichtswissenschaft* 4, no. 1 (1993): 141–147.

84. Butler, "Contingent Foundations," p. 35.

85. Butler, "Contingent Foundations," p. 42.

86. Butler, "Contingent Foundations," p. 43.

87. Butler, "Contingent Foundations," p. 40.

88. Butler, "Contingent Foundations," p. 40.

89. See above; italics added.

90. Butler, "Contingent Foundations," p. 39.

91. Axel Honneth, "Der Affekt gegen das Allgemeine: Zu Lyotards Konzept der Postmoderne," *Merkur* 38, no. 8 (1984): 900. For objections to Butler's generalized distancing from universalist conceptions of morality, see Alison Assiter, *Enlightened Women: Modernist Feminism in a Postmodern Age* (London, 1996), pp. 110–128.

92. Butler, "Contingent Foundations," p. 40.

93. Butler, "Contingent Foundations," p. 41.

94. See Herta Nagl-Docekal, "Das heimliche Subjekt Lyotards," in Manfred Frank, Gerard Raulet, and Willem van Reijen, eds., *Die Frage nach dem Subjekt* (Frankfurt/Main, 1987), pp. 230–246.

95. As Karin Hausen shows, the term *gender-specific character* started to be used at the turn from the seventeenth to the eighteenth century. See Hausen, "Die Polarisierung der 'Geschlechtscharaktere'—Eine Spiegelung der Dissoziation von Erwerbs- und Familienleben," in Werner Conze, ed., *Sozialgeschichte der Familie in der Neuzeit Europas* (Stuttgart, 1976), pp. 363–393.

96. Jean-Jacques Rousseau, *Emile: Or, on Education* (New York, 1979), p. 447f.

97. Immanuel Kant, *Observations on the Feeling of the Beautiful and Sublime*, trans. John T. Goldthwait (Berkeley, 1960), p. 81.

98. Kant, *Observations on the Feeling of the Beautiful and Sublime*, p. 78. Kant's remarks on women are, however, not uniform. See Ursula Pia Jauch, *Immanuel*

Kant zur Geschlechterdifferenz: Aufklärerische Vorurteilskritik und bürgerliche Geschlechtsvormundschaft (Vienna, 1988).

99. For an overview on the masculinization of reason in the history of European philosophy, see Genevieve Lloyd, *The Man of Reason: "Male" and "Female" in Western Philosophy* (Minneapolis, 1984).

100. "The fair sex has just as much understanding as the male," Kant claims. *Observations on the Feeling of the Beautiful and Sublime*, p. 78.

101. "Deep meditation and a long-sustained reflection," Kant remarks, "do not well befit" women (p. 78).

102. In the German-speaking realm this was undertaken, for instance, by Christine Kulke: "This rationality concept suggests that in a patriarchal order shaped by reason, women are the particular victims of reification and the deformation processes resulting from it." See Christine Kulke, "Von der instrumentellen zur kommunikativen Rationalität patriarchaler Herrschaft," in *Rationalität und sinnliche Vernunft: Frauen in der patrarchalen Realität* (Pfaffenweiler, 1988), pp. 58f. See also Kulke, "Die Politik instrumenteller Rationalität und die instrumentelle Rationalität von Politik: Eine Dialektik des Geschlechterverhältnisses?" in Herta Nagl-Docekal and Herlinde Pauer-Studer, eds., *Denken der Geschlechterdifferenz: Neue Fragen und Perspektiven der feministischen Philosophie* (Vienna, 1990), pp. 71–87; Kulke, "Rationaltät der Rationalisierung: Eine Rechtfertigung der Geschlechterpolitik," in Christine Kulke and E. Scheich, eds., *Zwielicht der Vernunft: Die Dialektik der Aufklärung aus der Sicht von Frauen* (Pfaffenweiler, 1992), pp. 59–70. But the feminist critique of reason should not adopt the concept of the dialectic of Enlightenment, since this leads to a contradiction. The problematization of the concept of reason of the Enlightenment happens here in such a general way that the preconditions of reason that make the criticism possible cannot be reflected any longer.

103. Brigitte Weisshaupt explains: "The aim . . . is a reasonable being, whose intellect does not exclude, but includes sensual experiences. The aim is also the transfer of immanent experiences of the multi-layered bodily and physical kind on the level of symbolic representation." See Brigitte Weisshaupt, "Schatten über der Vernunft," in Nagl-Docekal, *Feministische Philosophie*, p. 152. Weisshaupt sees the foundations for a theoretical elaboration of this aim in the "free unity of a communicatively liquified I-identity" described by Habermas and Wellmer (p. 149).

104. A dedifferentiation of the two questions distinguished here can be found in authors who plead not to see reason but the body in its gendered peculiarity as the location of knowledge. The critique of a virility that denies emotions shifts here into a questionable epistemology. This problem can be seen, for instance, in Grosz. She writes, alluding to Derrida, that "it is necessary to examine the subordinated, negative, or excluded term, body, as the unacknowledged condition of the dominant term, reason." See Elisabeth Grosz, "Bodies and Knowledges," p. 195. Jaggar's proposal to assign emotions an equal rank to reason as a place of scientific cognition also raises questions. See Alison M. Jaggar, "Love and Knowledge: Emotion in Feminist Epistemology," in Alison M. Jaggar and Susan R. Bordo, eds., *Feminist Reconstructions of Being and Knowing* (New Brunswick, N.J., 1989), pp. 145–171.

105. For a detailed discussion of this question, see Detlef Horster, ed., *Weibliche Moral: Ein Mythos?* (Frankfurt/Main, 1998).

106. A confusion of these two levels sometimes marks the feminist critique of Descartes and the Enlightenment conceptions of reason derived from his thinking. Paradigmatically Susan Bordo, *The Flight to Objectivity: Essays on Cartesianism and Culture* (Albany, N.Y., 1987). For a discussion of such misunderstanding, see the first chapter of this book.

Chapter 4

1. See the distinction suggested by Immanuel Kant between "innate and the acquired right. An innate right is that which belongs to everyone by nature, independently of any legal act that would establish a right; an acquired right is that for which such an act is required." Kant, *The Metaphysics of Morals*, trans. Mary Gregor (Cambridge, 1991), p. 63.

2. Herta Nagl-Docekal, "Feministische Ethik oder eine Theorie weiblicher Moral?" in Detlef Horster, ed., *Weibliche Moral: Ein Mythos?* (Frankfurt/Main, 1998), pp. 42–72; Nagl-Docekal, "Ein Postscriptum zum Begriff 'Gerechtigkeitsethik,'" in *Weibliche Moral*, pp. 142–153.

3. For an overview of this critique, see Robin May Schott, "Immanuel Kant," in Alison M. Jaggar and Iris M. Young, eds., *A Companion to Feminist Philosophy* (Oxford, 1998), pp. 39–48. See also the four essays published under the title "II Ethics" in Robin May Schott, ed., *Feminist Interpretations of Immanuel Kant* (University Park, Pa., 1997), pp. 77–172.

4. See, for example, Kant, *Metaphysics of Morals*, p. 186.

5. Immanuel Kant, *Groundwork on the Metaphysics of Morals*, trans. Mary J. Gregor (Cambridge, 1998), p. 38.

6. Kant, *Groundwork on the Metaphysics of Morals*, p. 62.

7. It must be "taken into consideration," Kant writes, that those affected by our actions "ought always at the same time to be rated as ends—that is, only as beings who must themselves be able to share in the end of the very same action" (*Groundwork on the Metaphysics of Morals*, p. 62).

8. On the feminist turn away from humanism, see Tina Chanter, "Postmodern Subjectivity," in Jaggar and Young, *Companion to Feminist Philosophy*, p. 267.

9. For such reasons, Susan Moller Okin argues in the context of her considerations on gender justice that feminist intentions will lead not to an antihumanist position, rather to a "humanist justice." Okin, *Justice, Gender, and the Family* (New York, 1989), pp. 170–186.

10. My thesis is in line with Nancy Holmstrom's call for a new feminist humanism. "The new feminist humanism," writes Holmstrom, "combines the respect for difference characteristic of progressive movements since the 1960s with the universalistic aspirations of earlier liberatory traditions." Holmstrom, "Human Nature," in Jaggar and Young, *Companion to Feminist Philosophy*, p. 288.

11. Kant, *Metaphysics of Morals*, p. 62.

12. Kant, *Metaphysics of Morals*, p. 62.

13. Kant, *Metaphysics of Morals*, p. 67.

14. Kant, *Metaphysics of Morals*, p. 63.

15. See Marilyn Frye, *The Politics of Reality: Essays in Feminist Theory* (Trumans-burg, N.Y., 1983); bell hooks, *Talking Back: Thinking Feminist, Thinking Black* (Boston, 1989); bell hooks, *Killing Rage/Ending Sexism* (New York, 1995); Audry Lorde, *Sister Outsider* (Trumansburg, N.Y., 1984); Esther Ngang-Ling Chow et al., eds., *Race, Class, and Gender: Common Bonds, Different Voices* (Thousand Oaks, Calif., 1996); Elizabeth Higginbotham and Mary Romero, eds., *Women and Work: Exploring Race, Ethnicity, and Class* (Thousand Oaks, Calif., 1997); Marianne Grünell and Sawitri Saharso, "bell hooks and Nira Yuval-Davis on Race, Ethnicity, Class, and Gender," *European Journal of Women's Studies* 6, no. 2 (1999): 203–218.

16. See Elizabeth Spelman, *Inessential Woman: Problems of Exclusion in Feminist Thought* (Boston, 1988); Dorothy Rosenberg, "Distant Relations: Class, 'Race,' and National Origin in the German Women's Movement," *Women's Studies International Forum* 19, no. 1–2 (1996): 112–124; Abby Wilkerson, "Ending at the Skin: Sexuality and Race in Feminist Theorizing," *Hypatia* 12, no. 3 (1997): 164–173.

17. Iris Marion Young, "Five Faces of Oppression," in *Justice and the Politics of Difference* (Princeton, 1990), pp. 39–65.

18. Young, "Five Faces of Oppression," p. 135.

19. Onora O'Neill, "Einverständnis und Verletzbarkeit: Eine Neubewertung von Kants Begriff der Achtung für Personen," in Herta Nagl-Docekal and Herlinde Pauer-Studer, eds., *Jenseits der Geschlechtermoral: Beiträge zur Feministischen Ethik* (Frankfurt/Main, 1993), pp. 335–368.

20. The same result is reached in the volume by Beate Rössler, ed., *Quotierung und Gerechtigkeit: Eine moralphilosophische Kontroverse* (Frankfurt/Main, 1993). See also Frigga Haug, "Paradoxien der feministischen Realpolitik: Zum Kampf um die Frauenquote," *Das Argument* 37, no. 4 (1995): 519–538.

21. The controversy that has continued to this day was triggered by Carol Gilligan, *In a Different Voice: Psychological Theory and Women's Development* (Cambridge, Mass., 1982).

22. See Eva-Maria Schwickert, "Carol Gilligans Moralkritik zischen Universalismus und Kontextualismus," *Deutsche Zeitschrift für Philosophie* 42, no. 2 (1994): 255–273.

23. The care that has traditionally been a woman's task still has to be provided, and the current debate on morality and law can be understood as comprehensive only when it recognizes this task. See Selma Sevenhuijsen, *Citizenship and the Ethics of Care: Feminist Considerations on Justice, Morality, and Politics* (London, 1998).

24. For a detailed presentation of this subdiscipline, see Herta Nagl-Docekal, "Bericht: Feministische Ethik," *Information Philosophie* 2 (1995): 24–31.

25. See Luce Irigaray, *Ethik der sexuellen Differenz* (Frankfurt/Main, 1984). Also see Friederike Kuster, "Ortschaften: Luce Irigarays Ethik der sexuellen Differenz," in Ernst Wolfgang Orth and Karl-Heinz Lembeck, eds., *Phänomenologische Forschung*, n.s. 1 (Freiburg, 1996), pp. 44–66.

26. Jacques Derrida and Christie McDonald, "Interview: Choreographies," in Derrida, *The Ear of the Other: Otobiography, Transference, Translation* (Lincoln, 1988), p. 194.

27. Annemarie Pieper argues along these lines when she proposes "the concept of an ethics" in which "a male and female moral sense are so integrated that they neither compete with one another nor are ranked above or below one another. Rather, they will fuse as two equally essential cornerstones of a true human morality. . . . Yet such an ethics that goes beyond gender antagonism will have to be an ethic of gender-specific morality nevertheless." Pieper, *Aufstand des stillgelegten Geschlechts: Einführung in die feministische Ethik* (Freiburg, 1993), pp. 8ff. For a comparable position, see Luce Irigaray, *An Ethics of Sexual Difference* (Ithaca, N.Y., 1993).

28. Derrida also intends the thought of a "new choreography" to escape "from an implacable destiny which immures everything for life in the figure 2." See Derrida and McDonald, "Interview: Choreographies," p. 194. See also John D. Caputo, "Derrida, Drucilla Cornell, and the Dance of Gender," in Ellen K. Feder, Mary C. Rawlinson, and Emily Zakin, eds., *Derrida and Feminism: Recasting the Question of Woman* (New York, 1997), pp. 141–160.

29. Susan Wolf, comment, in Charles Taylor and Amy Gutman, eds., *Multiculturalism: Examining the Politics of Recognition* (Princeton, N.J., 1994), pp. 75–86.

30. For a discussion of this problem from both perspectives, see Claire Wallace, "Eine Westfeministin geht in den Osten," *Transit* 9 (1995): 129–145; Hana Havelková, "Real existierender Feminismus," *Transit* 9 (1995): 146–158.

31. K. Anthony Appiah, "Identity, Authenticity, Survival: Multicultural Societies and Social Reproduction," in Taylor and Gutman, *Multiculturalism*, pp. 149–165.

32. For an overview of the different versions of the objections formulated thus far against essentialist thought patterns, see the section "Contemporary Discussions: Essentialisms and Anti-essentialisms" in Holmstrom, "Human Nature," pp. 284–288; Elizabeth Grosz, "Sexual Difference and the Problem of Essentialism," in *Space, Time, and Perversion: Essays on the Politics of Bodies* (New York, 1995). Barbara Holland-Cunz has demonstrated the many different meanings of the concept of essentialism. "How enigmatic the concept actually is, as employed today, can be read from the fact that from a poststructuralist perspective, historical-material positions appear to be essentialist, while a feminist view would see there a constructivist bias at work." Holland-Cunz, *Soziales Subjekt Natur: Natur- und Geschlechterverhältnis in emanzipatorischen politischen Theorien* (Frankfurt/Main, 1994), p. 49.

33. The expression *identity politics* is employed in differing ways in the contemporary debate. It indicates a politics which assumes that certain groups can be assigned a common identity; for some authors, it also refers to the fact that certain persons have common political goals because they share certain experiences. Jean Cohen uses this concept in regard to the diverse protest movements of the present day in "Strategy or Identity? New Theoretical Paradigms and Contemporary Social Movements," *Social Research* 52 (1985): 663–716. See also the chapter "Strange Multiplicity: Die Politik der Identität und Differenz im globalen Zusammenhang," in Seyla Benhabib, *Kulturelle Vielfalt und demokratische Gleichheit: Politische Partizipation im Zeitalter der Globalisierung* (Frankfurt/Main, 1999), pp. 13–32.

34. See Susanne Maurer, *Zwischen Zuschreibung und Selbstgestaltung: Feministische Identitätspolitik* (Tübingen, 1996); and Susan Bickford, "Anti-Anti-Identity

Politics: Democracy and the Complexities of Citizenship," *Hypatia* 12, no. 4 (1997): 111–131.

35. Victoria Baker, "Definition and the Question of 'Woman,'" *Hypatia* 12, no. 2 (1997): 205. Baker's critique refers specifically to Denise Riley, *Am I That Name? Feminism and the Category of "Women" in History* (Minneapolis, 1988).

36. For a similar argument, see Moira Gatens, *Imaginary Bodies: Ethics, Power, and Corporeality* (London, 1996), p. 77. That it is possible and necessary to free the concept "we" from all essentialist implications is also shown by Chantal Mouffe, "Für eine anti-essentialistische Konzeption feministischer Politik," *Deutsche Zeitschrift für Philosophie* 46, no. 5 (1998): 841–848.

37. See Marilyn Friedman, "Feminismus und moderne Formen der Freundschaft: Eine andere Verortung von Gemeinschaft," in Axel Honneth, ed., *Pathologien des Sozialen: Aufgaben der Sozialphilosophie* (Frankfurt/Main, 1994), pp. 184–204.

38. Another example is provided by the legal theorist Martha Minow, who demonstrates that in the course of deciding the composition of juries, the unspoken assumption often tips the scales that an objective judgment can be expected only of white men. Minow, "Equalities," *Journal of Philosophy* 88, no. 11 (1991): 633–644.

39. See Herta Nagl-Docekal, "Feministische politische Theorie: Ergebnisse und aktuelle Probleme," in P. Koller and K. Puhl, eds., *Current Issues in Political Philosophy: Justice in Society and World Order* (Vienna, 1997), pp. 236–252.

40. In the university systems of German-speaking countries, scholars are required to pass an additional qualification process—apart from the doctorate—to be eligible for senior faculty positions. This process, which requires, among other things, a book-length study, is called *habilitation* (—Trans.).

41. Catharine A. MacKinnon, "Geschlechtergleichheit: Über Differenz und Herrschaft," in Herta Nagl-Docekal and Herlinde Pauer-Studer, eds., *Politische Theorie: Differenz und Lebensqualität* (Frankfurt/Main, 1996), pp. 140–173.

42. In the U.S. debate, the "Sears case" achieved paradigmatic status regarding the problem of contradicting feminist demands in the realm of labor law. The controversy over this legal battle is assessed by Sieglinde Rosenberger in chapter 5, "Differenz im Dilemma," of her book *Geschlechter-Gleichheiten-Differenzen: Eine Denk- und Politikbeziehung* (Vienna, 1996), pp. 183–232.

43. See Anna Yeatman, "Jenseits des Naturrechts: Die Bedingungen für einen universalen Staatsbürgerstatus," in Nagl-Docekal and Pauer-Studer, *Politische Theorie*, pp. 315–349.

44. For a thorough presentation of the pro and con arguments on this topic, see Anne Phillips in chapter 3, "Quotas for Women," in *The Politics of Presence* (Oxford, 1995), pp. 57–84.

45. See also Seyla Benhabib and Linda Nicholson, "Politische Philosophie und die Frauenfrage," in Iring Fetscher and Herfried Münkler, eds., *Pipers Handbuch der Politischen Ideen* (Munich, 1985–1988), 5:513–562, esp. "Die neuzeitlichen Vertragstheorien und die Geschlechterfrage," pp. 527–548.

46. See the section "Rationality and gender blindness in the sciences" in Chapter 3 of this book.

47. Carole Pateman, *The Sexual Contract* (Stanford, 1988), p. 184. See also Pateman, "God Hath Ordained to Man a Helper: Hobbes, Patriarchy, and Conjugal Right," in Mary Shanley et al., eds., *Feminist Interpretations and Political Theory* (University Park, Pa., 1991), pp. 53–73. See also Erna M. Appelt, "Kann der Gesellschaftsvertrag feministisch konzipiert werden?" *L'Homme: Zeitschrift für feministische Geschichtswissenschaft* 8, no. 1 (1997): 64–77.

48. See especially Susan Moller Okin, *Justice, Gender, and the Family* (New York, 1989), chap. 5, "Justice as Fairness: For Whom?" pp. 89–109. See also Scott R. Sehon, "Okin on Feminism and Rawls," in *Philosophical Forum* 27, no. 4 (1996): 321–332.

49. For an introduction to the recent debate, see Birgit Sauer, *Die Asche des Souveräns: Staat und Demokratie in der Geschlechterdebatte* (Frankfurt/Main, 2001).

50. Alison M. Jaggar, *Feminist Politics and Human Nature* (Totowa, N.J., 1983), p. 28. For just one among the numerous comparably founded objections, see Elizabeth Frazer and Nicola Lacey, *The Politics of Community: A Feminist Critique of the Liberal-Communitarian Debate* (Toronto, 1993), esp. chap. 2, "Liberal Individualism: The Feminist Critique," pp. 41–77. On this debate, see Nira Yuval-Davis, "Mitglied einer Gemeinschaft oder vereinzeltes Individuum? Zur Citizenship-Debatte," *Das Argument* 39, no. 218 (1997): 59–70.

51. On this point feminist arguments are congruent with objections to liberalism formulated from a communitarian approach. See, for example, Michael Sandel, *Liberalism and the Limits of Justice* (Cambridge, Mass., 1982).

52. See Christine di Stefano, *Configurations of Masculinity: A Feminist Perspective on Modern Political Theory* (Ithaca, N.Y., 1991).

53. See Elizabeth H. Wolgast, *The Grammar of Justice* (Ithaca, N.Y., 1987); and Virginia Held, *Feminist Morality: Transforming Culture, Society, and Politics* (Chicago, 1993).

54. Charles Taylor, "Cross-Purposes: The Liberal–Communitarian Debate," in Nancy L. Rosenblum, ed., *Liberalism and the Moral Life* (Cambridge, Mass., 1989), pp. 103–130.

55. Will Kymlicka, *Contemporary Political Philosophy: An Introduction* (Oxford, 1990), p. 62.

56. Herlinde Pauer-Studer, "Der Begriff der Person und die feministische Ethik-Debatte," offers a similar critique of this type of objection in Dieter Sturma, ed., *Person: Philosophiegeschichte—Theoretische Philosophie—Praktische Philosophie* (Paderborn, 2001) pp. 377–400.

57. For a comprehensive presentation of this kind of reading, see Christine di Stefano, "Autonomy in the Light of Difference," in Nancy Hirschmann and Christine di Stefano, eds., *Revisioning the Political: Feminist Reconstructions of Traditional Concepts in Western Political Theory* (Boulder, 1996), pp. 95–116.

58. See Johann Gottlieb Fichte, *Der geschlossene Handelsstaat*, in *J. G. Fichtes Sämtliche Werke*, ed. I. H. Fichte, vol. 3 (Berlin, 1971). First edition, 1800.

59. Iris M. Young, *Justice and the Politics of Difference* (Princeton, N.J., 1990).

60. On the recent debate over the problem of violence (not only in the domestic sphere), see the special issue "Women and Violence," *Hypatia* 11, no. 4 (1996).

61. See Jean Cohen, "Redescribing Privacy: Identity, Difference, and the Abortion of Controversy," *Columbia Journal of Gender and Law* 1, no. 3 (1992): 43–77; Anita L. Allen, *Uneasy Access: Privacy for Women in a Free Society* (Totowa, N.J., 1988).

62. Marilyn Friedman also reaches this conclusion in "Autonomy and Social Relationships: Rethinking the Feminist Critique," in Diana Tietjens Meyers, ed., *Feminists Rethink the Self* (Boulder, 1997), pp. 40–61. But Friedman also points out that the way the term *autonomy* is commonly used in the contemporary Western cultural context calls for feminist criticism. The relationship between privacy and autonomy is also investigated by Beate Rössler, *Der Wert des Privaten* (Frankfurt/Main, 2001).

63. Marcia Baron presents a detailed analysis of this issue with reference to Kant: "Kantian Ethics and Claims of Detachment," in Schott, *Feminist Interpretations of Immanuel Kant*, pp. 145–170.

64. See Heidemarie Bennent, *Galanterie und Verachtung: Eine philosophiegeschichtliche Untersuchung zur Stellung der Frau in Gesellschaft und Kultur* (Frankfurt/Main, 1985); Ursula Pia Jauch, *Immanuel Kant zur Geschlechterdifferenz: Aufklärerische Vorurteilskritik und bürgerliche Geschlechtsvormundschaft* (Vienna, 1988); M. G. Clark and Lynda Lange, eds., *The Sexism of Social and Political Theory: Women and Reproduction from Plato to Nietzsche* (Toronto, 1979); Hannelore Schröder, *Die Rechtlosigkeit der Frau im Rechtsstaat* (Frankfurt/Main, 1979) (on Fichte).

65. Bennent, *Galanterie und Verachtung*, p. 92.

66. Okin, *Justice, Gender, and the Family*.

67. John Rawls, *A Theory of Justice* (Cambridge, Mass., 1971), pp. 128, 146.

68. For an overview of this debate, see Deborah L. Rhode, *Justice and Gender: Sexual Discrimination and the Law* (London, 1993). See also Sieglinde Rosenberger, "Privatheit und Politik," in Eva Kreisky and Birgit Sauer, eds., "Geschlechterverhältnisse im Kontext politischer Transformation," *Politische Vierteljahresschrift*, special issue, 28 (1997): 120–136. That the slogan "the personal is political" is used with widely varying meanings, some of them rather questionable, is illuminated by Alice Pechriggl, *Utopiefähigkeit und Veränderung: Der Zeitbegriff und die Möglichkeit kollektiver Autonomie* (Pfaffenweiler, 1993), pp. 132f.

69. See Cornelia Klinger, "Woman—Landscape—Artwork: Alternative Realms or Patriarchal Reserves?" in Herta Nagl-Docekal and Cornelia Klinger, eds., *Continental Philosophy in Feminist Perspective: Re-Reading the Canon in German* (University Park, Pa., 2000), pp. 147–174.

70. Jean-Jacques Rousseau, *Emile, or On Education* (New York, 1979), p. 365.

71. As Edith Saurer shows, it is also required in this context to reconsider the concept of love from a feminist perspective: Saurer, "Liebe, Geschlechterbeziehungen und Feminismus," *L'Homme: Zeitschrift für Feministische Geschichtswissenschaft* 8, no. 1 (1997): 6–20.

72. Benhabib and Nicholson, "Politische Philosophie und die Frauenfrage," p. 549.

73. Jaggar, *Feminist Politics and Human Nature*, p. 72. Brigitte Rauschenbach argues in a similar way in *Politische Philosophie und Geschlechterordnung: Eine Einführung* (Frankfurt/Main, 1998), esp. chap. 6/2, "Fetisch Lohnarbeit oder das Geheimnis des weiblichen Werts," pp. 153–160.

74. See Regine Becker-Schmidt, "Identitätslogik und Gewalt: Zum Verhältnis von Kritischer Theorie und Feminismus," *Beiträge zur Feministischen Theorie und Praxis* 24 (1989): 31–64.

75. See Birgit Sauer, "'Die Magd der Industriegesellschaft': Anmerkungen zur Geschlechtsblindheit von Staats- und Institutionentheorien," in Brigitte Kerchner and Gabriele Wilde, eds., *Staat und Privatheit: Aktuelle Studien zu einem schwierigen Verhältnis* (Opladen, 1977), pp. 29–54.

76. See Erna Appelt, Geschlect—Staatsbürgerschaft—Nation. Politische Konstruktionen des Geschlecterverhöltnisses (Frankfurt/Main, 1999).

77. In this connection, the feminist discussion is based mostly on T. H. Marshall's threefold typology of rights. See Marshall, *Class, Citizenship, and Social Development* (New York, 1964).

78. See Friedrich Kambartel, "Arbeit und Praxis," *Deutsche Zeitschrift für Philosophie* 41, no. 2 (1993): 239–249. See also Angelika Krebs, "Eine feministische Stellungnahme zu Kambartels 'Arbeit und Praxis,'" pp. 251–256; and Angelika Krebs, "Kann denn Liebe Arbeit sein?" in Koller and Puhl, *Aktuelle Fragen politischer Philosophie*, pp. 253–260.

79. See Nancy Fraser, "Die Gleichheit der Geschlechter und das Wohlfahrtssystem: Ein postindustrielles Gedankenexperiment," in Nagl-Docekal and Pauer-Studer, *Politische Theorie*, pp. 469–498.

80. Pateman, *Sexual Contract*, p. 7.

81. Carole Pateman, "Feminismus und Ehevertrag," in Nagl-Docekal and Pauer-Studer, *Politische Theorie*, pp. 174–222.

82. Pateman, *Sexual Contract*, p. 184.

83. Jean-Jacques Rousseau, *Vom Gesellschaftsvertrag oder Prinzipien des Staatsrechts*, in *Politische Schriften* (Paderborn, 1964), 1:79.

84. See Fred Dallmayr, "Die Heimkehr des Politischen," review of Chantal Mouffe, *The Return of the Political* (London, 1993), *Deutsche Zeitschrift für Philosophie* 44, no. 3 (1996): 517–522.

85. The lack of clarity addressed here can be seen, for example, in Jane Flax, "Jenseits von Gleichheit: Geschlecht, Gerechtigkeit und Differenz," in Nagl-Docekal and Pauer-Studer, *Politische Theorie*, pp. 223–250.

86. See Barbara Herman, "Could it be Worth Thinking About Kant on Sex and Marriage?" in Louise M. Anthony and Charlotte Witt, eds., *A Mind of One's Own*, (Boulder, Co., 1993), pp. 49–68.

87. John Rawls, "The Idea of Public Reason Revisited," *University of Chicago Law Review* 64, no. 3 (1997): 765–807.

88. For an example of an argument along these lines, see Seyla Benhabib, "The Universalized and the Concrete Other: Visions of the Autonomous Self" in Sandra Harding and Merrill B. Hintikka, eds., *Discovering Reality*, (Dordrecht, 1983) pp.121–137. See also Brigitte Rauschenbach, *Politische Philosophie und Geschlechterordnung: Eine Einführung* (Frankfurt/Main, 1998), pp. 114–119.

89. See the second section of Chapter 3 in this book.

90. Ruth Anna Putnam, "Why Not a Feminist Theory of Justice?" in Martha Nussbaum and Jonathan Glover, eds., *Women, Culture, and Development:. A Study of Human Capabilities* (Oxford, 1995), p. 310.

91. See especially Ronald Dworkin, *Taking Rights Seriously* (Cambridge, Mass., 1978). Regarding the thesis that a purely formal equality is insufficient to ensure full justice between the sexes, see also Herta Nagl-Docekal, "Feministische Politische Theorie," pp. 236–252.

92. For a discussion of this problem, also see Ute Gerhard, "Massstäbe für eine neue Verfassung: Über Freiheit, Gleichheit und die Würde der Frauen," in Ulrich K. Preuss, ed., *Zum Begriff der Verfassung: Die Ordnung des Politischen* (Frankfurt/Main, 1994), pp. 248–276.

93. With reference to Ronald Dworkin's argument that the principle of equality implies the demand to view all individuals "as equals," Drucilla Cornell calls for a feminist conception of equality. "The demand is for freedom and equality, for the recognition of each one of us as the node of representation for our own sexuality and therefore of our equivalent value, despite the forms with which we choose to represent our sexual difference. The state must show us equal concern by recognizing our equivalent value as persons who inevitably express their sexuate being." Cornell, *At the Heart of Freedom: Feminism, Sex, and Equality* (Princeton, N.J., 1998), p. 60. See Dworkin, *Taking Rights Seriously*, chap. 9.

94. That Rawls's conception can be used in this way is shown, among others, by Morris B. Kaplan, *Sexual Justice: Democratic Citizenship and the Politics of Desire* (New York, 1997), esp. pp. 28–39; Kaplan, *Intimacy and Equality: The Question of Lesbian and Gay Marriage* (Stony Brook, N.Y., 1993).

BIBLIOGRAPHY

Adorno, Theodor W. "Reconciliation Under Duress." In Ernst Bloch et al., eds., *Aesthetics and Politics*. London, 1977.

Allen, Anita L. *Uneasy Access: Privacy for Women in a Free Society*. Totowa, N.J., 1988.

Almond, Brenda. "Philosophy and the Cult of Irrationalism." In A. P. Griffiths, ed., *The Impulse to Philosophize*. Cambridge, Mass., 1992.

Antony, Louise M. "Quine as Feminist: The Radical Import of Naturalized Epistemology." In Louise M. Antony and Charlotte Witt, eds., *A Mind of One's Own: Feminist Essays on Reason and Objectivity*, pp. 185–226. Boulder, 1993.

Apel, Karl Otto. "Szientistik, Hermeneutik, Ideologiekritik" (Scientism, Hermeneutics, Critique of Ideologies). In *Viennaer Jahrbuch für Philosophie* (Viennese Yearbook of Philosophy), 1968, 1:15–45.

Apel, Karl Otto, and Matthias Kettner, eds. *Die eine Vernunft und die vielen Rationalitäten* (One Reason and Many Rationalities). Frankfurt am Main, 1996.

Appelt, Erna M. *Geschlecht-Staatsbürgerschaft-Nation: Politische Konstruktionen des Geschlechterverhältnisses* (Gender-Citizenship-Nation: Political Constructions of Gender Relations). Frankfurt am Main, 1999.

———. "Kann der Gesellschaftsvertrag feministisch konzipiert werden?" (Can the Social Contract Be Conceptualized in Feminist Terms?). *L'Homme: Zeitschrift für feministische Geschichtswissenschaft* 8, no. (1997): 64–78.

Appiah, K. Anthony. "Identity, Authenticity, Survival: Multicultural Societies and Social Reproduction." In Amy Gutman, ed., *Multiculturalism: Examining the Politics of Recognition,* pp. 149–163. Princeton, 1994.

Armour, Ellen T. "Questions of Proximity: 'Woman's Place' in Derrida and Irigaray." *Hypatia* 12 (1997): 63–78.

Assiter, Alison. *Enlightened Women: Modernist Feminism in a Postmodern Age*. London, 1996.

213

Baber, Harriet. "The Market for Feminist Epistemology." *Monist* 77, no. 4 (1994): 403–423.

Bachtin, Michail M. "The Problem of the Text in Linguistics, Philology and the Human Sciences." In *Speech, Genres and Other Late Essays*, edited by Caryl Emerson and Michael Holquist. Austin, 1986.

Barker, Victoria. "Definition and the Question of 'Woman.'" *Hypatia* 12, no. 2 (1997): 185–215.

Baron, Marcia. "Kantian Ethics and Claims of Detachment." In Robin May Schott, ed., *Feminist Interpretations of Immanuel Kant*, pp. 145–172. University Park, Pa., 1997.

Barta, Ilsebill. Foreword to *Frauen, Bilder, Männer, Mythen: Kunsthistorische Beiträge* (Women, Images, Men, Myths: Contributions from Art History), pp. 7–10. Berlin, 1987.

Beauvoir, Simone de. *Das andere Geschlecht: Sitte und Sexus der Frau.* Hamburg, 1968. English edition: *The Second Sex.* New York, 1989.

―――― "La femme et la création." In C. Francis and F. Gonhier, eds., *Les Ecrits de Simone de Beauvoir: La Vie—L'Ecriture.* Paris, 1979. English edition: "Women and Creativity." In Moi Toril, ed., *French Feminist Thought: A Reader*, pp. 17–32. Oxford, 1987.

Becker-Schmidt, Regine. "Identitätslogik und Gewalt: Zum Verhältnis von Kritischer Theorie und Feminismus" (The Logic of Identity and Violence: On the Relation between Critical Theory and Feminism), *Beiträge zur Feministischen Theorie und Praxis* (Contributions to Feminist Theory and Practice) 24 (1989): 51–64.

Benhabib, Seyla. "The Debate over Women and Moral Theory Revisited." In Herta Nagl-Docekal, ed., *Feministische Philosophie* (Feminist Philosophy), pp. 191–201. 2nd ed. Vienna, 1994.

――――. "Der verallgemeinerte und der konkrete Andere: Ansätze zu einer feministischen Moraltheorie." In Elisabeth List and Herlinde Studer, eds., *Denkverhältnisse: Feminismus und Kritik*, pp. 454–487. Frankfurt am Main, 1989. English edition: "The Universalized and the Concrete Other: Visions of the Autonomous Self." In S. Harding and M. B. Hintikka, eds., *Discovering Reality*, pp. 121–137. Dordrecht, 1983.

――――. *Kulturelle Vielfalt und demokratische Gleichheit: Politische Partizipation im Zeitalter der Globalisierung* (Cultural Diversity and Democratic Equality: Political Participation in the Age of Globalization). Frankfurt am Main, 1999.

――――. *Selbst im Kontext: Kommunikative Ethik im Spannungsfeld von Feminismus, Kommunitarismus und Postmoderne.* Frankfurt am Main, 1995. English edition: *Situating the Self. Gender, Community and Postmodernism in Contemporary Ethics.* Cambridge, U.K., 1992.

Benhabib, Seyla, and Linda Nicholson. "Politische Philosophie und die Frauenfrage" (Political Philosophy and the Woman Question). In Iring Fetscher and Herfried Münkler, eds., *Piepers Handbuch der Politischen Ideen* (Pieper's Handbook of Political Ideas), 5:513–562. Munich, 1985–1988.

Benhabib, Seyla, Judith Butler, Drucilla Cornell, and Nancy Fraser, eds. *Der Streit um Differenz: Feminismus und Postmoderne.* Frankfurt am Main, 1993. English edition: *Feminist Contentions: A Philosophical Exchange.* New York, 1995.

Benjamin, Walter. "Über den Begriff der Geschichte" (On the Notion of History). In *Illuminationen: Ausgewählte Schriften,* pp. 251–261. Frankfurt am Main, 1977. English edition: *Illuminations,* edited by Hannah Arendt. New York, 1969.

———. "Denkbilder" (Images of Thought). In *Werkausgabe* (Complete Works), 4:305–438. Frankfurt am Main, 1980.

Bennent, Heidemarie. *Galanterie und Verachtung: Eine philosophiegeschichtliche Untersuchung zur Stellung der Frau in Gesellschaft und Kultur* (Gallantry and Contempt: On the Social and Cultural Positioning of the Woman in the History of Philosophy). Frankfurt am Main, 1985.

Betzler, Monika. "'Objektivität' als epistemische Norm feministischer Erkenntnistheorie" ('Objectivity' as an Epistemic Norm in Feminist Epistemology). *Deutsche Zeitschrift für Philosophie* (German Journal of Philosophy) 5 (1998): 783–798.

Bickford, Susan. "Anti-Anti-Identity Politics: Democracy and the Complexities of Citizenship." *Hypatia* 12, no. 4 (1997): 111–131.

Bigwood, Carol. "Renaturalizing the Body (with a Little Help from Merleau-Ponty)." *Hypatia* 6, no. 3 (1991): 54–73.

Birkhan, Ingvild. "Das Vienna der Jahrhundertwende: Eine Wende für oder gegen die Frau? Überlegungen zu Weininger und Freud." In Herta Nagl-Docekal and Herlinde Pauer-Studer, eds., *Denken der Geschlechterdifferenz* (Thinking Gender Difference), pp. 41–70. Vienna, 1990. English edition: "Fin-de-siècle Vienna: A Movement for or Against Womanhood? Some Thoughts on Freud and Weininger." In Herta Nagl-Docekal and Cornelia Klinger, eds., *Continental Philosophy in Feminist Perspective: Re-Reading the Canon in German,* pp. 255–280. University Park, Pa., 2000.

Bock, Gisela. "Der Platz der Frauen in der Geschichte" (Women's Place in History). In Herta Nagl-Docekal and Franz Wimmer, eds., *Neue Ansätze in der Geschichtswissenschaft* (New Approaches in the Historical Sciences), pp. 108–127. Conceptus Studien 1. Vienna, 1984.

Bordo, Susan. "The Cartesian Masculinization of Thought." In *Signs: Journal of Women in Culture and Society* 11, no. 3 (1986): 439–456.

———. *The Flight to Objectivity: Essays on Cartesianism and Culture.* Albany, N.Y., 1987.

Bovenschen, Silvia. *Die imaginäre Weiblichkeit: Exemplarische Untersuchungen zu kulturgeschichtlichen und literarischen Präsentationsformen des Weiblichen* (Imaginary Femininity: Paradigmatic Investigations on the Forms of Literary Presentation of the Feminine). Frankfurt am Main, 1979.

Braidotti, Rosi. *Patterns of Dissonance: A Study of Women in Contemporary Philosophy.* Cambridge, U.K., 1991.

Brändli, Sabina. "'Die unbeschreibliche Beherrschung und Ruhe in Haltung und Geberden': Körperbilder des bürgerlichen Mannes im 19. Jahrhundert" (The Undescribable Restraint and Composure of Posture and Gesture: Body Images of the Bourgeois Man in the Nineteenth Century). *Österreichische Zeitschrift für Geschichtswissenschaften* (Austrian Journal for the Historical Sciences) 8, no. 2 (1997): 274–281.

Braun, Christina von Nichtich. *Logik, Lüge, Libido* (Non-Ego: Logic, Lie, Libido). Frankfurt am Main, 1990.

Brennan, Teresa. "Psychoanalytic Feminism." In Alison M. Jaggar and Iris M. Young, eds., *A Companion to Feminist Philosophy*, pp. 272–279. Oxford, U.K., 1998.

Bronfen, Elisabeth. *Nur über ihre Leiche: Tod, Weiblichkeit und Ästhetik*. Munich, 1992. English edition: *Over Her Dead Body: Death, Femininity and the Aesthetic*. New York: 1992.

Broude, Norma, and Mary D. Garrard. Introduction to *The Power of Feminist Art: The American Movement of the 1970s: History and Impact*. New York, 1994.

Browning, Cole Eve. *Philosophy and Feminist Criticism: An Introduction*. New York, 1993.

Burns, Steven. "Reason and Objectification." *Ethik und Sozialwissenschaften: Streitforum für Erwägungskultur* (Ethics and the Social Sciences: A Forum for Contention and the Culture of Pondering) 3, no. 4 (1992): 542–544.

Butler, Judith. *Das Unbehagen der Geschlechter*. Frankfurt am Main, 1991. English edition: *Gender Trouble: Feminism and the Subversion of Identity*. New York, 1990.

_____. "Gendering the Body: Beauvoir´s Philosophical Contribution." In Ann Garry and Marilyn Pearsall, eds., *Women, Knowledge and Reality: Explorations in Feminist Theory*, pp. 253–262. Boston, 1989.

_____. "Kontingente Grundlagen: Der Feminismus und die Frage der 'Postmoderne.'" In Seyla Benhabib, Judith Butler, Drucilla Cornell, and Nancy Fraser, eds., *Der Streit um Differenz: Feminismus und Postmoderne in der Gegenwart*, pp. 31–58. Frankfurt am Main, 1993. English edition: "Contingent Foundations." In Seyla Benhabib, Judith Butler, Drucilla Cornell, and Nancy Fraser, eds., *Feminist Contentions: A Philosophical Exchange*, pp. 127–144. New York, 1995.

_____. *Körper von Gewicht: Die diskursiven Grenzen des Geschlechts*. Frankfurt am Main, 1995. English edition: *Bodies That Matter*. New York, 1993.

_____. "Variationen zum Thema Sex und Geschlecht." In Gertrud Nunner-Winkler, ed., *Weibliche Moral: Die Kontroverse um eine geschlechtsspezifische Ethik* (Feminine Morality: The Controversy on a Gendered Ethics), pp. 56–78. Frankfurt am Main, 1991. English edition: "Variations on Sex and Gender: Beauvoir, Wittig and Foucault." In Seyla Benhabib and Drucilla Cornell, eds., *Feminism as Critique: Essays on the Politics of Gender in Late-capitalist Societies*, pp. 128–142. Cambridge, U.K., 1987.

Caputo, John D. "Derrida, Drucilla Cornell, and the Dance of Gender." In Ellen K. Feder, Mary C. Rawlinson, and Emily Zakin, eds., *Derrida and Feminism: Recasting the Question of Woman*, pp. 141–160. New York, 1997.

Chanter, Tina. "Postmodern Subjectivity." In Alison M. Jaggar and Iris M. Young, eds., *A Companion to Feminist Philosophy*, pp. 263–272. Oxford, U.K., 1998.

Chodorow, Nancy. *The Reproduction of Mothering: Psychoanalysis and the Sociology of Gender*. Berkeley, 1978.

Cixous, Hélène. "The Lough of the Medusa." In Elaine Marks and Isabelle de Courtivron, eds., *New French Feminism: An Anthology*, pp. 245–264. New York, 1981.

Clark, M. G., and Lange Lynda, eds. *The Sexism of Social and Political Theory: Women and Reproduction from Plato to Nietzsche*. Toronto, 1979.

Code Lorraine. "Is the Sex of the Knower Epistemologically Significant?" *Metaphilosophy* 12 (1981). Reprinted in Lorraine Code, *What Can She Know? Feminist Theory and the Construction of Knowledge,* pp. 1–26. Ithaca, N.Y., 1991.

_____. "What Is Natural about Epistemology Naturalized?" *American Philosophical Quarterly* 33 (1996).

_____. "Epistemology." In Alison M. Jaggar and Iris M. Young, eds., *A Companion to Feminist Philosophy,* pp. 173–184. Oxford, U.K., 1998.

Cohen Jean, "Strategy or Identity? New Theoretical Paradigms and Contemporary Social Movements." *Social Research* 52 (1985).

_____. "Redescribing Privacy: Identity, Difference and the Abortion of Controversy." *Columbia Journal of Gender and Law* 1, no. 3 (1992).

Comini, Alessandra. "Gender of Genius? The Woman Artists of German Expressionism." In Norma Broude and Mary Garrard, *Feminism and Art History: Questioning the Litany.* New York, 1982.

Cornell, Drucilla. *At the Heart of Freedom: Feminism, Sex and Equality.* Princeton, 1998.

Dallmayr, Fred. "Die Heimkehr des Politischen" (The Homecoming of the Political). *Deutsche Zeitschrift für Philosophie* (German Journal of Philosophy) 44, no. 3 (1996): 517–522. Review of Chantal Mouffe, *The Return of the Political.* London, 1993.

Danto, Arthur C. *Analytische Philosophie der Geschichte.* Frankfurt am Main, 1974. English edition: *Analytical Philosophy of History.* Cambridge, Mass., 1965.

Derrida, Jacques, and Christie McDonald. "Interview: Choreographies." In *The Ear of the Other: Otobiography, Transference, Translation.* Lincoln, 1988.

Detel, Wolfgang. *Macht, Moral, Wissen: Foucault und die klassische Antike* (Power, Morality, Knowledge: Foucault and Classical Antiquity). Frankfurt am Main, 1998.

Deuber-Mankowski, Astrid. "Woman: The Most Precious Loot in the 'Triumph of Allegory': Gender Relations in Walter Benjamin's The Arcades Project." In H. Nagl-Docekal and C. Klinger, eds., *Continental Philosophy in Feminist Perspective: Re-Reading the Canon in German,* pp. 281–302. University Park, Pa., 2000.

Di Stefano, Christine. "Autonomy in the Light of Difference." In Nancy Hirschmann and Christine Di Stefano, eds., *Revisioning the Political: Feminist Reconstructions of Traditional Concepts in Western Political Theory.* Boulder, 1996.

_____. *Configurations of Masculinity: A Feminist Perspective on Modern Political Theory.* Ithaca, N.Y., 1991.

Duden, Barbara. *Der Frauenleib als öffentlicher Ort* (Woman's Body as Public Space). Hamburg, 1991.

_____. *Geschichte unter der Haut* (History Underneath the Skin). Stuttgart, 1991.

_____. "Zur Exegese vergangener Körpererlebnisse: Ein Gespräch mit Barbara Duden" (On the Exegesis of Past Body Experiences: A Conversation with Barbara Duden). *Die Philosophin* (Woman Philosopher) 7 (1993): 63–68.

Duran, Jane. *Toward a Feminist Epistemology.* Savage, 1991.

Dworkin, Ronald. *Bürgerrechte ernst genommen.* Frankfurt am Main, 1990.

Ehalt, Hubert Ch. "Über den Wandel des Termins der Geschlechtsreife in Europa und dessen Ursachen" (On the Changing Date of Sexual Marturity in Europe and its Causes). In *Zwischen Natur und Kultur: Zur Kritik biologistischer Ansätze* (Between Nature and Culture: A Critique of Biologistic Approaches), pp. 93–168. Vienna, 1985.

Ernst, Waltraud. "Von feministischer Wissenschaftskritik zu feministischen Wissenschaftskonstruktionen" (From a Feminist Critique of Science to Feminist Constructions of Science). *Die Philosophin* (Woman Philosopher) 9 (1994): 9–25.

_____. *Diskurspiratinnen: Wie feministische Erkenntnisprozesse die Wirklichkeit verändern* (Pirates of Discourse: How Feminist Processes of Knowing Transform Reality). Vienna, 1999.

Evans, Judith. *Feminist Theory Today: An Introduction to Second-Wave Feminism.* London, 1995.

Falludi, Susan. *Backlash: The Undeclared War Against American Woman.* New York, 1991.

Farrington, Benjamin, ed. *Temporis Partus Masculus: An Untranslated Writing of Francis Bacon.* Centaurus 1. Copenhagen, 1952.

Fasching, Maria. *Zum Begriff der Freundschaft bei Aristoteles und Kant* (On the Notion of Friendship in Aristotle and Kant). Würzburg, 1990.

Felski, Rita. *Beyond Feminist Aesthetics: Feminist Literature and Social Change.* Cambridge, 1989.

"Feministische Theorie: Zwischenbilanzen" (Feminist Theory: Assessing the Current State). *Deutsche Zeitschrift für Philosophie* (German Journal of Philosophy) 46, no. 5 (1998): 780–848.

Fichte, Johann Gottlieb. *Der geschlossene Handelsstaat* (The Closed Trading Society). In I. H. Fichte, ed., *J. G. Fichtes Sämtliche Werke.* Vol. 3. Berlin, 1971. First published in 1800.

Firestone, Shulamith. *The Dialectic of Sex.* New York, 1970.

Flax, Jane. "Jenseits von Gleichheit: Geschlecht, Gerechtigkeit und Differenz" (Beyond Equality: Gender, Justice and Difference). In Herta Nagl-Docekal and Herlinde Pauer-Studer, eds., *Politische Theorie: Differenz und Lebensqualität* (Political Theory: Difference and the Quality of Life), pp. 223–250. Frankfurt am Main, 1996. English edition: In Gisela Bock and Susan James, eds., *Beyond Equality and Difference: Citizenship, Feminist Politics and Female Subjectivity.* London, 1993.

Foucault, Michel. "Nietzsche, die Genealogie, die Historie." In *Von der Subversion des Wissens*, pp. 83–109. Frankfurt am Main, 1987. English edition: "Nietzsche, Genealogy, History." In D. F. Bouchard, Ed., *Language, Counter-Memory, Practice: Selected Essays and Interviews by Michel Foucault.* Oxford, U.K., 1977.

_____. *Sexualität und Wahrheit.* Frankfurt am Main, 1983–1986. English edition: *The History of Sexuality.* New York, 1978.

Frank, Manfred. "Über Subjektivität: Rede an die Gebildeten unter ihren Reduktionisten" (On Subjectivity: Address to the Educated Among Its Reductionists). In Jörg Huber and Alois Martin Müller, eds., *Die Wiederkehr des Anderen* (The Return of the Other), pp. 83–101. Basel, 1996.

Fraser, Nancy. "Die Gleichheit der Geschlechter und das Wohlfahrtssystem: Ein postindustrielles Gedankenexperiment" (Gender Equality and the Welfare System: A Postindustrial Thought Experiment). In Herta Nagl-Docekal and Herlinde Pauer-Studer, eds., *Politische Theorie: Differenz und Lebensqualität*, pp. 469–498. Frankfurt am Main, 1996. English edition: "Talking About Needs: Interpretive Contests as Political Conflicts in Welfare Societies." In Cass R. Sunstein, ed., *Feminism and Political Theory.* London, 1990.

————. "The Uses and Abuses of French Discourse Theories for Feminist Politics." In Nancy Fraser and Sandra Lee Bartky, eds., *Revaluing French Feminism: Critical Essays on Difference, Agency and Culture,* pp. 177–194. Bloomington, 1992.

Fraser, Nancy, and Sandra Lee Bartky, eds. *Revaluing French Feminism: Critical Essays on Difference, Agency and Culture.* Bloomington, 1992.

Frazer, Elizabeth, and Nicola Lacey. *The Politics of Community: A Feminist Critique of the Liberal-Communitarian Debate.* Toronto, 1993.

Freud, Sigmund. *Neue Folge der Vorlesungen zur Einführung in die Psychoanalyse.* In *Studienausgabe.* Vol. 1. Frankfurt am Main, 1982.

———— "Totem und Tabu." In *Studienausgabe,* 9:287–444.

Friedman Marilyn. "Autonomy and Social Relationships: Rethinking the Feminist Critique." In Diana T. Meyers, ed., *Feminists Rethink the Self,* pp. 40–61. Boulder, 1997.

————. "Feminismus und moderne Formen der Freundschaft: Eine andere Verortung von Gemeinschaft" (Feminism and Modern Forms of Friedship: Dislocating the Community). In Axel Honneth, ed., *Pathologien des Sozialen: Aufgaben der Sozialphilosophie,* pp. 184–204. Frankfurt am Main, 1994. English edition: In M. Friedman and P. Weiss, eds., *Feminism and Community.* Philadelphia, 1995.

————. *The Politics of Reality: Essays in Feminist Theory.* Trumansburg, N.Y., 1983.

Garber, Marjorie. *Verhüllte Interessen: Transvestitismus und kulturelle Angst* (Veiled Interests: Transvestitism and Cultural Fear). Frankfurt am Main, 1993.

Gatens, Moira. "Ethologische Körper: Geschlecht als Macht und Affekt" (Ethological Bodies: Gender as Power and Affect). In Marie-Luise Angerer, ed., *The Body of Gender: Körper, Geschlecht, Identitäten* (The Body of Gender: Bodies, Gender, Identities), pp. 35–52. Vienna, 1995.

————. *Imaginary Bodies: Ethics, Power and Corporeality.* London, 1996.

Gerhard, Ute. "Frauenbewegung in der Flaute?" (Is the Women's Movement Currently in a Lull?). *Transit.: Europäische Revue* (Transit.: A European Review) 10 (1995): 117–135.

————. "'Illegitime Töchter': Das komplizierte Verhältnis zwischen Feminismus und Soziologie" (Illegitimate Daughters: The Complex Relationship Between Feminism and Sociology). In Jürgen Friedrichs, M. Rainer Lepsius, and Karl Ulrich Mayer, eds., *Die Diagnosefähigkeit der Soziologie* (Sociology's Diagnostic Competence), pp. 343–382. Opladen, 1998.

————. "Maßstäbe für eine neue Verfassung: Über Freiheit, Gleichheit und die Würde der Frauen" (Standards for a New Constitution: On Freedom, Equality and the Dignity of Women). In Ulrich K. Preuß, ed., *Zum Begriff der Verfassung: Die Ordnung des Politischen* (On the Concept of Constitution: The Order of the Political), pp. 247–276. Frankfurt am Main, 1994.

Gildemeister, Regine, and Angelika Wetterer. "Wie Geschlechter gemacht werden" (How Genders are Made). In Gudrun-Axeli Knapp and Angelika Wetterer, eds., *Traditionen: Brüche* (Traditions: Ruptures), pp. 201–254. Freiburg, 1992.

Gilligan, Carol. *In a Different Voice: Psychological Theory and Women's Development.* Cambridge, Mass., 1982. German edition: *Die andere Stimme: Lebenskonflikte und Moral der Frau.* Munich, 1984.

Giuliani, Regula. "Körpergeschichten zwischen Modellbildung und haptischer Hexis: Thomas Laqueur und Barbara Duden" (Histories of the Body Between Model Construction and Haptic Hexis: Thomas Laqueur and Barbara Duden). In Silvia Stoller and Helmuth Vetter, eds., *Phänomenologie und Geschlechterdifferenz* (Phenomenology and Gender Difference), pp. 148–165. Vienna, 1997.

Goodfield, June. *An Imagined World.* New York, 1981.

Gössmann Elisabeth, ed. *Archiv für philosophie- und theologiegeschichtliche Frauenforschung* (Archive for Women's Studies in the History of Philosophy and Theology). Munich, 1984.

Grawe, Ch. "Kultur, Kulturphilosophie" (Culture, Cultural Philosophy). In *Historisches Wörterbuch der Philosophie* (Historical Dictionary of Philosophy), 4:1309–1324. Darmstadt, 1976.

Greenson, Ralph. "Disidentifying from Mother: Its Special Importance for the Boy." *International Journal of Psychoanalysis* 49 (1968).

Greer, Germaine. *The Female Eunuch.* London, 1970.

Grimshaw, Jean. *Feminist Philosophers: Women's Perspectives on Philosophical Traditions.* Brighton, 1986.

Grosz, Elizabeth. "Bodies and Knowledges: Feminism and the Crisis of Reason." In *Space, Time and Perversion: Essays on the Politics of Bodies,* pp. 25–44. New York, 1995.

———. "Nietzsche and the Stomach for Knowledge." In Paul Patton, ed., *Nietzsche, Feminism and Political Theory,* pp. 49–70. London, 1993.

———. "Sexual Difference and the Problem of Essentialism." In *Space, Time, and Perversion: Essays on the Politics of Bodies,* pp. 45–58. New York, 1995.

———. *Volatile Bodies: Toward a Corporeal Feminism.* Bloomington, 1994.

Grünell, Marianne, and Sawitri Saharso. "bell hooks and Nira Yuval-Davis on Race, Ethnicity, Class and Gender." *European Journal of Women's Studies* 6, no. 2 (1999): 203–218.

Gulyga, Arsenij. *Immanuel Kant.* Frankfurt am Main, 1981.

Haanstra, B. *Fressen und gefressen werden* (To Feed and to Be Fed). Vienna, 1982.

Hagemann-White, Carol. "Wir werden nicht zweigeschlechtlich geboren . . . " (We are not born as two sexes . . .). In Carol Hagemann-White and Maria A. Rerrich, eds., *Frauen-Männer-Bilder* (Women-Men-Images), pp. 224–235. Berlin, 1988.

Hammer, Felix. *Leib und Geschlecht: Philosophische Perspektiven von Nietzsche bis Merleau-Ponty und Phänomenologischer Aufriß* (Body and Gender: Philosophical Perspectives from Nietzsche to Merleau-Ponty and a Phenomenological Sketch). Bonn, 1974.

Haraway, Donna. "In the Beginning Was the Word: The Genesis of Biological Theory." *Signs: Journal of Women in Culture and Society* 6, no. 3 (1981): 469–481.

———. *Modest Witness at Second Millennium: Female Man Meets Onco Mouse.* New York, 1997.

———. "The Promises of Monsters: A Regenerative Politics for Inappropriate/d Others." In Lawrence Grossberg et al., eds., *Cultural Studies.* New York, 1992.

———. *Simians, Cyborgs, and Women: The Reinvention of Nature*. London, 1991. German edition: *Die Neuerfindung der Natur: Primaten, Cyborgs und Frauen*. Frankfurt am Main, 1995.

Harding, Sandra. "Feminism, Science, and the Anti-Enlightenment Critiques." In Linda Nicholson, ed., *Feminism/Postmodernism*. New York, 1990.

———. "Geschlechtsidentität und Rationalitätskonzeptionen: Eine Problemübersicht." In Elisabeth List and Herlinde Studer, eds., *Denkverhältnisse: Feminismus und Kritik* (Thinking Conditions: Feminism and Critique), pp. 425–453. Frankfurt am Main, 1989. English edition: "Is Gender a Variable in Conceptions of Rationality? A Survey of Issues." In Carol C. Gould, ed., *Beyond Domination*, pp. 43–63. Totowa, N.J., 1983.

———. *Is Science Multicultural? Postcolonialisms, Feminisms and Epistemologies*. Bloomington, 1998.

———. "Ist die westliche Wissenschaft eine Ethnowissenschaft?" (Is Western Science an Ethnoscience?). *Die Philosophin* (Woman Philosopher) 5, no. 9 (1994): 26–44.

——— "Rethinking Standpoint Epistemology: What Is Strong Objectivity?" In Alcoff Linda/Potter Elizabeth, eds. Feminist Epistemologies, Oxford, U.K./ Malden, Mass., 1999, pp. 49–82.

———. *The Science Question in Feminism*. Ithaca, N.Y., 1986. German edition: *Feministische Wissenschaftstheorie: Zum Verhältnis von Wissenschaft und sozialem Geschlecht*. Hamburg, 1990.

Hartsock, Nancy. "The Feminist Standpoint: Developing the Grounds for a Specifically Feminist Historical Materialism." In Sandra Harding and Merrill B. Hintikka, eds., *Discovering Reality: Feminist Perspectives on Epistemology, Methodology and Philosophy of Science*, pp. 283–310. Dordrecht, 1983.

———. *Money, Sex and Power*. Boston, 1985.

Haslanger, Sally. "On Being Objective and Being Objectified." In Louise M. Antony and Charlotte Witt, eds., *A Mind of One's Own: Feminist Essays on Reason and Objectivity*, pp. 85–126. Boulder, 1993.

Haug, Frigga. *Sexualisierung der Körper* (The Sexualization of Bodies). Hamburg, 1988.

Hausen, Karin. "Die Polarisierung der 'Geschlechtscharaktere': Eine Spiegelung der Dissoziation von Erwerbs- und Familienleben" (The Polarization of Gender Characters: A Reflection of the Dissociation of Domestic and Wage Labor). In Werner Conze, ed., *Sozialgeschichte der Familie in der Neuzeit Europas* (The Social History of the Family in Europe's Modern Times), pp. 363–393. Stuttgart, 1976.

Hausen, Karin, and Helga Nowotny, eds. *Wie männlich ist die Wissenschaft?* (How Masculine are the Sciences?). Frankfurt am Main, 1986.

Havelková, Hana. "Real existierender Feminismus" (Real Existing Feminism). *Transit*. 9 (1995): 146–158.

Hegel, Georg Wilhelm Friedrich. *Enzyklopädie der philosophischen Wissenschaften*, sec. 410, In *Werke in zwanzig Bänden*, ed. Eva Markus and Michel Karl Markus. Vol. 10. Frankfurt am Main, 1971. English edition: *Encyclopedia of the Philosophical Sciences*. Pt. 1. Indianapolis, 1991.

Heinz, Marion, and Sabine Doyé, eds. *Feministische Philosophie: Bibliographie, 1970–1995* (Feminist Philosophy: Bibliography, 1970–1995). Bielefeld, 1996.

Heinz, Marion, and Meike Nordmeyer. *Feministische Philosophie: Bibliographie, 1996–1997* (Feminist Philosophy: Bibliography, 1996–1997). Bielefeld, 1999.

Held, Virginia. *Feminist Morality: Transforming Culture, Society and Politics.* Chicago, 1993.

Hempel, C. G. "Wissenschaftliche und historische Erklärungen." In Hans Albert, ed., *Theorie und Realität* (Theory and Reality), pp. 237–262. Tübingen, 1972. English edition: "Explanation in Science and History." In William H. Dray, ed., *Philosophical Analysis and History*, pp. 95–126. New York, 1966.

Herman, Barbara. "Ob es sich lohnen könnte, über Kants Auffassungen von Sexualität und Ehe nachzudenken?" *Deutsche Zeitschrift für Philosophie* (German Journal of Philosophy) 43, no. 6 (1995): 964–966. English edition: "Could It Be Worth Thinking About Kant on Sex and Marriage?" In Louise M. Anthony and Charlotte Witt, eds., *A Mind of One's Own*, pp. 49–68. Boulder, 1993.

Higginbotham, Elizabeth, and Mary Romero, eds. *Women and Work: Exploring Race, Ethnicity and Class.* Thousand Oaks, Calif., 1997.

Hirschauer, Stefan. *Die soziale Konstruktion der Transsexualität* (The Social Construction of Transsexuality). Frankfurt am Main, 1993.

Holland-Cunz, Barbara. *Soziales Subjekt Natur: Natur- und Geschlechterverhältnis in emanzipatorischen politischen Theorien* (The Social Subject Nature: Nature and Gender Relations in Emancipatory Political Theories). Frankfurt am Main, 1994.

Holmstrom, Nancy. "Human Nature." In Alison M. Jaggar and Iris M. Young, eds., *A Companion to Feminist Philosophy*, pp. 280–288. Oxford, U.K., 1998.

Honegger, Claudia. *Die Ordnung der Geschlechter: Die Wissenschaften vom Menschen und das Weib* (The Order of the Sexes: Human Sciences and the Woman). Frankfurt am Main, 1991.

Honig, Elsa Fine. *Women and Art.* Montclair, N.J., 1978.

Honneth, Axel. "Der Affekt gegen das Allgemeine: Zu Lyotards Konzept der Postmoderne" (The Affect Against the Universal: On Lyotard's Concept of Postmodernity). *Merkur* 38, no. 8 (1984): 8.

_____. *Kampf um Anerkennung: Zur moralischen Grammatik sozialer Konflikte.* Frankfurt am Main, 1992. English edition: *The Struggle for Recognition: The Moral Grammar of Social Conflicts.* Cambridge, Mass., 1996.

Hooks, bell. *Killing Rage/Ending Sexism.* New York, 1995.

_____. *Talking Back: Thinking Feminist, Thinking Black.* Boston, 1989.

Horster, Detlef, ed. *Weibliche Moral: Ein Mythos?* (Feminine Morality: A Mythos?). Frankfurt am Main, 1998.

Husserl, Edmund. *Gesammelte Werke* (Collected Writings) (Husserliana). Vol. 4. The Hague, 1950–.

Irigaray, Luce. *Das Geschlecht, das nicht eins ist.* Berlin, 1979.

_____. *Ethik der sexuellen Differenz.* Frankfurt am Main, 1984. English edition: *An Ethics of Sexual Difference.* Ithaca, N.Y., 1993.

_____. "Is the Subject of Science Sexed?" *Hypatia* 2, no. 3 (1987).

_____. *Speculum: Spiegel des anderen Geschlechts.* Frankfurt am Main, 1980. English edition: *The Speculum of the Other Woman.* Ithaca, N.Y., 1985.

Jaggar, Alison M. "Feminist Ethics: Projects, Problems, Prospects." In Herta Nagl-Docekal and Herlinde Pauer-Studer, eds., *Denken der Geschlechterdifferenz: Neue Fragen und Perspektiven der Feministischen Philosophie* (Thinking Gender Difference: New Questions and Perspectives in Feminist Philosophy), pp. 143–172. Vienna, 1990.

———. *Feminist Politics and Human Nature.* Totowa, N.J., 1983.

———. "Love and Knowledge: Emotion in Feminist Epistemology." In Alison M. Jaggar and Susan R. Bordo, eds., *Feminist Reconstructions of Being and Knowing.* New Brunswick, N.J., 1989.

Jaggar, Alison M., and Susan R. Bordo. Introduction to *Gender/Body/Knowledge: Feminist Reconstructions of Being and Knowing,* pp. 1–12. New Brunswick, N.J., 1989.

Jaggar Alison M., and Iris Marion Young, eds. *A Companion to Feminist Philosophy.* Oxford, U.K., 1998.

Jardine, Alice, and Alice Smith, eds. *Men in Feminism.* New York, 1987.

Jauch, Ursula Pia. *Immanuel Kant zur Geschlechterdifferenz: Aufklärerische Vorurteilskritik und bürgerliche Geschlechtsvormundschaft* (Immanuel Kant on Gender Difference: Enlightenment Criticism of Bias and Bourgeois Paternalism). Vienna, 1988.

Jeffreys, Sheila. *Anticlimax.* London, 1989.

Kambartel, Friedrich. "Arbeit und Praxis" (Labor and Praxis). *Deutsche Zeitschrift für Philosophie* (German Journal of Philosophy) 41, no. 2 (1993): 239–250.

Kant, Immanuel. *Beobachtungen über das Gefühl des Schönen und Erhabenen.* In *Werke in sechs Bänden,* 1:825–886. Edited by Wilhelm Weischedel. Darmstadt, 1960. English edition: *Observations on the Feeling of the Beautiful and Sublime.* Translated by John T. Goldwait. Berkeley, Calif., 1965.

———. *Die Metaphysik der Sitten.* In *Werke in sechs Bänden,* 4:309–636. Darmstadt, 1960. English edition: *The Metaphysics of Morals.* Translated by Mary Gregor. Cambridge, 1991.

———. *Grundlegung zur Metaphysik der Sitten.* In *Werke in sechs Bänden,* 4:11–106. Darmstadt, 1960. English edition: *Groundwork of the Metaphysics of Morals.* Translated by Mary Gregor. Cambridge, 1998.

———. *Kritik der Urteilskraft.* In *Werke in sechs Bänden,* 5:237–622. Darmstadt, 1960. English edition: *The Critique of Judgment.* Translated by James Creed Meredith. Oxford, U.K., 1952.

———. *Logik: Ein Handbuch zu Vorlesungen* (Logic: A Handbook for Lectures), sec. 81. In *Werke in sechs Bänden,* 3:421–586. Darmstadt, 1960.

———. *Zum ewigen Frieden.* In *Werke in sechs Bänden,* 6:195–254. Darmstadt, 1960. English edition: "To Perpetual Peace: A Philosophical Sketch." In *Perpetual Peace and Other Essays.* Translated by Ted Humphrey. Indianapolis, 1985.

Kaplan, Morris B. *Intimacy and Equality: The Question of Lesbian and Gay Marriage.* Stony Brook, N.Y., 1993.

———. *Sexual Justice: Democratic Citizenship and the Politics of Desire.* New York, 1997.

Keller, Evelyn Fox. *Liebe, Macht und Erkenntnis: Männliche oder weibliche Wissenschaft?* Munich, 1986. English edition: *Reflections on Gender and Science.* New Haven, 1985.

Klinger, Cornelia. "Bis hierher und wie weiter? Überlegungen zur feministischen Wissenschafts- und Rationalitätskritik" (Up to Here and Where to Now? Reflections on the Feminist Critique of Science and Rationality). In Marianne Krüll, ed., *Wege aus der männlichen Wissenschaft: Perspektiven feministischer Erkenntnistheorie* (Ways Out of Masculine Science: Perspectives of Feminist Epistemology), pp. 21–56. Pfaffenweiler, 1990.

———. "Das Bild der Frau in der patriarchalen Philosophiegeschichte: Eine Auswahlbibliographie" (The Image of the Woman in the Patriarchal History of Philosophy: A Selected Bibliography). In Herta Nagl-Docekal, ed., *Feministische Philosophie* (Feminist Philosophy), pp. 244–276. Vienna, 1990.

———. "Frau-Landschaft-Kunstwerk: Gegenwelten oder Reservoire des Patriarchats?" In Herta Nagl-Docekal, ed., *Feministische Philosophie* (Feminist Philosophy), pp. 63–94. Vienna, 1990. English edition: "Woman-Landscape-Artwork: Alternative Realms or Patriarchal Reserves?" In Herta Nagl-Docekal and Cornelia Klinger, eds., *Continental Philosophy in Feminist Perspective: Re-Reading the Canon in German,* pp. 147–174. University Park, Pa., 2000.

———. "Periphere Kooptierung: Neue Formen der Ausgrenzung feministischer Kritik—Ein Gespräch mit Cornelia Klinger" (Peripheral Cooptation: New Patterns of Marginalization—A Conversation with Cornelia Klinger). *Die Philosophin* (Woman Philosopher) 9, no. 18 (1998): 95–107.

———. "Von der Kritik an der 'ästhetischen Ideologie' über 'cunt art' und 'écriture féminine' zum Diskussionsstand einer feministischen Ästhetik heute" (From the Critique of the Aesthetic Ideology through Cunt Art and Écriture Féminine to the Current State of Feminist Aesthetics). *Deutsche Zeitschrift für Philosophie* (German Journal of Philosophy) 46, no. 5 (1998): 799–822.

Koertge, Noretta. "Feminist Epistemology: Stalking an Un-Dead-Horse." In Paul R. Gross et al., eds., *The Flight from Science and Reason.* Annals of the New York Academy of Sciences, vol. 775. New York, 1996.

Krebs, Angelika. "Eine feministische Stellungnahme zu Kambartels 'Arbeit und Praxis'" (A Feminist Response to Kambartel's Labor and Praxis). *Deutsche Zeitschrift für Philosophie* (German Journal of Philosophy) 41, no. 2 (1993): 251–256.

———. "Kann denn Liebe Arbeit sein?" (Can Love Be Labor?). In Peter Koller and Klaus Puhl, eds., *Current Issues in Political Philosophy: Justice in Society and World Order,* pp. 253–260. Vienna, 1997.

Kreisky, Eva, and Birgit Sauer. "Geschlechterverhältnisse im Kontext politischer Transformation" (Gender Relations in the Context of Political Transformation). *Politische Vierteljahresschrift* (Political Quarterly) 38, no. 28 (1997): 9-49.

Kristeva, Julia. *Die Chinesin.* Frankfurt am Main, 1982. English edition: "About Chinese Women." In Moi Toril, ed., *The Kristeva Reader,* pp. 138–159. New York, 1986.

———. *Die Revolution der poetischen Sprache.* Frankfurt am Main, 1978. English edition:: *Revolution in Poetic Language.* New York, 1984.

———. "Kein weibliches Schreiben? Fragen an Julia Kristeva" (No Feminine Writing? Some Questions for Julia Kristeva). Interview with R. Rossum-Guyon. *Freibeuter* (Pirate) 2 (1979): 79–84.

———. "La femme, ce n'ést jamais ça." Interview with Jacqueline Rose. *Polylogue* (Paris), 1977, pp. 517–524.

———. "Maternité selon Giovanni Bellini." *Polylogue* (Paris), 1977.

———. *Soleil noir: Dépression et mélancolie.* Paris, 1987.

———. "Stabat mater." In *Geschichten von der Liebe*, pp. 226–255. Frankfurt am Main, 1989. English edition: "Stabat Mater." In Moi Toril, ed., *The Kristeva Reader*, pp. 160–186. New York, 1986.

Krüger, Hans-Peter. *Zwischen Lachen und Weinen: Das Spektrum menschlicher Phänomene* (Between Loughing and Crying: The Spectrum of Human Phenomena). Berlin, 1999.

Kruks, Sonia. "Existentialism and Phenomenology." In Alison M. Jaggar and Iris M. Young, eds., *A Companion to Feminist Philosophy*, pp. 66–74. Oxford, U.K., 1998.

Krumholz, Linda, and Estella Lauter. "Annotated Bibliography on Feminist Aesthetics in the Visual Arts." *Hypatia* 5, no. 2 (1990): 158–172.

Kulke, Christine. "Die Politik instrumenteller Rationalität und die instrumentelle Rationalität von Politik: Eine Dialektik des Geschlechterverhältnisses?" (The Politics of Instrumental Rationality and the Instrumental Rationality of Politics: A Dialectic of Gender Relations?). In Herta Nagl-Docekal and Herlinde Pauer-Studer, eds., *Denken der Geschlechterdifferenz: Neue Fragen und Perspektiven der Feministischen Philosophie* (Thinking Gender Difference: New Questions and Perspectives of Feminist Philosophy), pp. 71–88. Vienna, 1990.

———. "Rationalität der Rationalisierung: Eine Rechtfertigung der Geschlechterpolitik" (The Rationality of Rationalization: A Justification of Gender Politics). In Christine Kulke and Elvira Scheich, eds., *Zwielicht der Vernunft: Die Dialektik der Aufklärung aus der Sicht von Frauen* (Twilight of Reason: The Dialectic of Enlightenment from the Perspective of Women), pp. 59–70. Pfaffenweiler, 1992.

———. "Von der instrumentellen zur kommunikativen Rationalität patriarchaler Herrschaft" (From the Instrumental to the Communicative Rationality of Patriarchal Domination). In *Rationalität und sinnliche Vernunft: Frauen in der patriarchalen Realität* (Rationality and Sensual Reason: Women in Patriarchal Reality), pp. 55–70. Pfaffenweiler, 1988.

Kuster, Friederike. "Ortschaften: Luce Irigarays Ethik der sexuellen Differenz" (Places: Luce Irigaray's Ethics of Sexual Difference). In Ernst Wolfgang Orth and Karl-Heinz Lembeck, eds., *Phänomenologische Forschung: Neue Folge* (Phenomenological Research: New Series) 1:44–66. Freiburg, 1996.

Kymlicka, Will. *Contemporary Political Philosophy: An Introduction.* Oxford, 1990.

Landweer Hilge. "Fühlen Männer anders? Überlegungen zur Konstruktion von Geschlecht durch Gefühle" (Do Men Feel Differently? Reflections on the Construction of Gender Through Emotions). In Silvia Stoller and Helmuth Vetter, eds., *Phänomenologie und Geschlechterdifferenz* (Phenomenology and Gender Difference), pp. 249–273. Vienna, 1997.

———. "Generativität und Geschlecht: Ein blinder Fleck in der sex/gender-Debatte" (Generativity and Gender: A Blind Spot in the Sex/Gender Debate). In Theresa Wobbe and Gesa Lindemann, eds., *Denkachsen: Zur theoretischen und in-*

stitutionellen Rede vom Geschlecht (Axes of Thought: On the Theoretical and In-stitutional Language About Gender), pp. 147–176. Frankfurt am Main, 1994.

————. "Geschlechterklassifikation und historische Deutung" (Classification of Gender and Historical Interpretation). In Klaus E. Müller and Jörn Rüsen, eds., *Historische Sinnbildung* (Historical Interpretation), pp. 142–164. Reinbek bei Hamburg, 1997.

————. "Kritik und Verteidigung der Kategorie Geschlecht: Wahrnehmungs- und symboltheoretische Überlegungen zur sex/gender-Unterscheidung" (Critique and Defense of the Category Gender: Reflections on the Perceptional and Sym-bolical Aspects of the Sex/Gender Distinction). *Feministische Studien* 2 (1993): 34–43.

Laqueur, Thomas. *Auf den Leib geschrieben: Die Inszenierung der Geschlechter von der Antike bis Freud*. Frankfurt am Main, 1992. English edition: *Making Sex: Body and Gender from the Greeks to Freud*. Cambridge, Mass., 1990.

Lauter, Estella. "Re-enfranchising Art: Feminist Interventions in the Theory of Art." *Hypatia* 5, no. 2 (1990): 91–106.

Leibniz, Gottfried Wilhelm. *Monadologie*. Jena, 1720.

Leland, Dorothy. "Lacanian Psychoanalysis and French Feminism." In Nancy Fraser and Sandra Lee Bartky, eds., *Revaluing French Feminism: Critical Essays on Dif-ference, Agency, and Culture,* pp. 113–135. Bloomington, 1992.

Lennon, Kathleen, and Margaret Whitford, eds. *Knowing the Difference: Feminist Perspectives in Epistemology*. New York, 1994.

Lindemann, Gesa. "Zeichentheoretische Überlegungen zum Verhältnis von Körper und Leib" (Sign-theoretical Reflections on the Relationship of Body and Lived Body). In Annette Barkhaus et al., eds., *Identität, Leiblichkeit, Normativität: Neue Horizonte anthroplogischen Denkens* (Identity, Corporeality, Normativity: New Horizons of Anthropological Thought), pp. 146–175. Frankfurt am Main, 1996.

Lindner, Ines, et al., eds. *Blick-Wechsel: Konstruktionen von Männlichkeit und Weib-lichkeit in Kunst und Kunstgeschichte* (Exchanging Glances: Constructions of Masculinity and Femininity in Art and Art History). Berlin, 1989.

List, Elisabeth. "Schmerz: Der somatische Signifikant im Sprechen des Körpers" (Pain: The Somatic Signifier in the Speech of the Body). In Jörg Huber and Alois Martin Müller, eds., *Die Wiederkehr des Anderen* (The Return of the Other), pp. 223–244. Basel, 1996.

————. "Schmerz: Selbsterfahrung und Grenzerfahrung" (Pain: Experiencing the Self and Its Limits). In Maria Wolf et al., eds., *Körper/Schmerz: Intertheoretische Zugänge* (Body/Pain: Intertheoretical Approaches), pp 143–160. Innsbruck, 1998.

————. "Theorieproduktion und Geschlechterpolitik: Prolegomena zu einer femi-nistischen Theorie der Wissenschaften" (Theory Production and Gender Politics: Prolegomena to a Feminist Theory of the Sciences). In Herta Nagl-Docekal, ed., *Feministische Philosophie* (Feminist Philosophy), pp. 158–183. Vienna, 1990. 2nd ed., 1994.

Lloyd, Elisabeth A. "Objectivity and the Double Standard for Feminist Epistemolo-gies." *Synthese* 104 (1955).

Lloyd, Genevieve. *Das Patriarchat der Vernunft: "Männlich" und "weiblich" in der westlichen Philosophie*. Bielefeld, 1985. English edition: *The Man of Reason: "Male" and "Female" in Western Philosophy*. Minneapolis, 1984.

———. "Rationality." In Alison M. Jaggar and Iris M. Young, eds., *A Companion to Feminist Philosophy*, pp. 165–172. Oxford, U.K., 1998.

Löffler, Winfried, and Edmund Runggaldier, eds. *Vielfalt und Konvergenz der Philosophie: Vorträge des V. Kongresses der Österreichischen Gesellschaft für Philosophie* (Plurality and Convergency in Philosophy: Papers of the Fifth Congress of the Austrian Society for Philosophy). Vienna, 1999.

Lomperis, Linda, and Sarah Stanbury, eds. *Feminist Approaches to the Body in Medieval Literature*. University Park, Pa., 1993.

Longino, Helen. *Science as Social Knowledge: Values and Objectivity in Scientific Inquiry*. Princeton, N.J., 1990.

———. "Subjects, Power, and Knowledge: Description and Prescription in Feminist Philosophy of Science." In Linda Alcoff and Elizabeth Potter, eds. Feminist Epistemologies, pp. 101–120. Oxford, U.K., 1999.

Lorde, Audry. *Sister Outsider*. Trumansburg, N.Y., 1984.

Lorenz, Konrad. *Das sogenannte Böse: Zur Naturgeschichte der Aggression* (The So-Called Evil: On the Natural History of Aggression). Vienna, 1963.

Lorey, Isabell. "Der Körper als Text und das aktuelle Selbst: Butler und Foucault" (The Body as Text and the Actual Self: Butler and Foucault). *Feministische Studien* (Feminist Studies) 2 (1993): 10–23.

Lyotard, Jean-François. "Das Erhabene und die Avantgarde" (The Sublime and the Avant-Garde). In Jacques LeRider and Gérard Raulet, eds., *Verabschiedung der (Post-)Moderne* (Dismissing [Post-]Modernity), pp. 251–274. Tübingen, 1987.

MacKinnon, Catharine A. "Geschlechtergleichheit: Über Differenz und Herrschaft." In Herta Nagl-Docekal and Herlinde Pauer-Studer, eds., *Politische Theorie: Differenz und Lebensqualität,* pp. 140–173. Frankfurt am Main, 1996. English edition: "Sex Equality: On Difference and Dominance." In *Toward a Feminist Theory of the State*. Cambridge, Mass., 1989.

———. *Nur Worte*. Frankfurt am Main, 1993. English edition: *Only Words*. Cambridge, Mass., 1993.

Maihofer, Andrea. *Geschlecht als Existenzweise* (Gender as a Mode of Existence). Frankfurt am Main, 1995.

Mainardi, Patricia. "Quilts: The Great American Art." In Norma Broude and Mary D. Garrard, eds., *Feminism and Art History: Questioning the Litany*. New York, 1982.

Maiworm, Angelika. *Räume, Zeiten, viele Namen: Ästhetik als Kritik der Weiblichkeit* (Spaces, Times, Multiple Names: Aesthetics as Critique of Femininity). Weingarten, 1984.

Mann, Patricia. *Micropolitics: Agency in a Postfeminist Era*. Minneapolis, 1994.

Margolis, Joseph. "Reconciling Analytic and Feminist Philosophy and Aesthetics." In Peggy Zeglin and Carolyn Korsmeyer, eds., *Feminism and Tradition in Aesthetics*. University Park, Pa., 1995.

———. "Reinterpreting Interpretation." *Journal of Aesthetics and Art Criticism* 47 (1989).

Marks, Elaine, and Isabelle de Courtivron, eds. *New French Feminisms: An Anthology.* New York, 1981.

———. "Why This Book?" In *New French Feminisms: An Anthology,* pp. IX-XIII. New York, 1981.

Marshall, T. H. *Class, Citizenship and Social Development.* New York, 1964.

Maruani, Margaret. "Die gewöhnliche Diskriminierung auf dem Arbeitsmarkt" (The Common Discrimination on the Labor Market). In Irene Dölling and Beate Krais, eds., *Ein alltägliches Spiel: Geschlechterkonstruktion in der sozialen Praxis* (An Everyday Game: Constructions of Gender in Social Praxis), pp. 48–72. Frankfurt am Main, 1997.

Matisons, Michelle Renée. "The New Feminist Philosophy of the Body: Haraway, Butler, and Brennan." *European Journal of Women's Studies* 5, no. (1998): 9–34.

Mattick, Paul, Jr. "Beautiful and Sublime: 'Gender Totemism' in the Constitution of Art." In Peggy Zeglin and Carolyn Korsmeyer, eds., *Feminism and Tradition in Aesthetics,* pp. 27–48. University Park, Pa., 1995.

Maurer, Susanne. *Zwischen Zuschreibung und Selbstgestaltung: Feministische Identitätspolitik* (Between Attribution and Self-Formation: Feminist Identity Politics). Tübingen, 1996.

McDowell, John. "Zwei Arten von Naturalismus" (Two Types of Naturalism). *Deutsche Zeitschrift für Philosophie* (German Journal of Philosophy) 45, no. 5 (1997): 687–710.

McNay, Lois. "The Foucauldian Body and the Exclusion of Experience." *Hypatia* 6, no. 3 (1991): 125–139.

Merleau-Ponty, Maurice. *Phänomenologie der Wahrnehmung.* Berlin, 1966. English edition: *The Phenomenology of Perception.* London, 1962.

Meyer, Ursula I., and Heidemarie Bennent-Vahle, eds. *Philosophinnen Lexikon* (Encyclopedia of Women Philosophers). 2nd ed. Aachen, 1996.

Meyers, Diana T. "The Subversion of Women's Agency in Psychoanalytic Feminism: Chodorow, Flax, Kristeva." In Nancy Fraser and Sandra Lee Bartky, eds., *Revaluing French Feminism: Critical Essays on Difference, Agency, and Culture,* pp. 136–161. Bloomington, 1992.

Millet, Kate. *Sexual Politics.* New York, 1970.

Minow, Martha, "Equalities." *Journal of Philosophy* 88, no. 4 (1991): 633–644.

Mitchell, Juliet. *Psychoanalysis and Feminism: Freud, Reich, Laing and Women.* New York, 1975.

Mitterauer, Michael. "Diktat der Hormone? Zu den Bedingungen geschlechtstypischen Verhaltens aus historischer Sicht" (Dictate of the Hormons? The Preconditions of Gender Typical Behavior from a Historical Perspective). In Hubert Ch. Ehalt, ed., *Zwischen Natur und Kultur: Zur Kritik biologistischer Ansätze* (Between Nature and Culture: A Critique of Biologistic Approaches), pp. 63–92. Vienna, 1985.

Moi, Toril. *Sexus, Text, Herrschaft.* Bremen, 1988. English edition: *Sexual/Textual Politics: Feminist Literary Theory.* London, 1985.

Moi, Toril, ed. *French Feminist Thought: A Reader.* Oxford, 1988.

Mouffe, Chantal. "Für eine anti-essentialistische Konzeption feministischer Politik" (For an Anti-Essentialist Politics). *Deutsche Zeitschrift für Philosophie* (German Journal of Philosophy) 46, no. 5 (1998: 841–848.

Nabakowski, G., H. Sander, and P. Gorsen, eds., *Frauen in der Kunst* (Women in Art). Vol. 2. Frankfurt am Main, 1980.

Nagl-Docekal, Herta. "Anknüpfungen und Einsprüche: Ein Versuch, auf sehr unterschiedliche Kommentare zur Feministischen Philosophie einzugehen" (Picking Up and Objecting. An Attempt to Respond to Some Very Different Comments on Feminist Philosophy). *Ethik und Sozialwissenschaften* (Ethics and The Social Sciences) 3, no. 4 (1992): 577–592.

_____. "Bericht: Feministische Ethik" (Report: Feminist Ethics). *Information Philosophie* 2 (1995): 24–31.

_____. "Das heimliche Subjekt Lyotards" (The Hidden Subject in Lyotard). In Manfred Frank, Gerard Raulet, and Willem von Reijen, eds., *Die Frage nach dem Subjekt* (The Issue of the Subject), pp. 230–246. Frankfurt am Main, 1987.

_____. *Die Objektivität der Geschichtswissenschaft* (The Objectivity of the Historical Sciences). Vienna, 1992.

_____. "Ein Postskriptum zum Begriff 'Gerechtigkeitsethik'" (A Postscript on the Concept 'Ethics of Justice'). In Detlef Horster, ed., *Weibliche Moral: Ein Mythos?* (Feminine Morality: A Mythos?), pp. 142–153. Frankfurt am Main, 1998.

_____. "Feministische Ethik oder eine Theorie weiblicher Moral?" (Feminist Ethics or a Theory of Feminine Morality?). In Detlef Horster, ed., *Weibliche Moral: ein Mythos?* (Feminine Morality: A Mythos?), pp. 42–72. Frankfurt am Main, 1998.

_____. "Feministische politische Theorie: Ergebnisse und aktuelle Probleme" (Feminist Political Theory: Results and Current Issues). In Peter Koller and Klaus Puhl, eds., *Current Issues in Political Philosophy: Justice in Society and World Order*, pp. 236–252. Vienna, 1997.

_____. "Für eine geschlechtergeschichtliche Perspektivierung der Historiographiegeschichte" (Rewriting the History of Historiography From a Gender-Historical Perspective). In Wolfgang Küttler, Jörn Rüsen, and Ernst Schulin, eds., *Geschichtsdiskurs.* Vol. 1, *Grundlagen und Methoden der Historiographiegeschichte* (Discourse on History, Vol. 1, Foundations and Methods of the History of Historiography), pp. 233–256. Frankfurt am Main, 1993.

_____. "Rezension zu Judith Butler, 'Das Unbehagen der Geschlechter'" (Review of Judith Butler, "Gender Trouble"). *L'Homme: Zeitschrift für Feministische Geschichtswissenschaft* (L'Homme: Journal of Feminist History) 4, no. 1 (1993): 141–147.

_____. "Von der feministischen Transformation der Philosophie" (On the Feminist Transformation of Philosophy). *Ethik und Sozialwissenschaften* (Ethics and the Social Sciences), 3, no. (1992): 523–531.

_____. "Was ist feministische Philosophie?" (What is Feminist Philosophy?). In *Feministische Philosophie* (Feminist Philosophy), pp. 7–38. Vienna, 1990.

Nelson, Jack, and Lynn Hankinson Nelson. "No Rush to Judgment." *Monist* 77, no. 4 (1994): 486–508.

Nelson, Lynn Hankinson. "Epistemological Communities." In Linda Alcoff and Elizabeth Potter, eds., *Feminist Epistemologies,* pp. 121–160. Oxford, U.K., 1999.

_____. *Who Knows: From Quine to a Feminist Empiricism.* Philadelphia, 1990.

Newman, Barnett. "The Sublime Is Now." In *Selected Writings and Interviews,* edited by John P. O'Neill. New York, [1948] 1990.

Ngang-Ling Chow, Esther, et al., eds., *Race, Class and Gender: Common Bonds, Different Voices.* Thousand Oaks, Calif., 1996.

Nicholson, Linda. "Was heißt 'gender'?" (What is the Meaning of "Gender"?). In Institut für Sozialforschung (Institute of Social Research), ed., *Geschlechterverhältnisse und Politik* (Gender Relations and Politics), pp. 188–220. Frankfurt am Main, 1994.

Nierhaus, Irene. *Raum, Geschlecht, Architektur* (Space, Gender, Architecture). Sonderzahl, 1999.

Nochlin, Linda. "Why Have There Been No Great Women Artists?" In Thomas B. Hess and Elizabeth C. Baker, eds., *Art and Sexual Politics.* New York, 1973.

Nussbaum, Martha. "Menschliches Tun und soziale Gerechtigkeit: Zur Verteidigung des Aristotelischen Essentialismus" (Human Agency and Social Justice: A Defense of the Aristotelian Essentialism). In Micha Brumlik and Hauke Brunkhorst, eds., *Gemeinschaft und Gerechtigkeit* (Community and Justice), pp. 323–360. Frankfurt am Main, 1993.

———. Review of Louise M. Antony and Charlotte Witt, eds., *A Mind of One's Own: Feminist Essays on Reason and Objectivity. Times Literary Supplement* 41, no. 17 (1994).

Nye, Andrea. *Philosophy and Feminism at the Border.* New York, 1995.

———. *Words of Power: A Feminist Reading of the History of Logic.* New York, 1990.

Oakley, Ann. *Sex, Gender and Society.* London, 1972.

Okin, Susan Moller. *Justice, Gender and the Family.* New York, 1989.

Oliver, Kelly. "Julia Kristeva's Feminist Revolutions." *Hypatia* 8, no. 3 (1993): 94–114.

O'Neill, Onora. "Einverständnis und Verletzbarkeit: Eine Neubewertung von Kants Begriff der Achtung für Personen." In Herta Nagl-Docekal and Herlinde Pauer-Studer, eds., *Jenseits der Geschlechtermoral: Beiträge zur Feministischen Ethik,* pp. 335–368. Frankfurt am Main, 1993. English edition: "Between Consenting Adults." *Philosophy and Public Affairs* 14, no. 3 (1985).

Parzer, Elisabeth C. "Was kommt nach der modernen Rationalität?" (What Comes After Modern Rationality?). *Die Philosophin* (Woman Philosopher) 5, no. 9 (1994): 59–72.

Pateman, Carole. "Feminismus und Ehevertrag." In Herta Nagl-Docekal and Herlinde Pauer-Studer, eds., *Politische Theorie: Differenz und Lebensqualität* (Political Theory: Difference and the Quality of Life), pp. 174–222. Frankfurt am Main, 1996. English edition: "Feminism and the Marriage Contract." In *The Sexual Contract,* pp. 154–188. New York, 1988.

———. "God Hath Ordained to Man a Helper: Hobbes, Patriarchy and Conjugal Right." In Mary Shanley et al., eds., *Feminist Interpretations and Political Theory.* University Park, Pa., 1991.

———. *The Sexual Contract.* Stanford, 1988.

Pauer-Studer, Herlinde. "Der Begriff der Person in der feministischen Ethik-Debatte" (The Concept Person in the Feminist Debate on Ethics. In Dieter Sturma, ed., *Person: Philosophiegeschichte-Theoretische Philosophie-Praktische Philosophie*

(Person: History of Philosophy-Theoretical Philosophy-Practical Philosophy), pp. 377–400. Paderborn, 2001.

_____. "Staatsbürgerstatus und feministische Kritik" (Citizen Status and Feminist Critique). In Matthias Kaufmann, ed., *Integration oder Toleranz? Minderheiten als philosophisches Problem* (Integration or Tolerance? Minorities as a Philosophical Problem), pp. 290–301, Freiburg, 2001.

Pechriggl, Alice. *Utopiefähigkeit und Veränderung: Der Zeitbegriff und die Möglichkeit kollektiver Autonomie* (Utopian Competency and Change: The Notion of Time and the Possibility of Collective Autonomy). Pfaffenweiler, 1993.

Phillips, Anne. *The Politics of Presence.* Oxford, 1995.

Pieper, Annemarie. *Aufstand des stillgelegten Geschlechts: Einführung in die feministische Ethik* (Revolt of the Pacified Sex: An Introduction to Feminist Ethics). Freiburg, 1993.

_____. *Gibt es eine feministische Ethik?* (Is There a Feminist Ethics?). Munich, 1998.

Pinnick, C. L. "Feminist Epistemology: Implications for Philosophy of Science." *Philosophy of Science* 61 (1994).

Plessner, Helmuth. *Die Stufen des Organischen und der Mensch* (The Steps of the Organic and the Human Being). Berlin, 1975.

_____. "Lachen und Weinen" (Loughing and Crying). In *Gesammelte Schriften VII: Ausdruck und menschliche Natur* (Collected Writings VII: Expression and Human Nature). Frankfurt am Main, 1982.

Plumwood, Val. *Feminism and the Mastery of Nature.* London, 1993.

Pollock, Griselda. "Women, Art and Ideology: Questions for Art Historians." *Women's Studies Quarterly* 15, no. 1–2 (1987).

Postl, Gertrude. *Weibliches Sprechen: Feministische Entwürfe zu Sprache und Geschlecht* (Feminine Speaking: Feminist Sketches on Language and Gender). Vienna, 1991.

Putnam, Ruth Anna. "Why Not a Feminist Theory of Justice?" In Martha Nussbaum and Jonathan Glover, eds., *Women, Culture and Development: A Study of Human Capabilities,* pp. 298–331. Oxford, 1995.

Radcliffe, Janet Richards. "Why Feminist Epistemology Isn't." In Paul R. Gross et al., eds., *The Flight from Science and Reason.* Annals of the New York Academy of Sciences, 775:385–412. New York, 1996.

Rauschenbach, Brigitte. *Politische Philosophie und Geschlechterordnung: Eine Einführung* (Political Philosophy and the Order of the Sexes). Frankfurt am Main, 1998.

Rawls, John. "The Idea of Public Reason Revisited." *University of Chicago Law Review* 64, no. 3 (1997).

_____. *A Theory of Justice.* Cambridge, Mass., 1971.

Recki, Birgit. *Aura und Autonomie: Zur Subjektivität der Kunst bei Benjamin und Adorno* (Aura and Autonomy: On the Subjectivity of Art in Benjamin and Adorno). Würzburg, 1988.

Rensch, B. "Geschlechtlichkeit" ("Sexuality"). In *Historisches Wörterbuch der Philosophie* (Historical Dictionary of Philosophy), 3:443–444. Darmstadt, 1974.

Rhode, Deborah L. *Justice and Gender: Sexual Discrimination and the Law.* London, 1993.

Riley, Denise. *Am I That Name? Feminism and the Category of "Women" in History.* Minneapolis, 1988.

Rössler Beate. *Der Wert des Privaten* (The Value of Privacy). Frankfurt am Main, 2001.

Rössler, Beate, ed. *Quotierung und Gerechtigkeit: Eine moralphilosophische Kontroverse* (Quotation and Justice: A Moral-Philosophical Controversy). Frankfurt am Main, 1993.

Rooney, Phyllis. "Gendered Reason: Sex Metaphor and Conceptions of Reason." *Hypatia* 6, no. 2 (1991): 77–103.

Rose, Hilary. "Hand, Brain and Heart: A Feminist Epistemology for the Natural Sciences." *Signs: Journal of Women in Culture and Society* 9, no. 1 (1983): 73–90.

Rosenberg, Dorothy. "Distant Relations: Class, 'Race' and National Origin in the German Women's Movement." *Women's Studies International Forum* 19, no. 1–2 (1996).

Rosenberger, Sieglinde. *Geschlechter-Gleichheiten-Differenzen: Eine Denk- und Politikbeziehung* (Genders-Equalities-Differences: A Relation of Thought and Politics). Vienna, 1996.

_____. "Privatheit und Politik" (Privacy and Politics). In Eva Kreisky and Birgit Sauer, eds., *Geschlechterverhältnisse im Kontext politischer Transformation* (Gender Relations in the Context of Political Transformation). *Politische Vierteljahresschrift* (Political Quarterly) special issue 28 (1997): 120–136.

Rosser, Sue V. "Feminist Scholarship in the Sciences: Where Are We Now and When Can We Expect a Theoretical Breakthrough?" In Nancy Tuana, ed., *Feminism and Science*, pp. 3–16. Bloomington, 1989.

Rousseau, Jean-Jacques. *Emil oder über die Erziehung.* Paderborn, 1971. English edition: Emile or On Education. New York, 1979.

_____. *Vom Gesellschaftsvertrag oder Prinzipien des Staatsrechts.* In *Politische Schriften.* Vol. 1. Paderborn, 1964. English edition: "Of the Social Contract or Principles of Political Right." In *Of the Social Contract and Discourse on Political Economy.* New York, 1984.

Rullmann, Margit, ed. *Philosophinnen* (Women Philosophers). Vol. 1, *Von der Antike bis zur Aufklärung* (From Antiquity to Enlightenment); vol. 2, *Von der Romantik bis zur Moderne* (From the Romantic Era to Modernity). 2nd ed. Zürich, 1994.

Sandel, Michael. *Liberalism and the Limits of Justice.* Cambridge, Mass., 1982.

Sauer, Birgit. "Die Magd der Industriegesellschaft: Anmerkungen zur Geschlechtsblindheit von Staats- und Institutionentheorien" (The Maid of Industrial Society: Remarks on the Gender Blindness in Theories of the State and Institutions). In Brigitte Kerchner and Gabriele Wilde, eds., *Staat und Privatheit: Aktuelle Studien zu einem schwierigen Verhältnis* (State and Privacy: Current Studies on a Complex Relationship), pp. 29–54. Opladen, 1997.

Saurer, Edith. "Liebe, Geschlechterbeziehungen und Feminismus" (Love, Gender Relations and Feminism). *L'Homme: Zeitschrift für Feministische Geschichtswissenschaft* (L'Homme: Journal for Feminist History) 8, no. 1 (1997): 6–21.

Schaeffer-Hegel, Barbara, and Barbara Watson-Franke, eds. *Männer-Mythos-Wissenschaft: Grundlagentexte zur feministischen Wissenschaftskritik* (Men-Mythos-

Science: Fundamental Texts on the Feminist Critique of Science). Pfaffenweiler, 1988.

Scheich, Elvira, ed. *Vermittelte Weiblichkeit: Feministische Wissenschafts- und Gesellschaftstheorie* (Mediated Femininity: Feminist Theory of Science and Economy). Hamburg, 1996.

Schiebinger, Londa. *The Mind Has No Sex? Women in the Origins of Modern Science.* Cambridge, Mass., 1989.

Schlesier, Renate. *Mythos und Weiblichkeit bei Sigmund Freud* (Mythos and Femininity in Sigmund Freud). Frankfurt am Main, 1990.

Schmitz, Bettina. *Arbeit an den Grenzen der Sprache: Julia Kristeva* (Work at the Limits of Language: Julia Kristeva). Königstein, 1998.

_____. "Heimatlosigkeit oder symbolische Kastration? Subjektivität, Sprachgenese und Sozialität bei Julia Kristeva und Jacques Lacan" (Homelessness or Symbolic Castration? Subjectivity, Speech Genesis and Sociability in Julia Kristeva and Jacques Lacan). In Jan Beaufort and Peter Prechtl, eds., *Rationalität und Prärationalität* (Rationality and Prerationality), pp. 337–353. Würzburg, 1998.

Schmitz, Hermann. *System der Philosophie* (System of Philosophy). Vol. 11/1, *Der Leib* (The Lived Body). Bonn, 1965.

Schott, Robin May. "Immanuel Kant." In Alison M. Jaggar and Iris M. Young, eds., *A Companion to Feminist Philosophy*, pp. 39–48. Oxford, U.K., 1998.

Schott, Robin May, ed. *Feminist Interpretations of Immanuel Kant.* University Park, Pa., 1997.

Schröder, Hannelore. *Die Rechtlosigkeit der Frau im Rechtsstaat* (The Rightlessness of the Woman in the Constitutional State). Frankfurt am Main, 1979.

_____. "Olympe de Gouges, 'Erklärung der Rechte der Frau und Bürgerin' (1791): Ein Paradigma feministisch-politischer Philosophie" (Olympe de Gouges, Declaration of the Rights of the Woman and Citizen [1791]: A Paradigm Case of Feminist Political Philosophy). In Herta Nagl-Docekal, ed., *Feministische Philosophie* (Feminist Philosophy), pp. 202–228. Vienna, 1994.

Schwickert, Eva-Maria. "Carol Gilligans Moralkritik zwischen Universalismus und Kontextualismus" (Carol Gilligan's Critique of Morality Between Universalism and Contextualism). *Deutsche Zeitschrift für Philosophie* (German Journal of Philosophy) 42, no. 2 (1994): 255–274.

Seblatnig, Heidemarie. *Einfach den Gefahren ins Auge sehen: Künstlerinnen im Gespräch* (Simply Facing the Dangers: Women Artists in Conversation). Vienna, 1988.

Sehon, Scott R. "Okin on Feminism and Rawls." *Philosophical Forum* 27, no. 4 (1996).

Sen, Amartya. *Inequality Reexamined.* Cambridge, Mass., 1995.

_____. "More Than 100 Million Women Are Missing." *New York Review of Books* 37, no. 20 (1990).

Sevenhuijsen, Selma. *Citizenship and the Ethics of Care: Feminist Considerations on Justice, Morality and Politics.* London, 1998.

Sichtermann, Barbara. *Wer ist wie? Über den Unterschied der Geschlechter* (Who Is How? On Gender Difference). Berlin, 1987.

Simek, Ursula. "'Es ist die schönste Familie, die man sich denken kann': Die Familie als musikalische Akademie" (This Is the Finest Family One Can Think Of: The

Family as Musical Academy). In Hana Havelková, ed., *Gibt es ein mitteleuropäisches Ehe- und Familienmodell?* (Is There a Middle-European Model of Marriage and Family?), pp. 87–96. Prague, 1995.

Simmel, Georg. "Das Relative und das Absolute im Geschlechter-Problem" (The Relative and the Absolute in the Issue of the Sexes) [1911]. In *Schriften zur Philosophie und Soziologie der Geschlechter* (Writings on the Philosophy and Sociology of the Sexes), pp. 200–223, Frankfurt am Main, 1985.

Smith, Dorothy. "Women's Perspective as a Radical Critique of Sociology." *Sociological Inquiry* 44 (1974).

Spanier, Bonnie B. *Im/partial Science: Gender Ideology in Molecular Biology*. Bloomington, 1995.

Spelman, Elizabeth. *Inessential Woman: Problems of Exclusion in Feminist Thought*. Boston, 1988.

Stanton, Donna C. "Difference on Trial: A Critique of the Maternal Metaphor in Cixous, Irigaray, and Kristeva." In Allen Jeffner and Iris Marion Young, eds., *The Thinking Muse: Feminism and Modern French Philosophy*, pp. 156–179. Bloomington, 1989.

Stein, Edith. *Zum Problem der Einfühlung* (On the Problem of Empathy). Halle, 1917.

Stoller, Robert J. *Sex and Gender*. London, 1968.

Stoller, Silvia. "Merleau-Ponty im Kontext der feministischen Philosophie" (Merleau-Ponty in the Context of Feminist Philosophy). In Regula Giuliani, ed., *Merleau-Ponty und die Kulturwissenschaften* (Merleau Ponty and the Cultural Sciences), pp. 199–226. Munich, 2000.

Suchsland, Inge. *Julia Kristeva*. Frankfurt am Main, 1992.

Tanesini, Alessandra. *An Introduction to Feminist Epistemologies*. Oxford, U.K., 1999.

Taylor, Charles. "Aneinander vorbei: Die Debatte zwischen Liberalismus und Kommunitarismus." In Axel Honneth, ed., *Kommunitarismus: Eine Debatte über die moralischen Grundlagen moderner Gesellschaften* (Communitarianism: A Debate on the Moral Foundations of Modern Societies), pp. 103–130. Frankfurt am Main, 1993. English edition: "Cross-Purposes: The Liberal-Communitarian Debate." In Nancy L.Rosenblum, ed., *Liberalism and the Moral Life*, pp. 159–182. Cambridge, Mass., 1989.

Taylor, Charles, ed. *Multikulturalismus und die Politik der Anerkennung* (Multiculturalism and the Politics of Recognition). Frankfurt am Main, 1997.

"Third Wave Feminisms." *Hypatia* 12, no. 3 (1997).

Trettin, Käthe. "Is a Feminist Critique of Logic Possible?" In Herta Nagl-Docekal and Cornelia Klinger, eds., *Re-Reading the Philosophical Canon: Feminist Critique in German*, pp. 175–200. University Park, Pa., 2000.

Tuana, Nancy, ed. *Re-Reading the Canon: Feminist Interpretations of Plato (1994), Kant (1997), Hegel (1996), Foucault (1996) und Derrida (1997)*. University Park, Pa., 1998.

Waithe, Mary Ellen, ed. *A History of Women Philosophers*. Vols. 1–4. Dordrecht, 1989–.

Wallace, Claire. "Eine Westfeministin geht in den Osten" (A Western Feminist Goes East). *Transit*. 9 (1995): 129–145.

Wallach, Joan Scott. *Gender and the Politics of History.* New York, 1988.

Waniek, Eva. "(K)ein weibliches Schreiben" ([No] Feminine Writing). *Die Philosophin* (Woman Philosopher) 5 (1992): 45–59.

_____. *Hélène Cixous: Entlang einer Theorie der Schrift* (Hélène Cixous: Along a Theory of Writing). Vienna, 1993.

Weber, Jutta. "Sprechen wovon sich nicht sprechen läßt? Zum Naturbegriff in der aktuellen feministischen Debatte" (Speaking About What One Cannot Speak About?) *Feministische Studien* (Feminist Studies) 2 (1997): 109–120.

Weigel, Sigrid. "Die Verdoppelung des männlichen Blicks und der Ausschluß von Frauen aus der Literaturwissenschaft" (The Duplication of the Male Gaze and the Exclusion of Women from the Study of Literature). In Karin Hausen and Helga Nowotny Helga, eds., *Wie männlich ist die Wissenschaft?* (How Masculine Are the Sciences?), pp. 43–61. Frankfurt am Main, 1998.

Weir, Alison. "Identification with the Divided Mother: Kristeva's Ambivalence." In Oliver Kelly, ed., *Ethics, Politics and Difference in Julia Kristeva's Writing.* New York, 1993.

_____. *Sacrificial Logics: Feminist Theory and the Critique of Identity.* New York, 1996.

Weisshaupt, Brigitte. "Schatten über der Vernunft" (A Shadow over Reason). In Herta Nagl-Docekal, ed., *Feministische Philosophie* (Feminist Philosophy), pp. 136–157. Vienna, 1990.

Wellner, Uli. "Zur Biologie der Geschlechterdifferenzierung" (On the Biology of the Differentiation of the Sexes). In Heide Kellner, ed., *Geschlechtsunterschiede* (Gender Differences), pp. 93–126. Weinheim, 1979.

Welton, Donn, ed. *Body and Flesh: A Philosophical Reader.* Malden, Mass., 1998.

Wendell, Susan. *The Rejected Body: Feminist Philosophical Reflections on Disability.* New York, 1996.

Whelan, Imelda. *Modern Feminist Thought: From the Second Wave to "Post-Feminism."* New York, 1995.

White, Hayden. *Metahistory: Die historische Einbildungskraft im neunzehnten Jahrhundert in Europa.* Frankfurt am Main, 1991. English edition: *Metahistory: The Historical Imagination in Nineteenth-Century Europe.* Baltimore, 1973.

Whitford, Margaret. "Luce Irigaray's Critique of Rationality." In Morwenna Griffiths and Margaret Whitford, eds., *Feminist Perspectives in Philosophy,* pp. 109–130. London, 1988.

Wilkerson, Abby. "Ending at the Skin: Sexuality and Race in Feminist Theorizing." *Hypatia* 12, no. 3 (1997): 164–173.

Winnicot, Donald W. "Die Theorie von der Beziehung zwischen Mutter und Kind." In *Reifungsprozesse und fördernde Umwelt,* pp. 47–71. Frankfurt am Main, 1984. English edition: *The Maturational Process and the Facilitating Environment.* London, 1965.

Wolf, Susan. "Kommentar" (Commentary). In Charles Taylor, ed., *Multikulturalismus und die Politik der Anerkennung* (Multiculturalism and the Politics of Recognition), pp. 79–93 Frankfurt am Main, 1997.

Wolff, Janet. *Aesthetics and the Sociology of Art.* London, 1983.

Wolgast, Elizabeth H. *The Grammar of Justice.* Ithaca, N.Y., 1987.

"Women and Violence." *Hypatia* 11, no. 4 (1996).

Woolf, Virginia. *A Room of One's Own*. Cambridge, U.K., [1929] 1995.

Yeatman, Anna. "Jenseits des Naturrechts: Die Bedingungen für einen universalen Staatsbürgerstatus." In Herta Nagl-Docekal and Herlinde Pauer-Studer, eds., *Politische Theorie: Differenz und Lebensqualität* (Political Theory: Difference and the Quality of Life), pp. 315–349. Frankfurt am Main, 1996. English edition: "Beyond Natural Right: The Conditions of Universal Citizenship." In *Postmodern Revisionings of the Political*, pp. 57–79. New York, 1994.

Young, Iris Marion. "Five Faces of Oppression." In *Justice and the Politics of Difference*, pp. 39–65. Princeton, 1990. German edition: "Fünf Formen der Unterdrückung." In Herta Nagl-Docekal and Herlinde Pauer-Studer, eds., *Politische Theorie: Differenz und Lebensqualität* (Political Theory: Difference and the Quality of Life), pp. 99–139. Frankfurt am Main, 1996.

_____. *Justice and the Politics of Difference*. Princeton, 1990.

_____. "Werfen wie ein Mädchen: Eine Phänomenologie weiblichen Körperverhaltens, weiblicher Motilität und Räumlichkeit." *Deutsche Zeitschrift für Philosophie* (German Journal of Philosopphy) 41, no. 4 (1993): 707–726. English edition: "Throwing Like a Girl: A Phenomenology of Feminine Body Comportment, Motility, and Spatiality." In *Throwing Like a Girl and Other Essays in Feminist Philosophy and Social Theory*, pp. 141–159. Bloomington, 1990.

Yuval-Davis, Nira. "Mitglied einer Gemeinschaft oder vereinzeltes Individuum? Zur Citizenship-Debatte" (Community Memberor Isolated Individual? On the Citizenship Debate). *Das Argument* 39, no. 218 (1997): 59–70.

INDEX

Abilities, 16, 69
  See also Cultural abilities
Abjection of the other, 16
Action, 9, 11, 13, 16, 32
  behavior and, 4, 5–6
  decisionmaking and, 8
  moral, 6, 21
  norms and, 7
  not-acting and, 50
  responsible/immoral, 7
  sexist forms of, 85
  socio-technological, 115
Adorno, 85, 130
Aesthetics, viii, xviii, xx, 119, 121
  analytical/phenomenological
    approach to, 83, 84
  feminist, 41–42, 43, 45, 67, 73–85,
    92
  masculine connotations of, 81
  phenomenological, 83, 84
  philosophical, 73, 83, 158
  theory, 79, 85
Affirmative action, 136, 156
Allocation model, 3
Alternatives, 63, 69
Anal fantasy, 117
Analogies, 6
Anatomical theory, 35
Androcentrism, 23, 89, 91, 93–94, 106,
    121, 154, 158, 167

alternative to, 102–3
as bad science, 90
challenging, 95, 97, 98, 101, 109
ideologies of, 93
problem of, 103, 153
science and, 92
Androgyny, 44
Anthropology, philosophical, viii, xx,
    158
Antiessentialism, 100, 123
Anti-imperialist impulse, 126
Anti-Logos weapon, 67, 71
Antimasculinist impulse, 126
Appiah, Anthony, 149
Architecture, textiles and, 82–83
Argumentation, xx, xxi, 33, 42, 77, 82,
    88, 90, 99, 104, 106, 121, 140,
    145, 157, 169, 170
  binary thinking and, 16
  construtivist-inspired, 101
  feminist, 109
  in normative realm, 107–8
  philosophical terrain of, 28
  process of, 102, 107
Aristotle, xix, 7
Art
  applied, 43, 82
  asymmetry in, 42–43
  avant-garde, 74
  feminine, 67

237

feminist, 84, 85
gendered, 41–45
genuine, 43, 82
history, 42–43
masculinity and, 58
mediation and, 68
objectivity and, 80
philosophical analysis of, 80
politics and, 84
sublime and, 78
symbolic order and, 67
theories, 79
truth and, 78, 80
uterus, 67
women and, 42, 43, 48, 45, 56, 57,
    65, 83
Artists, 81
female, 43
Freud and, 45–58
historical situatedness of, 78
women, 56, 57, 83
Asymmetries, 45, 69, 99, 137, 145,
    152, 155, 162, 167
in art, 42–43
gender, xvii, 121, 153, 169
overcoming, xv, 2–3, 134
social, 140, 168, 170
Austin, speech/action and, 16
Autonomy, 122, 165
awareness of, 113
empowerment for, 160
interpretation of, 159
philosophical concept of, 160
self-determination and, 160
Avant la lettre (de Beauvoir), 39

Bacon, Francis, 110–11, 112
Baker, Victoria: on logic of definitions,
    149–50
Beautiful, sublime and, 74–75, 76, 77
Behavior, 37, 38, 50
action and, 4, 5–6
animal, 3, 4, 5
decisionmaking and, 4–5
detached, 87, 113, 129
dichotomous code of, 25
everyday, 131

expression and, 15
gender-specific, 23, 98–99, 129, 130
involuntary, 4, 6
masculine, 130, 132
moral, 6, 74, 76, 146
patterns of, 6, 8–9, 24, 129, 130,
    151
racist, 151
sexual, 13, 31, 34
social, 108
Being a body, having a body and, 12
Benhabib, Seyla, 79
Benjamin, Walter: on historiography, 43
Bennent, Heidemarie: on Rousseau, 161
Binary oppositions, 21, 118, 121
discrimination and, 15–18
feminist criticism of, 16, 17
theory of sexuality and, 120
Biochemical theory, 5, 35
Biological determinism, 3, 14, 44, 46,
    54
defending, 4–5
Biological features, 7, 13–14, 31
Biologism, 22, 23
Bisexuality, 25
Bluestocking, 88
Body, xx-xxi, 22
alternative description of, 33
as close object, 12
differences in, 11, 31, 33, 37
gendered, 11
girl's, 48–49
independent, 36–37
lived, 12, 20
male/female, 15, 26, 34
as physical body/lived body, 12
sentient, 12
Bourgeois, citoyen and, 165, 166
Bourgeois family model, 44, 66
Bourgeois society, 54, 162, 166
Butler, Judith, xx, 13–14, 28, 29, 130
antiessentialist motive of, 123
on discourse theory, 125
feminine identity and, 123
on Freud's theories, 14
on heterogeneity, 123
on heterosexuality, 33

on instrumental subject, 164
moral philosophy and, 122, 124
normative foundations and, 126–27
on social norms, 27
universalist tradition and, 124, 125

Cartesianism, 18–22
Castration, 50, 61, 62
   complex, 51, 52, 55
   mutual, 63
   punishment and, 52
Characterization, 16, 150
   sexual, 30, 50, 130, 164
Charpentier, Constance Marie, 42
Children, women and, 64, 155, 158
Chodorow, Nancy, 112, 113, 159
Citizenship, 33
   women and, 152–70
Citoyen, bourgeois and, 165, 166
Civil codes, 152
Civil law, 140
Civil rights, 33, 140, 163
Cixous, Hélène, xx, 70, 72, 120
   on artists, 68–69
   asymmetry and, 69
   critique by, 66
   on écriture féminine, 63, 64–65
   on equality, 67
   Lacan and, 59, 60, 61, 62, 66
   on oedipal phase, 61–62
   on phallogocentrism, 62
   symbolic order and, 59
Classical theory, 83
   feminist criticism of, 77, 78, 79
   interpretation of, 80
Clément, Catherine, 59
Clitoris, 52, 117
   apostrophized, 49
   masturbation, 56
   as penis-equivalent, 48
Code, Lorraine, 91
Cognition, 13, 19, 20, 21, 132
Cognitive subject, cognized object and,
   19
Cole, Eve Browning: on embodied self,
   20
Communication, 64, 80, 100, 102

Community, 158, 168
Conceptual continuity, 79
Conjugal relations, 111, 112
Constitution theory, 29, 31, 32, 35
Construction, 19–20, 31, 35, 90
Contextuality, science and, 103
Contract, 159
   feminism and, 157
   unjust, 137–38
Contract partners, 157–58, 160
Contract theory, 104, 156, 165, 169
   bourgeoisie and, 166
   contradictory evaluation of, 157
   implications of, 163
   patriarchal features of, 163–64
   point of departure for, 158–59
   reformulation of, 170
   women and, 161
Contractualism, 166, 168, 170
Cooking, cultural history of, 10
Corporeality, 24, 28, 29, 33, 35, 54, 63
   constructive design of, 36
   experienced, 12
   human, 38
   as issue of freedom, 9–15
   repression of, 132
   sexually differentiated, 22
   shaping/creation of, 30, 36
Creativity, 44, 85
   feminine form of, 58–73
   imaginary and, 63
Cult of the genius, deconstruction of,
   42, 78
Cultural abilities, 41, 45, 55, 59, 66, 67
   vagina-passivity-lack of, 57
   sexual drives and, 47, 68
Cultural imperialism, 123, 125, 144
Culture, 13, 103, 109, 114, 118
   alternative, 149
   diversity of, 25
   farming and, 36
   hegemonic, 149
   language and, 66
   masculinity and, 66
   nature and, 15, 27, 36, 39
   participation in, 69
   patriarchally structured, 93

phallus and, 70
women and, 9, 67

David, Jacques-Louis: Charpentier and, 42
De Beauvoir, Simone, 28, 39, 67
Decisionmaking, 122, 126, 159, 161
    action and, 4, 8
    behavior and, 4–5
    free, 136, 145
    political, xiv, 17
    process of, 102
Deconstruction, 42, 46, 78
De-differentiation, 109, 131
Definition
    logic of, 149–50
    power of, 122
De gustibus non est disputandum, 80
Democracy, 102, 156
    feminism and, 152
Derrida, Jacques, 16, 147, 165
    binary thinking and, 15
    on genders/sexuality, 24
    phallocentrism and, 61, 118
    on sexual difference, 25
De Saussure, 120, 165
Descartes, Rene, 18, 19, 20, 127
Development
    historical, 9, 79, 88
    identity, 24, 165
    infantile, 47, 49, 50, 51, 55, 61, 63, 68, 111, 113
    sexual, 47, 49, 68
Dichotomy, 18, 20, 37–38
Difference, 153, 154, 155
    acknowledgment of, 127
    biological, 9, 24
    corporeal, 11, 31, 33, 35, 37
    cultural sensitivity to, 148
    development of, 51
    ethics of, 147
    gender, 82, 87, 113, 114
    language and, 17
    opposition and, 25
    recognition of, xvi, 160, 169
    sexual, 30–31, 35, 37, 46, 56
Difference of the sexes, 27, 45, 73, 127
    biological, 23, 33, 98, 99, 138

feminist authors and, 58
    physical, 11, 26, 29, 57
Differentiation, 17, 32, 33, 38, 82
    language acquisition and, 66
    terminological, 77
    See also De-differentiation
Discourse, 19, 27, 28, 29
    ethics, 123, 125
    feminist, 20, 83
    philosophical, 97
    public, 122
    racial, 32
    scientific, 106
Discovery, 92, 104–5
Discrimination, 83, 90, 105, 107, 133, 137–43, 147, 150, 152–53, 155, 158, 167
    binary oppositions and, 15–18
    challenging, 1, 134–35, 139, 154, 156, 168, 170
    factual, 99
    feminist critique of, 15
    feminist we and, 151–52
    forms of, 17, 140, 142
    justice and, 169
    moral duty and, 140
    problem of, 139, 142, 148
    reverse, 169
    sex, xviii, 45, 142, 151, 153, 168, 170
Disenfranchisement, 115–16
Disinterested delight, 81, 85
Division of labor, 109, 127
    feminist rejection of, 8
    gendered, 129, 131, 162
    as given by nature/wanted by nature, 2
    moral, 146
    traditional, 64, 108, 153
Domestic domain, public domain and, 2
Domestic labor, 160, 162, 163
Dominance, 163
    challenging, 134
    patriarchal, 61, 88, 90, 110, 130, 164
Duden, Barbara, 12, 13
Duras, Colette, 62, 65
Duras, Marguerite, 62, 65

Duty
  inclination and, 131
  moral, 137, 140
Dworkin, justice and, 158

Economic decisions, feminist politics
  and, 134
Economic theory, 127, 134, 163
Écriture féminine, 59, 62, 64, 68, 72,
  73, 117
Education
  art, 42, 44
  equal access to, 152
  moral, 140
  women's, 33, 96, 128, 134
Egalitarian programs, 73, 127
Eia Mater, fons amoris, 72
Emile (Rousseau), 75, 77, 128
Emotions
  detached, 127–32
  reason and, 130, 131, 132
Engels, Friedrich, 162
Enlightenment, xvi, 2, 3, 126
  justice of, 107
  law of, 55
  philosophy of, 141, 158, 159
Environmental crisis, 112, 116
Epistemology, xviii, 28, 101, 102, 103,
  131, 132
  feminine, 146
  feminist, 91, 92, 94
  naturalized, 94
Equality, 96, 122, 130, 131, 145–46,
  156
  achieving, 157
  concept of, 126, 135–36, 169, 170
  political/juridicial conceptions of, 58
  women's liberation movement and,
  67
Equal rights, xiv, 89, 131, 145
Ernst, Waltraud: on social determinism,
  99
Erogenous zones, 48, 117
Essentialism, 58, 99, 139, 150
  feminist *we* and, 149
Ethics, xiv, xviii, 6, 21, 158
  discourse, 123, 125
  feminist, 131, 146, 147

Ethnocentrism, 94, 124, 125
Eurocentrism, 94, 144
Exclusionary mechanisms, 2, 45, 153
Expressions, 38
  behavior and, 15

Farming, culture and, 36
Felski, Rita, 85
Female body, ambiguity of, 118–19
Feminine, 65, 68, 69–70
  feminist and, 84
  rejection of, 73
Feminine care, masculine justice and,
  146
Femininity, 64, 72, 150
  ambiguity/ambivalence and, 122
  artistic creativity and, 59
  cliché, 69
  psychoanalysis and, 48
  sentimental design of, 127–28
Feminism, vii, xiv-xv, 67, 84, 123
  commitment to, 152
  contract and, 157
  democracy and, 152
  French, 59, 61, 73
  philosophy and, ix, xvii
  rejecting, xv, xvii
  science and, 89, 92
Feminist Art movement, 73
Feminist criticism, 9, 23, 60, 61, 67,
  70, 73, 74, 76, 77, 82, 87, 91, 94,
  95, 97, 99, 101, 106, 109, 116,
  117, 126, 127, 128, 129, 131,
  135, 136, 154
  asymmetry and, 162
  beginning of, 142
  contract partners and, 160
  core concern of, 1
  gender hierarchy and, 159–60
Feminist perspective, 81, 83, 85, 111,
  115, 132, 141, 155, 161
Feminist philosophy, vii-viii, xvi, 45, 73
  central issues of, viii, xviii-xix, 133
  definition of, xiii, xviii
  fighting off, xxi
  identification of, xx
  innovation of, xiv
  rejection of, xvii

Feminist politics, ix, 123, 135, 138–39,
    141–42
  challenge by, 134
  consequences for, 150
  goals of, 104
  labor law and, 155
  legislation/economic decisions and,
    134
  reasoning for, 169
  theory of, viii-ix, 133
Feminist project, 156, 159
Feminists, 83, 91, 130, 143, 157
  agenda, 78, 152
  feminine and, 84
  self-determination and, 160
Feminist theory, xvi, xix, 15, 38, 41, 57,
    82, 95, 113, 122, 135, 137,
    142–43, 155, 158, 165
  discrediting, xxi
  philosophical discourse and, 97
  psychoanalysis and, 59
  reevaluation of, xx
Feminist we, 141–52
  discrimination and, 151–52
  essentialism and, 149
  oppression and, 150
Fichte, 160
Flesh, 29, 30
Fossey, Dian, 98, 102
Foucault, Michel, 19, 27, 31, 94, 95, 142
Frankfurt School, 163
Fraser, Nancy: on post-feminism, xvii
Freedom, 22, 31, 34
  assembly, 169
  biological determinism and, 4–5
  corporeality and, 9–15
  diminishing, 137
  empirical sciences and, 5
  nature and, 21
  philosophical theories of, 4, 5
  speech, 169
French feminism, 59, 61, 73
Freud, Sigmund, 51, 56, 66, 121
  on active/passive schema, 50
  bourgeois society and, 54
  castration and, 52, 62
  criticism of, 46–47, 55, 57–58, 117

cultural achievements and, 47, 68
  female sexuality and, 64, 117, 120
  on femininity, 48
  feminist theory and, 57
  on heterosexual relationship, 53
  on masturbation/children, 48, 49
  phallic phase and, 49
  on sex/men, 49–50
  sex drive and, 14
  on sublimation, 47
  theory of, 41, 50, 55
  on vagina, 49
  women artists and, 45–58
Friedman, Marilyn: on friendships, 151
Fundamental thesis, 12, 106

Gender, 98, 107
  art and, 43
  clichés, 82
  design of, 69, 75, 147
  reflections on, 129
  sex and, 15, 22–39
  studies, 90, 100
  work and, 24
Gender blindness, 154, 168, 169
  science and, 88–110
Gender hierarchies, xx, 99, 146–47, 164
  feminist criticism and, 159–60
Gender-neutral laws, 153, 154, 156
Gender relations, 43, 45, 57, 111, 133,
    146
  bourgeois construction of, 56, 77
  culture and, 9, 11
  demand for, 152
  divergence of, 3
  hierarchical, 168
  naturalistic argumentation and, 9
  social history of, 11
  subtext of, 74
Gender roles, xv, 8, 22, 155
  rejection of, 150
  stabilization of, 156
Genealogy, 94
Genet, Jean, 65, 69
Genitals, 47, 52, 53
Genius, 56, 74
  cult of, 42, 78

Gilligan, Carol, 90
  on feminine care/masculine justice, 146
  feminine morality and, 131
Given by nature, 2, 3
Goodall, Jane, 98, 102
Goodfield, June, 116
Grammar, 59, 120
Great men, history and, 92–93
Grosz, Elizabeth, 29, 30, 39

Habilitation fellowships, 155
Haraway, Donna, 28, 90
Harding, Sandra, 89, 90, 105
  on masculine thinking, 99
  on objectivity, 93
  on positivist definition, 108
  strong objectivity and, 107–8
Hartsock, Nancy, 99
Having a body, being a body and, 12
Hegel, Friedrich: on corporeality, 36
Hegemony, 65, 66, 68, 124, 149
Heidegger, Martin, 61
Hempel, 34
Herder, 8
Heterogeneity, 65, 101, 109, 123
Heterosexualism, 14, 15, 33, 44
Hierarchy of the sexes, xvi, xix, 21, 83, 88
  ideas/structures of, 54
  understanding of, 53
History, 103
  great men and, 92–93
  intellectual, 42, 43
  nature and, 136
  philosophy of, 158
  women and, 104
Hobbes, Thomas, 156
Honneth, Axel, 125
Horkheimer, 130
Humanities, 34, 121
  science and, 89, 116
Husserl, 11

I, 20, 21, 22
  perceiving/acting, 19
Ideal, 22–23, 50
Identities, 123, 150
  common, 139, 149

development of, 24, 165
feminine, 122
gender, 24, 113, 126
imaginary, 60
masculine, 57, 111
question of, 90
religious, 135
Identity with, 118
Imaginary, 63, 65
Indifferent delight, 81
Individuality, 105, 158
Infantile development, 51, 61, 63, 68,
  111, 113
  sexual, 47, 49, 50, 55
Injustice, 152, 156
  critique of, xviii, 166
  double, 137–38
Insiders, outsiders and, 165
Instrumentalization, 137, 144, 164
Interpretations, 11, 26, 110
Irigaray, Luce, xx, 123
  on female body, 118–19
  feminist critique by, 117
  history of philosophy and, 119
  Lacan and, 59, 60
  Logos and, 118, 119, 120, 121
  on reason, 117–18
Irrationality, 16, 121
Isolation, 113, 151
"Is the Sex of the Knower
  Epistemologically Significant?"
  (Code), 91

Jaggar, Alison M., 39, 101, 162
Judgment, 75, 79, 80, 87
  critical, 16, 73, 99
  normative, 110
Justice, 106, 107, 108, 119, 131,
  158
  between the sexes, 141, 157, 167,
  169
  concepts of, 104, 127
  discrimination and, 169
  morally based, 141
  principles of, 105, 167
  theories of, 36, 157, 167–68
Justification, 92, 108

Kahlo, Frida, 44
Kant, Immanuel, 5, 79, 135, 138, 139, 144
  on beautiful/sublime, 74–75, 76, 78
  contracts and, 137, 156
  disinterested delight and, 85
  on duties of love, 145
  indifferent delight and, 81
  intellectual women and, 128
  interest and, 81
  marriage contract and, 164
  moral philosophy and, 124, 136, 137, 160, 165
  politics/morality and, 85
  practical reason and, 125
  on rights, 140
  sex roles and, 76, 81
  thing-in-itself and, 22
Keller, Evelyn Fox, xx, 111, 113–14
  on Bacon, 112
  criticism of, 116
  on domination, 115
  interpretation by, 110
  object-relations theory and, 114
  object status and, 115
  on science, 114
Klinger, Cornelia, 73
Knowledge, 27, 32, 101
  feminine, 98–99
  power and, 95, 96
  situatedness of, 94
Körper, 12, 20
Kristeva, Julia, 59
  on egalitarian programs, 73
  on language of love, 72
  polarization and, 71
  semiotic and, 70, 72
  symbolic and, 70
Kymlicka, Will, 158

Labor law, xiv, 155, 163
Labor unions, 155
Lacan, Jacques, 61, 66, 70, 117
  castration and, 62
  Derridean reading of, 59
  on femininities, 72
  French feminism and, 59
  imaginary and, 63

  language acquisition and, 59
  phallus/penis and, 60
Landweer, Hilge, 13
Language, 26, 34
  acquisition, 59, 60, 66
  alternative, 120
  anthropomorphizing, 6
  art and, 80
  capacity for, 66
  critique of, 18
  culture and, 66
  differentness and, 17
  everyday, 35, 37, 106
  feminine, 73, 118–19
  games, 46, 64
  gender-neutral, 162–63
  Logos and, 120
  masculinity and, 66, 120, 129
  morality and, 16–17
  order and, 59–60
  patterns of, 4, 142
  phallus and, 70
  philosophy of, 27, 29, 31, 32
  potential of, 29, 32
  reason and, 129
  science and, 35
Laqueur, Thomas, 26, 34, 35
Law
  civil, 140
  international, 141
  moral, 135, 140, 141
  philosophy of, 126, 127, 135, 141, 156, 166–67
  positive, 140
Law of the father, voice of the mother and, 65
Lectures on the Introduction to Psychoanalysis (Freud), 46
Legal theory, xviii, 136, 156
  feminist, 153
  social contract and, 157
Legitimization, 2, 93
Leib, 12
L'Enclos, Madame, 128
Liberal tradition, masculine character of, 159
Libido, 58–59
  development of, 48, 50, 55

female, 50, 56, 59, 62, 63, 64, 65, 68
 male, 59, 65, 68
Literature, 43, 70
Locke, John, 156
Logic, 17, 87, 97
Logos, 61, 116–22
Lorenz, Konrad, 6
Love, 48, 70, 116
 duties of, 145
 language of, 72
Lyotard, 78

MacKinnon, Catherine, 17, 153–54
Maihofer, on penis/phallus, 27
"Male Birth of Time, The" (Bacon),
 110
Man, 35
 as ideal type, 22–23
 patriarchal images of, 44
 woman and, 1, 14
Margolis, Joseph: on interpretation, 80
Marriage, 164
 gay/lesbian partnerships and, 170
Marx, Karl, 94, 162, 163
Masculine, 44, 108
 objective and, 88
Masculine bias, 89, 93, 94, 112, 147
Masculine justice, feminine care and,
 146
Masculinity, 44, 56, 57, 82
 art and, 58
 bourgeois ideals of, 78
 culture and, 66
 language and, 66, 129
 reason and, 88, 129
 science and, 95, 110–16
Masturbation, 48, 49, 56
Materiality, 28, 29
Maternal, 69, 123
Maturity, 38, 113, 114
Mein Leib, 20
Men's business, 1
Menstruation, 12
Merleau-Ponty, Maurice, 13, 37
Metaphysics, 21, 76
Michelangelo, 41
Mill, Harriet Taylor, xiii
Mill, John Stuart, xiii

Minorities, 149
Misogyny, xix, 90–91, 101, 142
Mitchell, Juliet: on Freud, 46
Modernity, 130, 156, 157
Morality, xvii, 18, 76, 108, 119,
 133–41, 160
 animal, 7
 behavior and, 6
 feminine, 131
 gendered, 77
 language and, 16–17
 law and, 141
 phylogenic genesis of, 6, 7
 politics and, 85
 universalistic conception of, 122,
  123, 125, 135–36, 143, 144, 145
Moral law, 128, 136, 140, 145, 160
Moral philosophy, 131, 134, 135, 136,
 138, 141, 145, 146, 151, 165, 168
 history of, 147
 quotas and, 156
 tradition of, 124, 125
Moral reproach, 16, 18–22
Mother, 49
 children and, 64
Mozart, Wolfgang Amadeus, 41
Multiculturalism, xiv, 101, 149
Music history, 43, 95
Mutuality, 114, 164

Naturalism, 3–4, 9, 14, 26–27, 33, 77,
 84
Natural sciences, 34, 116
Nature, 47–48, 110
 culture and, 15, 27, 36, 39
 domination of, 112, 114, 115, 116
 female, 149–50
 freedom and, 21
 given by, 2, 3
 history and, 136
 intention of, 2, 7, 8
 philosophy of, 31
 real, 114
 science/technology and, 111
 sexual functions and, 57
 structure and, 23
 wanted by, 2
Neutral formulations, 154–55

New Introductory Lectures on Psychoanalysis (Freud), 58
Newton, Sir Isaac, 104
Nietzsche, Friedrich, 94
Normative concepts, 23, 28, 110, 122–23
Norms, 7–8, 64, 125, 126
  action and, 7
  behavior, 24
  disciplinary, 30, 32, 34
  ethical, 6
  gender, 11, 37, 38
  juridicial, 30, 32
  medical, 30, 32
  naturalization of, 14, 34
  realities and, 33
  regulating, 31, 32
  relationship configurations and, 8
  social, 2, 3, 5, 7, 23, 27, 35
Nozick, justice and, 158
Nussbaum, Martha: on feminist critique, 97

Object, subject and, 18, 114, 115
Objectivity, 113
  art and, 80
  concept of, 23, 103, 104
  impairment of, 93
  masculine, 88
  reformulating, 105, 106
  revision of, 104
  scientistic conception of, 105–6
  strong, 105, 107–8
  term, 102–3, 107
Object-relations theory, 108, 111, 112, 114, 159, 160
Objet trouvé, 80–81
Observations on the Feeling of the Beautiful and the Sublime (Kant), 74–75, 77
Oedipal phase, 50–51, 54, 56, 61–62
O'Neill, Onora, 144
Okin, Susan Moller, 161
One-sex model, 26, 34, 35
Ontology, 27, 29, 123, 158
Oppression, 139–40, 151
  feminist *we* and, 150

five faces of, 144
  paternalism and, 159
Order
  language and, 59–60
  reality and, 33
Order of the sexes, 1–9, 11, 138
  challenging, 55, 156
  scholarship and, 93
  traditional, 166, 167
Organism, theory of, 18, 22
Orientation, 35, 87
  sexual, 13, 101, 107, 167, 170
Other, 17, 113

Painting, women and, 43
Participation, 66–67, 69, 160
Pateman, Carole, 166
  on contract theory, 163–64
  on feminism/contract, 157
  gender hierarchy and, 164
Paternalism, 148, 159
Patriarchy, 74, 81, 83, 109, 166
  critique of, 11, 142
  legitimating, 2
  Logos and, 121
Penis, 50, 52–53, 61
  phallus and, 27, 59, 60
Penis envy, 51, 54, 56, 117
Penislessness, 52–53, 55, 61
Pergolesi, 71
Phallic, 51, 62, 66, 67, 70
Phallic phase, 48, 49, 50, 52, 56
Phallocentrism, 62, 118, 119, 120, 121
Phallogocentrism, 61, 62
Phallus, 61, 65, 67, 68, 69, 71
  image of, 118
  language/culture and, 70
  penis and, 27, 59, 60
  symbolic order and, 60, 63, 66
Phenomenological, 83, 84
Philosophy, 32, 79, 131, 132, 160
  Enlightenment, 141, 158, 159
  history of, 28, 73–74, 82, 97, 119, 120, 122, 127
  morality and, 124
  postmodern, 78

subject, 74
terminology, 80
theory, 21
See also Feminist philosophy
Physical, centrality of, 12, 13–14, 20
Physiological theory, 35
Plato, xix, 61
Plessner, on independent body, 36–37
Plurality, 100, 101, 102
Poetry, 65, 71
Political correctness, 18, 152
Political theory, 127, 160, 165
Politics, 101, 127, 145, 148, 159–60
  art and, 84
  emancipatory, 143
  gender, 44
  identity, 149
  morality and, 85
  postcolonial, 106
  racist, 32
  women and, 161
  See also Feminist politics
*Portrait du Mlle. Charlotte du Val
  d'Ognes,* case of, 42
Positivism, 93, 103, 108
Postcolonialism, 126
Post-feminism, xv, xvi, xvii
Postmodernism, 28, 44, 46, 127
Poststructuralism, 125, 126
Poulain de la Barre, François, xiii
Poverty, feminization of, xiv
Power, 144
  criticism of, 21, 32, 33
  dissimulated effect of, 27
  interconnections of, 31
  knowledge and, 95, 96
  male monopoly on, 117–18
  relations, 11, 124
  ruse of, 124–25
Pregnancy, 10–11, 12, 22
Prejudice, 74, 93–94, 145
Pre-oedipal phase, 63, 70
Prima philosophia, 36
Privacy, concept of, 160
Private domain, public domain and,
  161–62
Procreativity, 49, 69

Psychic, 47, 57, 162
Psychoanalysis, 41, 45, 47, 54, 55, 70,
  90, 113, 116–17
  classics of, 62
  femininity and, 48
  feminist objections to, 46, 59
  man/woman typology and, 68
Psychology, 20, 108, 159
Public domain, private domain and, 2,
  161–62
Putnam, Ruth Anna, 104, 109
  theory of, 107, 167–68

Quality of life, xv
Quine, naturalized epistemology and,
  94
Quota systems, 145, 146, 156

Race, 107
Racism, 32, 33, 94, 144
Radical agenda, 26, 126
Rationality, 68, 125
  cultivation of, 87–88
  instrumental, 130
  irrationality and, 16
  masculine connotations of, 96
  poetic mode and, 65
  reason and, 132
  science and, 88–110
  scientific, 110, 112, 115, 116, 119,
   122
  universalist conceptions of, 79
Rawls, 157, 168
  justice and, 158
  objection to, 104, 167, 169
  theory of, 161, 167
Reason, xxi, 104
  capacity for, 127, 128
  challenging, 92–97, 130, 131
  concept of, 87, 119, 120, 127, 132
  emotion and, 130, 131, 132
  feminist critique of, 87, 88, 116,
   117–18, 122, 127–30, 132
  language and, 129
  masculinity and, 88, 129, 132
  normative judgments and, 110
  patriarchal power and, 88

practical, 125
rationality and, 132
reflections on, 129
sense and, 131
subject and, 122–27
Reductionism, 38, 131, 132
Relationships, 8, 13, 151
*Reproduction of Mothering:
Psychoanalysis and the Sociology of
Gender, The* (Chodorow), 112
Res cogitans, 19
res extensa and, 18
Research, 90, 101
empirical, 3, 5, 32, 34, 119
ethnological, 3
feminist, 2, 23, 44, 46, 105–6, 107,
109–10
historical, 3
methods, 91
normative aspect of, 106
scientific, 7, 37
situatedness of, 103
theoretical foundation of, 109–10
Res extensa, 21, 22
res cogitans and, 18
Respect, 136, 139, 147
Rights, 25, 140
civil, 33, 140, 163
equal, xiv, 89, 131, 145
fundamental, 106, 135
group, 151
human, 101
men's, 159
minority, xiv, 101
political, 163, 164
social, xiv, 156, 163
voting, 89, 152
women's, 134, 159
Right to vote, 152
universal franchise and, 89
Rose, Hilary, 99
Rousseau, Jean-Jacques, 75, 160, 161
bourgeois society and, 162
on competition/compensation,
166
contract theory of, 156
intellectual women and, 128

Kant and, 77
on social contract, 164

Scholarship
aim of, 103
masculine bias in, 89, 91
order of the sexes and, 93
political dimension of, 96
value-free, 106
women and, 90, 98, 100–101
Science
androcentrism and, 92
contextuality and, 103
criticism of, 97, 98, 114
democratic, 103–4
empirical, 119
everyday language and, 35
feminism and, 89, 103
feminist criticism of, 94, 97, 101,
104, 110
gender blindness and, 88–110
humanities and, 89, 116
logic of, 120
masculinity and, 93, 95, 110–16
nature and, 111
positivist concept of, 94, 95
power aspect of, 114
rationality and, 88–110
technology and, 110–11
theory of, viii, xix, xx, 31, 106
unified concept of, 92, 93
value-free, 93
women and, 129
Scientism, 110, 115, 119
Scientistic paradigm, 104, 106
Self, other and, 113
Self-confidence, 63, 149
Self-contradiction, performative, 15, 95,
120
Self-determination, 137, 139, 140, 149,
150
autonomy and, 160
feminists and, 160
principle of, 161
right of, 166
surrender of, 56
women and, 165–66

Self-legislation, 159, 164
Self-understanding, 3–4, 21, 45
Semiotic, 72
  symbolic and, 70, 71
Sense, reason and, 131
Separation, 113, 114
Sex
  anatomical distinction of, 30, 54–55
  civil rights and, 33
  classification by, 138
  components of, 37
  constitution of, 29
  discursive origin of, 27, 30
  education and, 33
  gender and, 15, 22–39
  income and, 33
  men and, 49–50
  psychical consequences of, 54–55
  social relevance of, 53
Sex characteristics, 10, 37
  biological, 38
  bodily, 46
  sexual relation and, 13
Sex drive, 14, 47, 51, 68
Sexes
  art history and, 42–43
  character of, 76, 77
  difference of, 10, 11, 23, 26, 27, 29,
    33, 45, 57, 58, 73, 98, 99, 127,
    138
  hierarchy of, xvi, xix, 21, 42, 53, 54,
    83, 88
  interrelations of, 77
  judgments of, 75
  order of, 1–9, 11, 55, 93, 138, 156,
    166, 167
  polarization of, 72, 130
  relation of, 9, 10, 14–15, 85
  social locations of, 99
  struggle of, 63
Sexts, 62
Sexual contract, social contract and, 164
Sexual development, 47, 49, 68
Sexual exploitation, 15, 166
Sexuality
  female, 49, 64, 117, 118, 120, 121
  internal links of, 13

phallic, 51
theory of, 24, 120
Sexual orientation, xvii, 13, 14, 89,
  101, 107, 167
  discrimination and, 170
Sexual relations, 15, 24, 117
  sex characteristics and, 13
Sexual violence, 152, 160
Sherman, Cindy, 44
Simmel, Georg, 88
Situatedness, 79, 95, 103
Sleeping, cultural history of, 10
Smith, Dorothy, 99
Social construction, 22, 28, 56, 57
Social contract
  individuality and, 158
  sexual contract and, 164
  theories of, 152–70
Social environment, 4, 105
Social history, 42, 43
Socialization, 38, 54, 55, 114
Social life, xiv, 44, 151
Social order, 7, 8, 67, 168
  bourgeois conception of, 127–28
  middle-class, 26
  patterns of, 59
  principle of, 163
Social position, 33, 128
Social roles, 2, 26
Social sciences, 34
Speech-act theory, 16–17
Spirit, 21
Stabat Mater (Pergolesi), 72
Stein, Edith, 11, 12
Strong objectivity, 105, 107–8
Subject, 20, 21, 82
  object and, 18, 114, 115
  reason and, 122–27
Subjectivity, 87, 113
Sublimation, 47, 48
Sublime, 78, 81
  beautiful and, 74–75, 76, 77
Subordination, 55, 60, 84, 88, 112,
  115, 144, 161, 162–63
  challenging, 134
  formulating, 53
Super-ego, 50, 51, 55–56

Symbolic, semiotic and, 70, 71
Symbolic order, 22, 28, 59, 61, 62, 68,
    71
  art and, 67
  feminist criticism of, 67
  human culture/social life and, 60
  identification of, 69
  imaginary fusion and, 65
  phallus and, 63, 66
  semiotic and, 72

Taylor, Charles, 147, 149, 158
Technology, 12
  nature and, 111
  science and, 110–11
"Temporis Partus Masculus" (Bacon),
    110
Terminological distinction, 21, 22
Theories, 127
  argumentative examination of, 107
  origin of, 59, 92, 104
  practice and, 34
  value-free, 105–6
"Theory of Justice, A" (Rawls), 167
Thing-in-itself, 22
Things, utility value of, 81
Thought
  abstract, 87
  essentialist patterns of, 100
  female, 98, 100
  feminist, 108
  masculine, 99, 108–9
  patriarchal, 76, 89, 91, 120, 166
  poststructuralist, 125
  sexist forms of, 85
  status, 96
  unconscious, 47
Transcendental pragmatics, 123, 125
Transformation, 111, 122
Trettin, Käthe, 97
Truth, 78, 79
Two-sex model, 26

Universal, 89, 91, 125, 214
Universal franchise, 91
  right to vote and, 89

Universalism, 79, 125, 150
Uterus art, 67

Vagina, 49
Veil of ignorance, 167, 168
Verbalization, 13
Victim, perpetrator and, 142
Virtue, 74, 75, 146, 147
  masculine/feminine, 69, 76–77
Voice of the mother, law of the father
    and, 65
Vote, right to, 89, 152

Wanted by nature, 2, 3, 7
We. See Feminist we
Weber, Max, 130
Wolf, Susan, 147
Wolff, Janet, 84
Woman
  as ideal type, 22–23
  man and, 1, 14
  nature of, 2, 48
  patriarchal images of, 44
  term, 35, 49, 123, 138, 149
"Woman Question in Science, The"
    (Harding), 90
Women
  discrimination against, 42, 89–90
  disparaging, 52–53
  intellectual, 128
  nature of, 57, 58
  representation of, 43, 44, 90
Women artists
  discrimination against, 83
  feminist perspective on, 57
  Freud's theory of, 56
Women's liberation, xix, 67, 112, 115,
    161
Woolf, Virginia, 67
Work, 24, 162
  women's, 1, 2, 145
Writing
  feminine, 64–65, 73, 146
  phallic, 67

Young, Iris, 143, 144, 160